The Fluid Text

The Fluid Text

A Theory of Revision and Editing for Book and Screen

John Bryant

Ann Arbor

THE UNIVERSITY OF MICHIGAN PRESS

2005   2004   2003   2002   4   3   2   1

A CIP catalog record for this book is available from the British Library.

Library of Congress Cataloging-in-Publication Data

Bryant, John, 1949–
The fluid text : a theory of revision and editing for book
and screen / John Bryant.
p.   cm. — (Editorial theory and literary criticism)
Includes bibliographical references and index.
ISBN 0-472-09815-2 (cloth : alk. paper) —
ISBN 0-472-06815-6 (pbk. : alk. paper)
1. Editing.   I. Title.   II. Series.

PN162 .B79   2002
808'.027—dc21   2002003605

In Memory of Doris H. Bryant
(1924–2001)
and
Some of the Women She Touched
Paula, Cerise, Emma, Eliza, and Liana

Contents

Acknowledgments

My first inkling that literary works are fluid texts came in college at the University of Chicago while studying Whitman with James E. Miller Jr., whose parallel text edition of "Song of Myself" continues to inspire me in finding ways of giving readers access to textual fluidity. Later, in 1973 and still at Chicago, I found myself unexpectedly entangled in a textual project involving Swinburne manuscripts under the direction of Jerome J. McGann, himself newly entangled in editing Byron. Later still, while researching Melville, I would drift uptown to the Newberry Library to confer with Harrison Hayford, who from time to time would drift down from Northwestern to conduct the making of his magisterial edition of *The Writings of Herman Melville*. These scholars and friends—along with others, including Walter Blair and Hamlin Hill—shaped and encouraged my early respect and interest in textual editing. But it was not until the discovery in 1983 of the *Typee* manuscript that I was able to find a textual project of my own, and one that would take me deeper into Melville manuscripts and the problem of textual fluidity in general. At this point and for years to come, I received the generous guidance and encouragement from Hayford as well as manuscript specialist Robert C. Ryan and textual scholar and theorist G. Thomas Tanselle. I am also indebted to Leslie Morris of the Houghton Library, Harvard University, and especially Mimi Bowling, former head of the manuscripts division at the New York Public Library, whose warmth of spirit and generosity in giving me access to the *Typee* manuscript and other papers surely hastened my labors in transcription and manuscript analysis.

Numerous individuals helped me in writing *The Fluid Text*. Chief among them is George Bornstein, who as general editor of the series in which this book appears, gave enthusiastic support throughout the entire process. Peter Shillingsburg gave a crucial, thorough reading of a "final" draft, and his insightful commentary guided me through revisions that made this a much better book than it was. LeAnn Fields, my editor at the University of Michigan Press, was also instrumental in helping me shape this volume into a sharper and yet (I hope) more pleasurable reading experience. Since 1996, I have also profited enormously from the critiques and conversations of various members of the Society for Textual Scholarship, especially Robin Schulze, who read several chapters closely and critically, as well as Hans Walter Gabler, D. C. Greetham, Donald Reiman, Martha Nell Smith, and Marta Werner. I have also enjoyed helpful feedback from various scholars and colleagues: G. Thomas Couser, Wyn Kelley, John Klause, Steven Olsen-Smith, Geoffrey Sanborn, Haskell Springer, John Unsworth, Paula Uruburu, Shari Zimmerman, and in particular Lee Zimmerman, whose well-argued doubts about the critical relevance of textual fluidity have forced me to sharpen my arguments to his satisfaction, almost.

Let me also thank my graduate and undergraduate students at Hofstra University whose excitements and bewilderments over innumerable textual fluidities brought up in various classes (one entitled "The Fluid Text") and in their papers have helped me immeasurably in gauging the limits and potentials of fluid text discourse, analysis, and editing. A "final" draft of this book was achieved during a 1998 sabbatical leave provided by Hofstra University, whose Provost, Herman Berliner, and Dean of Liberal Arts and Sciences, Bernard J. Firestone, have given constant encouragement. But, of course, the greatest grant-giver in this project and my life is my wife, Virginia Blanford. During this sabbatical our good friend Linda Spungen died, leaving us her newly adopted child Liana Meiling, now our adopted daughter. Things change. This book about reading and editing revision is suffused with the memory of our friend.

Introduction

The Fluid Text

The fluid text is a fact, not a theory.

This claim may be mystifying if you are unclear about my use of *fluid;* or arrogantly retrogressive if you suspect that I may be some fogy putting *fact* as a chip on my shoulder to upbraid critical theorists (and I am not); or philosophically naive for carelessly assuming that facts do "in fact" exist as something more objective than selected bits of data shaped by a theory. I anticipate this unease over words like *fluid, fact,* and *theory,* but I need them to make a point about *text.*

Simply put, a fluid text is any literary work that exists in more than one version. It is "fluid" because the versions flow from one to another. Truth be told, all works—because of the nature of texts and creativity— are fluid texts. Not only is this fluidity the inherent condition of any written document; it is inherent in the phenomenon of writing itself. That is, writing is fundamentally an arbitrary hence unstable hence variable approximation of thought. Moreover, we revise words to make them more closely approximate our thoughts, which in turn evolve as we write. And this condition and phenomenon of textual fluidity is not a theoretical supposition; it is fact.

Literary works invariably exist in more than one version, either in early manuscript forms, subsequent print editions, or even adaptations in other media with or without the author's consent. The processes of authorial, editorial, and cultural revision that create these versions are inescapable elements of the literary phenomenon, and if we are to understand how writing and the transmission of literary works operate in the processes of meaning making, we need first to recognize this fact of fluidity and also devise critical approaches, and a critical vocabulary, that will allow us to talk about the meaning of textual fluidity in writing and in culture.

In due course, and despite my claim that the fluid text is a fact not a theory, I will be theorizing about the fluid nature of literary phenomena in ways that I hope will be useful to scholars, critics, teachers, and those lucky enough to see themselves as all three. My goal is to challenge our tendency to define a material text—and by that I mean the physical writing on the page—as a fixed thing, and to suggest new ways of reading, interpreting, and teaching. This is not an easy task because literary theory and critical practice of the past century have built their work upon the general assumption that, while the texts we read may be infinitely interpretable, the material texts themselves ("received" from publishers and scholars and frozen into print) are, for all intents and purposes, static and that multiple versions of a given work are either anomalous corruptions with no real critical relevance or at best simply "other" texts to be treated separately. Modern readers, including critics and even many scholars, typically assume that the "job" of textual scholarship— we dare not call it art—is to sift through this corruption and "otherness" and establish an authoritative or definitive text for common use. But when we inspect the causes of this "textualterity" (to lift for a moment another critic's portmanteau),[1] we find more than just the accidents of textual transmission; we begin to envision a fuller phenomenon, tied to historical moments but always changing and always manifesting one set of interests or another. The very nature of writing, the creative process, and shifting intentionality, as well as the powerful social forces that occasion translation, adaptation, and censorship among readers—in short, the facts of revision, publication, and reception—urge us to recognize that the only "definitive text" is a multiplicity of texts, or rather, the fluid text.

No doubt readers gravitate to so-called definitive texts because they desire the cultural creature comforts that definitive texts propose to offer: authenticity, authority, exactitude, singularity, fixity in the midst of the inherent indeterminacy of language. We are happy to acknowledge that any single text can yield up multiple interpretations; but the mind resists the thought that single literary works are themselves multiform, that they exist in various and varied physical states, each capable of yielding its own set of interpretations. We assume that because there once was a body called William Shakespeare, there is similarly only one body of work called "Shakespeare," and we expect *Lear* to be *Lear*. And yet there are variant *Lears*, not simply because that play has been interpreted differently in essays and books or even in multiple performances, but because the text of *Lear* in the Folio is radically different from that in the Quarto. Still, we expect one *Lear*, indeed want one *Lear*, and hundreds of years of editing have worked toward trying to insist upon one *Lear*.

Similarly, and to use the test text before us in this book, we want there to be one book by Herman Melville called *Typee*, even though the history of that literary work shows that the writer conceived of it and printed it in different versions. Now, it is easy enough to show that this gravitation toward a fixed or "definitive" text is an enormous blindness in our critical thinking[2] but quite another thing to ask scholars, critics, and teachers to take on yet another layer of indeterminacy in the process of reading by embracing rather than denying the fact of something called the fluid text. But that "little lower layer" of indeterminacy (as the writer of *Moby-Dick* might say) is a richer one that allows us a sharper vision of the evolution of texts and how writers, readers, and cultures interact.

Here, then, are some "facts" about the "fluidity" of literary phenomena. Writing is a process,[3] and a literary work evolves through various stages of revision in that process from the earliest creative moments of mental transcription (when writers make up words in the mind and transfer them on the page) to moments of publication and on to moments of adaptation in other media. The literary work also appears in different material manifestations throughout its existence: working drafts, fair copies, proofs, and authorized commercial editions. But textual fluidity does not end here. In the hands of readers a text's material presence changes in other ways through censorings, bowdlerizations, translations, adaptations, and even scholarly editions. These variant material manifestations of a literary work are not the exceptional cases; they are the rule, from the Bible to Chaucer, Shakespeare, and Donne; from Wordsworth to Eliot, Yeats, Joyce, and Marianne Moore; from *Moby-Dick* and *Clotelle* (our first African-American novel) to *The Red Badge of Courage*, various works by Faulkner, and Raymond Carver's early tales; from Dickinson and Whitman to Mary Shelley, Virginia Woolf, and Anne Frank. The list of fluid texts is so full as to constitute all of literature.[4] In fact, a good game to play is to try to find a text that is *not* fluid, one that has *not* changed materially, and in significant ways, over the years for some reason or another. I have seen changes carved on gravestones and am thus inclined to stick to my claim that the fluid text is a fact not a theory.

The textual condition—encompassing the processes of creation, editing, printing, and adaptation—is fundamentally fluid not because specific words lend themselves to different meanings or that different minds will interpret the words fixed on a page in different ways, but because writers, editors, publishers, translators, digesters, and adapters change those words materially. Moreover, these material revisions can attest not simply to localized fine-tunings but to new conceptualizations of the entire work. Thus, a literary work invariably evolves, by the collaborative forces of individuals and the culture, from one version to another. If we are to know the textual condition, we must get to the versions of a text, and there we will also find an even deeper condition of creativity within a culture. But the problem is that we generally have only partial access—often no access—to those versions. That is, the erasures, cancellations, and insertions on a manuscript, or the blue-pencilings of an editor, which are the manifestations of revision, are frequently lost to us, so that the prepublication versions of a work in particular come to us as hypotheticals. We can only speculate, then, on the flow of thought that eventuated in these inferred versions, and speculation is not a comfortable place to be. The irony is that the more one perceives the variable materiality of a text—let us say even a mere scrap of revised manuscript—the more one begins to focus on the immaterial processes of change that create the variances, the flow of texts. Our perception of texts as material objects ineluctably leads to an apperception of fluidity. But how does one treat this textual condition culturally, critically, pedagogically, and editorially?

The multiplicity of versions is not a condition one can wish away, for authorial, editorial, and cultural revision is in the nature of literary phenomena; nor is it merely a corruption to "correct" (unless the variation happens to be an obvious error, like the word *obvous* earlier in this sentence). Rather, it is something to celebrate, study, and interpret. In one important instance from the *Typee* manuscript, we find Melville altering the words *savage* and *native* to *islander*. This single pattern of material difference in word choice may have "triggered" an expansion in Melville's awareness of internalized imperialist structures he was beginning to call into question as he wrote. More certain is that the pattern implies a *strategy of revision* that can be a critical "sign" of Melville's expanding consciousness and rhetorical condition. Of course, readers of a print-text version of *Typee* that provides no textual apparatus will see only the word *islander* and not its hidden variant *(savage);* thus, these changes and strategies, as well as the fragile and tentative nature of textuality, are not an issue to them and do not affect their ways of reading. Nevertheless, once we are made aware that a given print-text *(islander)* is just the trace of an earlier process of revision (involving *savage*), we lean into that print-text more closely with a new set of worries and wonders. What are the variant meanings of the variant texts; what is the meaning of their difference; what are the causes of this revision; is there any meaning in the fact that this pattern of revision occurred here and not there? And what, we might also ask, was Melville thinking? What was the *intent* behind the revision?

The problems of pursuing the critical relevance of textual fluidity are admittedly monumental. It can be argued that even with manuscript evidence in hand, the reader has no real access to Melville's thought processes, which like all mental acts are irretrievable. Writers, editors, and censorious readers may be the efficient causes of revision throughout the history of a text, and we might to some extent plumb their intentions, but the process of revision itself can only be inferred from fossil texts residing in certain documents, and like paleoanthropologists we must resort to supplying fabricated flesh and bone to render an approximation of evolution. Like them, we can only construct a history. How, then, might our investigation of the fluidity behind a print-text seriously impact upon one's reading of that print-text?

Fluidity is an inherent condition of textuality familiar to all textual scholars, less so to the interpreters of texts: theorists, critics, and historicists. As a result, interpretive communities have yet to establish critical standards for the discussion of the phenomenon. Some refer to this condition of fluidity as *textual instability,* but this phrasing implies a teleological perspective I want to avoid.[5] A text may vary radically from one version to the next, yielding significant interpretive differences. And our tendency is to want to stabilize this instability and determine once and for all the primacy of one version (usually the latest one before printing occurs) over the other. The teleological assumption, here, is that revision is a mode of aesthetic improvement and the fulfillment of an author's previously inchoate but now realized intentions. But in many cases, such as Melville's wavering between the words *savage* and *islander,* the change is essentially multivalent, revealing the writer's human condition of doubt that is inherently perhaps irresolvably ambivalent (not resolvably unstable), and one that if made known to readers becomes a sign of a culture's deepest ambivalences as well. Melville wavers, perhaps, because in 1845 at the time he composed *Typee* he was (through the process of writing itself) interrogating certain "savageries" of his past life in Polynesia just as his reaction to Western culture's savage imperialism against island cultures was beginning to call into question complacent assumptions about the idea of civilization. In this and innumerable other instances print-texts conceal radically irresolvable textual fluidity.

Scholars have also referred to textual fluidity as *indeterminacy,* which is a fair expression for Melville's *savage/islander* quandary, but this term also has its limitations, for we know that writers and editors can be quite determined in their word choice with one audience in mind at one moment, and quite determined at a later time or circumstance in changing that wording. Some of Shakespeare's plays, if we give authority to his so-called foul papers and previously much maligned quarto editions, include a vast array of variants suggesting the playwright's and players' attempts to accommodate different audiences. The rhetorical strategies inherent in these revisions are anything but indeterminate. Nor was Wordsworth indeterminate or unstable (for a poet, at any rate) when he took fifty years to write his *Prelude,* which exists in at least three authorial versions; and Whitman's sequential editions of *Leaves of Grass* from 1855 to 1892 were quite determinate both in their adding and dropping of poems and in their revisions of surviving poems.

I prefer to call these apparent instabilities and indeterminacies *textual fluidities* because the surviving variant texts, when taken together, give us a vivid material impression of the *flow* of creativity, both authorial and editorial, that constitutes the cultural phenomenon of writing. Notice that I extend the "flow of creativity" beyond the prepublication realms of the single writer writing in relative isolation to embrace subsequent postpublication kinds of "writers," namely editors. By *editor* I mean anyone—friends, family, professional and scholarly editors, publishers, even adapters—who in the course of the history of a given work lays hands upon that text to shape it in new ways. By making this extension into what is now referred to as the *social text,* I do not want to diminish the exciting creative impulses of individual writers as manifest in their manuscripts or authorized print-text revisions; I simply want to expand the horizon of creativity, normally a preserve for the writers who originate literary works, to include those readers who also materially alter texts. Our acceptance of this community of single writers and collaborators is crucial to fluid-text analysis, but current editorial theory, both intentionalist and materialist, tends—I think unnecessarily—to segregate these different kinds of creators. In chapters 1, 2, and 3, I draw upon elements in both theories to argue for a more integrated approach.

One point I hope to make is that if in the study of fluid texts we admit to a larger and broader community of writers, we must become all the more vigilant in not allowing ourselves to homogenize that community of collaborators. To understand the nature and specifics of "multiple authorship," we need to know who wrote what and when; we need to clarify one set of intentions from another. This means addressing two controversial matters: collaboration and intentionality.

Our most immediate notion of "collaboration" is that texts come into being with two or more individuals laboring together shoulder to shoulder (like lyricist and composer at the piano) as a single sensibility, but in fact that practice almost never happens.[6] Most collaboration derives from conflict. Indeed, a major cause of textual fluidity derives from the conflicting sensibilities of collaborators, both friendly and adversarial. Collaborators act primarily as "second readers," the first reader being the writer writing. That is, these second readers take a writer's work and provide new perspectives by suggesting changes; in some cases, they demand changes. Often they get those changes. It is well known that successive editors, male and female, have altered (some might say mutilated) Dickinson's poems, that Dreiser's friends urged him to cut *Sister Carrie* drastically; that Pound helped Eliot carve away lengthy portions of *The Waste Land;* that Maxwell Perkins molded Thomas Wolfe's novels out of cartloads of typescript; that Richard Wright desexed *Native Son* for the Book-of-the-Month Club, that Gordon Lish pared Raymond Carver down to a minimalist; and that various posthumous Hemingway books are the product of marketplace editors. In virtually all these cases, the "collaborators" do not work together from the inception of the project; rather, the collaboration begins with one person acting as an editor to shape what a principal writer has written. Thus, I am nervous about bestowing upon such editorial figures the status of authorial collaborator, since authorship implies a kind of unified, originary role not played by most collaborators. I would rather call these agents of textual fluidity *editors,* but this is problematic because we think of editors (erroneously I think) as functionaries in the marketplace or academe, not creative associates to whom a writer goes for feedback and suggested revision, midwives, not birth-mothers. Nevertheless, I plan to stick to this word *editor* (rather than collaborator) and use it in this broader sense in hopes that it will allow us to look more carefully at the complex of interacting intentions between writer and editor in the flow of their sometimes synergistic sometimes oppositional creativities.

I have also found that one cannot talk about fluid texts without some consideration of intentionality. This, of course, is heresy. One need not rehearse the history of criticism to realize that modern approaches to literature—formalism, poststructuralism, new historicism—have removed creative process, intentionality, and (most famously) authorship itself from the playing fields of interpretation. If texts cohere, deconstruct, or reveal the imprint of ideology, they do so, according to current theory, because of the nature of signification or of a reader's response or of a culture's "political unconsciousness," not through the conscious agency of an individual writer. It is, of course, a truism that we cannot retrieve the creative process, nor, according to the "intentional fallacy," can we use some magically derived sense of an writer's intentions as a validation of or substitute for an interpretation of a text.[7] But in the past century, some advocates of this tenet have grown so doctrinaire as to commit what might be called the Intentional Fallacy Fallacy, which is essentially to imagine that because intentions have no critical relevance·they are not even discussable.[8] Of course, intentions exist; they are an unalienable element in letters, love, and law, and once announced or perceived in some way, they tend to be the *only* topic of discussion. With the fluid text featured in this book, I will be speculating on intentions quite a bit in order to construct, not retrieve, the history of a process of writing called *Typee*. And to do this, I need to establish the ways in which concepts such as intention, creativity, and writer (if not "author") are not only discussable but have critical utility.

To be sure, recognition of the intentional fallacy has helped facilitate the largely positive transformation of literary interpretation from the worship of canonized "geniuses" into an act of analysis, but certain babies have been tossed out with that belletristic bathwater. While a reader's interpretation exists independently from a writer's intentions, we know that the writer intended certain acts of revision, and that if articulated in our critical pursuits, even as a speculation, these intended

acts of revision have no less of a place in the discourse on literary meaning than any other set of hermeneutic acts we might construct while
contemplating a string of words. But textual fluidity offers a more
focused perspective on intentionality that allows us to sharpen the
dimensions of speculation. Fluid texts are the material evidence of *shifting* intentions. Indeed, the fact of revision manifests the intent to alter
meaning. We may not presume to know precisely what Melville
intended to mean by *savage* or *islander,* but we know that his change
from one to the other is itself conscious and meaningful. This awareness
enables us to place more useful boundaries on speculation. And, with
our construction of a strategy out of Melville's intended revision in
mind, we can also more carefully speculate upon the ways our awareness
of textual fluidity may affect the ways we read a text and a culture.

A fluid text bodies forth concrete instances of an idiosyncratic individual negotiating idiosyncratically with an audience. Such idiosyncrasies
cannot represent a culture, but as a particularized instance of cultural
engagement, they may be seen in their peculiarity as a concrete enactment of a culture. Thus, textual fluidities are more than just small
moments in (an otherwise critically irrelevant) biography; they are a
graphic manifestation of the discourses of self, word, and society. Despite
this critical potential, most critics are in denial about the fluid text. Of
course, critics of various generations have drawn upon evidence of revision to glimpse (what Foucault appropriately reviled as) "the author in
the workshop" or promote a particular biographical reading. My purpose
here is to explore deeper critical and cultural potentials derived from revision implicit in textual fluidity. Exactly why textual fluidity has been
largely ignored may have a great deal to do with the problem of access.
Evidence of textual fluidity often exists in rare books and unique manuscripts that are hard enough to locate let alone use without collation and
transcription. Moreover, the mechanics and economics of publishing
such scholarly materials effectively are often prohibitive, even in the computer age. Despite efforts in the past decades to make textual fluidity
more accessible in the graduate schools if not among the general public,
fluid texts have not been analyzed much as fluid texts because scholarly
editions (the repositories of textual fluidity) tend to showcase single
"clear reading" texts; the evidence of revision is invariably marginalized
in the editorial notes and apparatus. But the critical denial of textual
fluidity is also rooted in deeper matters, such as the dismissal of "authorship" in current poststructuralist and new historicist theory.

Concluding his seminal essay "Structure, Sign, and Play in the Discourse of the Human Sciences" with a focus on the "freeplay" of signification, Jacques Derrida distinguishes two "interpretations of interpretation." There is the "ethic of nostalgia for origins," which "dreams of deciphering, a truth or an origin which is free from freeplay."[9] Here, critical interpretation is the manifestation of our desire to locate and give priority to meanings associated with a "negative," that is, the "absent origin" or central, creative author of the signifiers themselves. But there is also a mode of interpretation that decenters meaning, that is a positive denial of the relevance to meaning of the creative moment, one that takes pleasure in *"given and existing, present, pieces"* of signification, one that "affirms freeplay and tries to pass beyond man and humanism" (533). The transcendent goal for that "being" called "man" in Derrida's formulation is the dream of "full presence," which is both the "origin and end of the game" of interpretation. Derrida does not specify if this human is a writer or reader, for that distinction finally does not matter; each is both. Writers are their own first readers; readers "write out" their interpretations. Thus, Derrida does not so much deny the historical fact of the creative process as deem it irrelevant to freeplay. That is, the conditions of genesis do not lend any special power to the word created; therefore, the freeplay of meaning "surrenders itself to *genetic* indetermination," and the author becomes an absence.

Textual critics who are mindful of authorial intentionality as well as the inherent indeterminacy of material texts have worried over the deconstructionist dismissal of the author for the simple reason that textual scholarship generally reinforces deconstructionist principles.[10] Not only is language seen to be an imperfect intermediary between a writer's intangible thought and the concrete expression of his or her text, but the processes of writing, as engaged in by single writers, clearly enact the aporetic nature of language.[11] That is, one of the most vivid instances of "freeplay" in human endeavor occurs at the moment of genesis, when a writer writes but then revises and revises, as if to ritualize in ceaseless, revisionary, creative acts the inadequacy of words to approximate thought. Fluid texts, insofar as their material versions register these breakdown revisionary acts, are, from the moment of genesis and on into print, a constant "deferral" of the literary work itself. Thus, the history of textual revision and versions can be seen as an enactment of deconstruction. Rather than ignore writers writing, we need to inspect their creative acts if only to experience in some commensurate critical way their breakdowns. As an immersion in continuous creativity, fluid-text analysis is, paradoxically, a transcendence beyond "man and humanism"; it is a way of engaging more fully in freeplay.

Moreover, the analysis of fluid texts is a historicizing of freeplay. The realities of the fluid text strongly argue for a resurrection of the writer in our critical thinking, and for a form of historicism that can accommodate creative process and the forces that drive textual fluidity. This resurrection is really a transmigration, for if current theory has buried the Author, we need more fully to acknowledge the advent of the Writer. *Author* is a title conferred, late or soon, upon an individual whose writings have circulated to such an extent that the culture concedes and confers upon it a reputation, and while many have achieved this status in greater or lesser degree, the title itself is an acknowledgment of status and "authority." But whereas an "author" appears only at the moment of cultural recognition, a "writer" is simply *one who writes* and is born at the moment of his or her act of writing, not through the conferring of the status of social recognition. An author is a social construct; a writer is one who performs a human process. Of course, all authors are writers (except, I suppose, for plagiarists and those who hire their writing out), but if we want to know about the personal and social causes of revision and versions of texts, we must study the processes of writing, which are inseparable from the person writing and worry elsewhere about the sociology of Authorship. Current theory has killed the author, and with good reason, but the writer never died. The question, of course, is whether this individual writes to achieve idiosyncratic ends or is an unconscious social function.

In "What Is an Author?" Michel Foucault energetically unearths the Author in order to rebury the concept in the graveyard of traditional historicism. Although he does not distinguish writer from author, he deconstructs idiosyncratic authorship as a valid measure of a culture. It is a culture's discourse, not the individual voice, that carries meaning; thus, he asks along with Beckett, "What difference does it make who is speaking?"[12] In reaction to all members of the Party Nostalgic, who long for glimpses into "the author's workshop," he rightly denies the author's status as "an inexhaustible world of significations"; the author is only one of various conduits of cultural meaning, "a functional principle" that necessarily "limits, excludes, and chooses." Indeed, the individual author or our allegiance to that authority "impedes the free circulation, the free manipulation, the free composition, decomposition, and recomposition of fiction" (274). Perhaps Foucault comes not so much to bury authors as to dismiss mere author-worship in order to reach higher orders of creativity, the engendering forces of language, ideology, and cultural discourse. An author is not a who; an author is a how—a function. But, even though the author is a functionary, the functionality of that function is in the process of writing, which is the site at which cultural discourse is necessarily manifested through the utterly unique and idiosyncratic mechanisms of a writer. The critical goal for Foucault and other new historicists is not to access the individual talent or genius of the writer; rather it is "to grasp the subject's points of insertion, modes of functioning, and system of dependencies" (274). But can we grasp a "subject's point of insertion" into the cultural discourse without comprehending the subjective inserter? The importance of knowing "who is speaking" is that such knowledge of genesis permits us a closer inspection of the means by which individuals transcribe, transform, translate ideology into language. Knowing this cultural process is a matter of knowing how *and* who. Just as the study of fluid texts enables us to enact the freeplay of language, so, too, can our analysis of textual fluidity—writing, revision, and versions—help us historicize the cultural functionality of creative process: the insertions of self into discourse, the modes of revision, the interdependency of writer and culture.

I hope this book will show that the notion of textual fluidity is compatible with current critical approaches. But some modifications are in order. To be sure, a writer's "presence" in a text is in that individual's "absence," but when we turn from print-texts to manuscript, and in particular a working draft such as the *Typee* manuscript, that paradoxical absence is felt all the more vividly, and it is not an undifferentiated blank. A cancellation or insertion in manuscript is the visible sign of altered intentions. When we observe a revision, we "see" the vestige of a writer's changings, and in this way the writer's absence takes on more presence, or more precisely, we begin to perceive layerings of absence. A revision has a beginning, middle, and end, and its end does not negate the beginning or middle. A revision occupies space and reflects the passage of time; it reveals options and choices; it has direction. It is a chord of dissonances and harmonies, and not a single note. A writer's revision presents us with multiple texts vying for position on the page. In revision, writers exist, it may be said, not in the linear sequence of their words but in the shifting tides of the language they use, in their *choice* of words and the distance between one choice and the next. This is a different order of absence, and of presence.

Deconstruction and new historicism need not abandon their separately derived myths of the Death of the Author. But in light of the realities of literary production, they need to expand their horizons of textuality to include the full panoply of material variation that constitutes the fluid text. After all, the variants in a working draft manuscript, or in revised or expurgated editions, or in translations and adaptations deconstruct along the same principles as any single, materially frozen print-text. The only difference is that a fluid text deconstructs more complexly, and more vividly. Moreover, these fluidities enable us to construct more fully the historical moment of the interpenetrations of an individual writer and a culture's discourse. If we allow textual fluidity the critical validity it merits, then we are obliged to give renewed status to the writer. Thus, if we want to know how language works and how to historicize linguistic processes, we must inspect writers writing and revising as well as readers reading.

For Melville, these acts of writing and revision were a process of "unfolding," which he first articulated in a June 1851, letter to Hawthorne. Pausing in the "flurry" of finishing *Moby-Dick* to write his friend, Melville considered his "development" up to that point.

> Until I was twenty-five, I had no development at all. From my twenty-fifth year I date my life. Three weeks have scarcely passed, at any time between then and now, that I have not unfolded within myself. But I feel that I am now come to the inmost leaf of the bulb, and that shortly the flower must fall to the mould.[13]

Here is one recently established Author writing to a more fully established Author, but more importantly it is a writer writing to a writer about writing.

The passage is most often cited as evidence of Melville's ominous exhaustion as he worked to finish the unfinishable *Moby-Dick*. But it also establishes Melville's conception of the birth date of his artistic "life." This biographical moment is not the death of his father in childhood, not his whaling years, or even that month he spent living among the "cannibals" of Taipivai, but the moment in 1845 at age twenty-five when he began to write. Of course, Melville had written before: letters, adolescent love poems now lost, even two published short stories. But in his twenty-fifth year, just back from four years at sea, Melville was another person altogether and ready to write anew, and to dive: he wrote *Typee*. While that book strikes us as a freshman endeavor lacking the depth and complexity of *Moby-Dick*, Melville clearly proclaims that the composition of this work triggered in him a series of "unfoldings" that would culminate in *Moby-Dick*. In the past, scholars have taken Melville at his word and characterized his confession of exhaustion as an admission of artistic depletion evident in his subsequent works, which never quite equal *Moby-Dick*. But readers today need to know that Melville's exhaustion after so much unfolding was only temporary. Melville may have tired of the "growing" he self-mockingly complained of in another letter to Hawthorne, but he never tired of growth, and he never tired of writing. Melville was a relentless writer, more than an Author, by which I mean he succeeded far better in the practice of composition than in playing the role of a literary representative of the culture (although he played that role when it suited his mood and has come to play that role, posthumously). With his Whale behind him he went on writing, pursuing new Krakens (as he called his next novel, *Pierre*), and astonishingly enough new kinds of writing: tales, then poems, then prose & poem concoctions. He never ceased writing; he never ceased unfolding.[14]

For Melville, writing was an act of expansion revealing layer upon layer of hidden consciousnesses; it was self-genesis. He feared that in completing *Moby-Dick* he was nearing the last unfolding—the "naught" at the center of the bulb of his being—and we are drawn to *Moby-Dick* because of its dalliance with this nothingness. However, we are also drawn to *Typee* as Melville's first unfolding, a plunge into new aesthetic, sexual, and political worlds formerly unexplored, undeveloped, within the young man. As a single print-text, *Typee* gives no real sense of this "development." But as a fluid text, *Typee*'s many versions, in particular its working draft manuscript, reveals material evidence of the twenty-five-year-old struggling with words, readers, and himself. In its numerous textual fluidities we find Melville unfolding.

My study of Melville's unfoldings in *Typee* is in three parts—theoretical, historical, and editorial—and it is projected to appear in two books, the volume you now hold and a second entitled *Melville Unfolding*. I apologize for the confusion. This complex formatting makes sense if you know the course of my project and the recent development of computer technology.

I began my study soon after the discovery of the three-chapter *Typee* manuscript in 1983. My plan was simply to transcribe this fragment so that fellow Melville scholars could read it. It was to be a local venture. But I soon found that "reading" a fluid text such as this required a fairly sophisticated pair of "trifocals." Moreover, I came to feel that conventional methods of transcription were inadequate to the task of rendering a writer's revisions, especially if the object is to make those revisions and their interpretive meanings accessible to students, critics, even general readers—all of whom I have discovered have an automatic fascination with revision. They fix on these fluidities like Ishmael gazing at the sea: meditation and fluid texts are wedded forever. Furthermore: I came to feel that the current debates among textual scholars, while stimulating, did not always hit the mark in addressing the problem of the relevance of textual fluidity, revision, and versions in critical thinking and literary analysis. Inevitably, my attempts to transcribe a manuscript and teach it drew me into critical and editorial theory. Those same attempts to understand the *Typee* manuscript led me to a deeper investigation of Melville's method of composition, his use of sources, his strategies of writing, self-expression, and concealment, even his evolving sexuality and political ideology. In a sense, I found that I could offer a narrative of Melville's revision that was in fact not only a history of the composition of the entire work but of the young writer's growth as an artist.

Thus, and to return, this project has three dimensions. Part 1 initiates a theoretical discourse on the fluid text, which offers a vocabulary that enables me to articulate in part 2 a narrative of Melville's revisions of *Typee*. And the evidence for all this is located in an innovative "fluid-text edition" of the *Typee* manuscript in part 3. Parts 2 and 3 constitute *Melville Unfolding* and appear together in one print volume, along with an electronic component complementing part 3's editorial apparatus. The present volume, *The Fluid Text*, is designed for those readers interested primarily in the project's theoretical dimension. It uses the *Typee* manuscript as a case study to exemplify problems concerning textual scholarship, editing, and critical interpretation, as they relate to theoretical investigation of the fluid text. *The Fluid Text* does not include the fuller historical and editorial studies of parts 2 and 3.

The following chapters in *The Fluid Text* perform a number of important steps. In the first three chapters, I try to integrate useful conceptions of textuality as they have emerged in the recent textual debate between intentionalist and materialist editors. In chapters four and five, I draw upon European genetic editorial theory to explore the nature of revision in an attempt to provide a critical vocabulary for the literary and cultural analysis of fluid texts. The remainder of the book responds to a call Peter Shillingsburg issues toward the end of *Resisting Texts:* "If it is practically impossible simultaneously to establish a single standard text and to acknowledge multiplicity and indeterminacy, then I think we should seriously consider some major alterations in the way we present scholarly editions" (185). In chapter 6, I examine the additional "impossibility" (or near impossibility) of reading textual fluidity and argue that while fluid texts will always involve a struggle for readers, the "pleasures of the fluid text" are profound and worth pursuing. Accordingly, in chapter 7, I argue that editors of fluid texts must strategize creatively in order to make their editions not only accessible but pleasurable and more self-consciously critical. They must at the very least involve a "synergy of book and screen."

Those wishing to plunge deeper into the exhilarating "mess" of the *Typee* manuscript and its tracings of Melville's process of unfolding are invited to continue on to *Melville Unfolding.* This is a historical construction of the composition of *Typee.* In particular I examine three unfoldings as they are manifested in three inferred versions located in the revisions found on the working draft. What I have found in this analysis is fascinating evidence of Melville's attempts to "colonize" his sexualities in the context of his increased awareness of the ideologies of Pacific imperialism. Here, I also offer a "fluid-text edition" of the *Typee* manuscript, including photofacsimiles and a transcription of Melville's manuscript itself along with individual revision narratives for each of the five hundred or so revision sites found in the manuscript. In addition, I have prepared an electronic version of the manuscript that renders Melville's revision graphically and works synergistically with the print transcription.

My hope is that, taken together, both *The Fluid Text* and *Melville Unfolding* will give a fair reckoning of how we may proceed beyond textual debate to a new integration of scholarship and reading, of freeplay and the history of freeplay, of intentions and texts, of the processes of creativity and the realities of cultural discourse. But I hope they will also give a more concrete presence to an absence called Melville, one who in his twenty-fifth year embarked upon the writing of a book that was an unfolding of himself, which became the trigger for further unfoldings as he continued to write, and which have in turn triggered ceaseless unfoldings in generations of readers. Fluid texts are a fact, not a theory, and they are the fact of our own unfolding.

CHAPTER ONE

The Textual Debate

Intended Texts and Social Texts

*I see no other possibility but a version
like mine, which wavers between personal
interpretation and a resigned rigor.*

—Jorge Luis Borges, on translating
Leaves of Grass

Our first awareness of textual fluidity may come accidentally when we chance upon a typo, or what seems to be a typo, in the book we are reading. The word or line does not seem quite right. Perhaps some printer has made an error, and we are reminded that writing is finally a mechanical process whose transformations are not always exact. Or the wording is readable but oddly unexpected, and we wonder if the writer really meant it, in which case we experience an equally unanticipated encounter with the problem of intentionality. In either case, we generally move on. But our fullest exposure to a fluid text is through textual scholarship and scholarly editions of literary works.

While most assume that textual scholarship is the means by which fixed texts are established, it is, in fact, a discipline for the effective management of fluid texts. It is also a method for making sense of textual fluidities, and as a "making" of sense, it reflects the judgments of the makers of texts, both the originating writer and subsequent editors; it is, therefore, inescapably critical. And the nature of textual editing is itself the focus of critical debate. We cannot fully understand the nature of fluid texts, and how they are to be managed, without understanding the

18 ⚭ THE FLUID TEXT

disciplines of textual scholarship and the logics of editorial theory. In particular, we need to inquire into the ways in which a fluid text is a confluence of public events and private intentions.[1]

Textual scholarship and editing are professional phenomena that occur when people recognize that a particular document is so artistically compelling, historically important, critically relevant, or even financially promising that they want to see it reproduced. This is why certain texts, like *Moby-Dick,* may be edited and others, like Melville's recently discovered Christmas mailing list, may not. Since art, criticism, historicism, and the market are "sometime things," favored works will come and go; new texts and new kinds of text will enter the canon; and editors will clamber to get these texts to the public. There was a time between 1851 and 1892 when few read *Moby-Dick* or saw it as being particularly relevant, and no new editions of it were published.[2] That has changed. A time may come when Melville's mailing list becomes relevant to a critical argument, and those arguing the point will want to quote the list. Merely as a service to readers, they might consider reproducing the list in facsimile, but certain list items are bound to be indecipherable even in a blowup, and those concerned will naturally consider transcribing the list into a readable form to accompany the facsimile.

In making a transcription, editors will inevitably come face to face with matters of intentionality. The list might have names crossed out or squeezed in; check marks may appear next to names; the names may have an apparent or not so apparent order; additional text (such as a draft of a line from "Bartleby") may be inscribed on the same sheet of paper as the list. Indeed, the document appears to be an accretion of various intentions stemming from various times. But how will these matters of intentionality be conveyed in the transcription? And other questions will emerge: who are these people, why are they on this list, when was the list compiled, is it really a Christmas list? The editor will also have to consider how the transcription itself will be displayed: Is it accurate, intelligible, comprehensive, and, we must add, demonstrable of the critical arguments that make the list relevant in the first place? In time, one fact will become clear: editing, even the editing of a simple list, is more than a mere service to readers; it is a critical act and one that calls textuality itself into question.

In confronting the physicality of the working draft manuscript of *Typee* for the first time, I found myself as a critic having to look more deeply into textual scholarship and the principles of textuality. Wanting to quote from the manuscript, I needed to transcribe. Trying to transcribe, I had to decipher scribbles, cancellations, and insertions. Transcription is the seemingly simple conversion of handwriting into print, a presumably mechanical matter. But the manuscript text before me soon became an object that defied perception. Such a vexatious "not-me" challenges our self-satisfied assurances that text-objects are definable, much less interpretable. I have gazed at Melville's handwriting now for over ten years, and each time I return to a passage of his writing, it requires a period of retraining for me to make it readable. I read a crucial, illegible word in the *Typee* manuscript as "promotion"; whereas Hershel Parker sees it as "peroration."[3] The word Melville intended is one word only; the scribble we both "see" is the same; but the readings we give to it vary with our differing rhetorical agendas. I doubt that Parker and I, or anyone, will be able to resolve this issue; all we can do is engage in a discourse upon the intended text, and its intentionality is defined by that discourse.

In deciphering this and other scribbles, one has no recourse but to speculate upon intended meanings, to take leaps. Not only did I find that I had to take leaps to identify words, I also found myself hypothesizing about hidden words suggested by "false starts" or partially executed words on the manuscript page, and partially or totally obscured words lurking beneath cancellation lines. And with a myriad of cancellations and insertions on each manuscript page, I also confronted the issue of revision and the sequence of Melville's revisions. The difficulty of "mere" transcription gave me new insight into the problematic physicality of words. Wanting to know the critical nature of Melville's scribbles and revisions—his textual fluidities—is what seduced me into becoming a textual scholar.

Rather than custodians, textual scholars are the managers and explainers of the fluid text. They assemble and record the available evidence of textual fluidity in a literary work. In their editions they display these materials as fully as their principles of selection will allow, rendering them in one way or another depending upon the degree of showcasing they wish to provide. And they justify their arrangements with arguments based on historical, aesthetic, even political and psychological reasonings. Exactly how an editor might manage an edition—whether to emphasize one, two, or all moments of intentionality throughout a literary work—is a principal problem confronted by all textual scholars. And these protocols depend upon the way we conceptualize a literary work, perhaps as a coherent whole, or as a single moment in a process of writing, or as the entire writing process itself, insofar as it is possible to conceive and then render such processes. If we are to edit the fullness of a fluid text, we are obliged to develop protocols, even ways of reading and modes of analysis, that can elucidate the revision as revision. This means devising new display strategies for the fluid-text edition (a matter to be discussed in chapter 7). But it also means revisiting some fundamental questions of textual scholarship: what is a literary work, and what is the relation of an edition to that conception of the work?

The field of textual scholarship is presently engaged in a penetrating textual debate that is posing these and other problems. It is also affecting our discussions of the ontology of literary works, historicism itself, and the way critics do business. In chapters 2 and 3, I want to analyze certain specifics of this debate as found in the works of G. Thomas Tanselle and Jerome J. McGann, and eventually propose a synthesis of conflicting views that may help us better envision a way to edit, critique, and teach the fluid text. For the moment, however, we can explore some of the broader features of the textual debate through the example of *Typee*.

The Textual Debate and Typee

The central controversy, which may be loosely defined as a conflict between intentionalists and materialists, is a debate over the validity of "the critical edition." General readers are likely to call a critical edition a "definitive" text, established for all time by scholars, and complemented with notes and critical essays in the back. This is a double misconception: no edition, critical or otherwise, can be "definitive," and an edition is "critical" not simply because publishers bind the primary text along with secondary criticism. The critical edition is a genre of scholarly editing in which a text is constructed usually after the inspection, and sometimes the conflation, of significant versions of the work; it is also a text that is invariably emended along certain principles so as to bring it closer to an announced notion of intentionality. This approach differs from diplomatic and facsimile editing, which attempts to reproduce, without conflation or emendation, a singular occurrence or physical version of a work, like a particular manuscript, or a first or revised edition so as to render the text as closely as possible to the historic original. There are subgenres of critical editing, such as the variorum, which displays all textual variants of a work on the reading page; or the eclectic edition, which prints a "clear reading text" based on an emended copy-text and displays variants in an appended, textual apparatus; or the "genetic edition," which integrates coded, sequentialized variants into the reading text. These are all *critical* because editorial judgment is required in constructing the edition. Without a doubt, a fluid-text edition can be nothing other than a critical edition, but as I hope to show, it will have to expand considerably upon the present protocols of critical editing.

For intentionalists, a critical edition may be designed to approximate a writer's intentions at a given moment in the writing process and is itself the end product of a process of historical "construction." Once editors decide to make a critical edition of a work, they will first collate all of the relevant historical versions of that work and assemble a list of the variant texts (or textual fluidities) found throughout the versions. And there can be many such variants due to various reasons: the accidents of printers, the censorings of publishers, or the revisions of the writer. The critical editor's role is to judge which of these variants is authorial or otherwise, and which to showcase. On the basis of some given criterion of intentionality, the editor will also select one complete version of the work (let's say, a set of corrected page proofs or the first printed edition) to be a *copy-text*. This is a version one chooses because one can argue that it more reliably represents the writer's intentions than the others, and it is the one upon which the editor bases the edition.

But what about the significant variant readings in the other, non-copy-text versions that have some claim to being at certain points in the text better representatives of the writer's intention than what appears in the copy-text? If, for instance, the editor feels that a variant word or phrase taken from a particular point in, let's say, the second edition has more authority than what appears at the corresponding point in the first-edition copy-text, the editor may then, with regard to the announced criterion of intentionality, change or "emend," the copy-text wording at this one point to this particular second-edition wording. Such emendations may occur in hundreds of places throughout a critical edition. The final product, then, is a conflated or eclectic text, which consists mostly of the copy-text but which also contains several substitute wordings, or emendations, seamlessly inserted at various places into that copy-text. These emendations may be a comma, just one word, or as much as a line, paragraph, or even chapter substituted for the reading found in the copy-text. Presumably, the substituted variant text comes closer to the form of authorial intention that the editor hopes to construct than the version found in the copy-text.

It is, however, important to note that since a literary work evolves through several aesthetically valid stages of a writer's intention in both manuscript and print, one editor is likely to disagree with another on the choice of copy-text and the degree of emendation. Thus, we can envision a variety of different critical editions of the same work, each deriving from a different editor's different assumptions of which phase of intentionality is most worth reproducing, which copy-text to use, and which variants to honor. Hence, for this reason, no critical edition can be "definitive"; all are the products of judgment and the object of debate. Even so, publishers, and readers have erroneously labeled certain critical editions definitive, and this inevitable slippage (see chap. 3) is one cause of the materialist's complaint about the scholarly genre of the critical edition.

Of modern editors, W. W. Greg is best known for his development of the critical edition in Renaissance studies, and Fredson Bowers extended the genre to nineteenth-century American texts. In the past two decades, the critical edition's ablest defender has been G. Thomas Tanselle, who has been most illuminating in adapting received editorial principles to meet challenges posed by equally capable defenders in the materialist camp of textual editing. Not surprising is the fact that these challenges stem from disagreements over the importance of fluid texts and how they may be edited and displayed. Chief among the challengers is Jerome J. McGann, who along with others intrigued by his notion of "social text," argues that the eclectic nature of critical editions focusing solely upon final intentions (as many such editions do) effectively dehistoricizes the literary work. Because an eclectic critical edition does not reprint as its reading text an actual historical version of a work (let's say a first or a revised edition published in the writer's lifetime), but conflates copy-text and emendations to make a new version (one, in fact, that the writer never authorized), this new, conflated version seems to transcend the historical moment in which the work appeared. It is a well-crafted, scholarly patchwork of texts designed typically to approach a form of an author's socially unimpeded intentions, but does so at the expense of all other historical versions and their potentially meaningful moments in the social history of the work.

As it happens, the modern editing of *Typee* provides a good example of the intentionalist-materialist debate over the strengths and limitations of the critical edition.

Melville first published *Typee* in England with John Murray in February 1846. Based on a four-week adventure in 1842 on the Marquesan island of Nuku Hiva and his "residence" during that time among the allegedly cannibalistic inhabitants of the island's remote valley of Taipivai, Melville's travel book romance was an instant success, securing Melville an immediate, international reputation. In March 1846, the American publisher John Wiley issued a separate American edition, a resetting of the British text, minus five or so lusty passages deemed unsuitable by Wiley. These first British and American editions vary in numerous other nonconsequential ways, but the biggest change in the text of *Typee* was to come in the fall of 1846, when, in response to criticisms from the evangelical press about Melville's antimissionary stance, Melville relented to Wiley's request for further expurgations of *Typee* in over one hundred places. These expurgations included the excision of several half-chapters and one whole chapter as well as numerous single lines and phrases. Wiley also added to this revised version of the American edition specific changes Melville requested as well as his brief sequel, "The Story of Toby" (which recounts his partner Richard Tobias Greene's escape from Taipivai). In Britain, John Murray declined to follow any of the American expurgations in his subsequent printings of *Typee,* but he did add "The Story of Toby" and kept publishing *Typee* on his side of the Atlantic in its augmented but unrevised and uncensored version. Thus, throughout the nineteenth and well into the twentieth century Americans read their reduced version of *Typee* and the British read their fuller version. Two cultures; two *Typees.*

What is significant about this fluid text is that Melville intended two texts at two times, and each intended text is in some way shaped by external forces, also intentional: those of censorious editors and angry readers. In 1968 scholars Harrison Hayford, Hershel Parker, and Tanselle himself published their Northwestern-Newberry (NN) critical edition of *Typee,* which gives a full accounting of this textual history.[4] Their decision was to use an early printing of the British edition as copy-text, thus effectively restoring the American expurgations, and to emend that British copy-text with variants from the American texts if the American variants could be shown to represent Melville's politically and economically unencumbered intentions. The goal of this edition was to construct a text that represents the "private Melville"[5] or "what Melville actually desired rather than what he acquiesced to at the publisher's request" (*Typee*, 309), and to emend "only when a convincing argument can be made that the change reflects Melville's own wishes regarding the artistic integrity of the book, apart from any practical considerations involving public response, sales, or the editorial policy of the publisher" (316).

In reading this critical edition, readers first come upon the editors' 271-page "clear reading text" of *Typee*. The idea of such a text is to permit a pleasurable reading unencumbered by any footnotes or editorial interventions. Although no attempt is made to recreate the typography or layout of an original, historical edition, this clear reading text in a sense emulates what might be considered a first-time or unself-conscious (i.e., nonscholastic) reading experience. In the NN *Typee* the reading text is followed by 101 pages of scholarship: Leon Howard's historical note, the editors' textual note, a transcription of the one leaf of the *Typee* manuscript then known to exist, and the edition's textual apparatus, including lists of all variants and emendations to the copy-text. With the apparatus, readers can inspect the editors' judgments in emendation and in effect assemble on their own the two American versions of *Typee* not selected as copy-text. By all accounts the NN edition of *Typee* is a remarkable accommodation of the general reader's need for a coherent text and the scholar/critic's desire for a full record of textual fluidity.

Even though its goal of approaching the "private Melville" is clear enough, the edition necessarily exhibits varying degrees of judgment in its textual emendations within that criterion of privacy, from the unarguable to the highly debatable. Let's look at three exemplary emendations to the *Typee* copy-text.

In one instance, the editors substitute the word *country* found in the American revised edition of the novel for the word *valley*, which appears in the first British edition copy-text. The change seems to be an indifferent, hence probably Melville's intentional, respecification of the terrain, but the reasoning for accepting it is based on a logic derived from our understanding of how the revised edition was created. To perform the expurgations, printers had to break apart and reassemble the original American plates of type. With any major reshifting of type such as this, typographical errors are an inevitability, especially in the vicinity of the reset areas. If a change in text is found near any of those lines printers had to break apart and reset in order to accommodate Wiley's expurgations, that change is most likely a result of the printer's error (or intervention) in resetting the type. But since the change to *country* occurs in an otherwise unreassembled set of pages, the likelihood is that printers did not make a hasty corruption but had to have made a special effort to alter *valley* to *country,* and such an effort would have most likely have been demanded by Melville himself, and the change was, therefore, probably made at Melville's insistence. Moreover, since the change from *valley* to *country* does not seem to be induced by any desire to appease the religious, political, or economic demands of publishers, it is deemed to be a more precise fulfillment of Melville's final private intention.

The same logic of reset lines applies in the more important case of Melville's "L-word." Here, the phrase *literally interpreted* used in copy-text to refer to Tommo's understanding of the Polynesian language is emended in the American revised version to a virtual antonym, *liberally interpreted.* The assumption is that the change from *literally* to *liberally* was a correction on Melville's part and not the result of any external political coercion or rethinking. But linguistically and from a reader's perspective, the change is so fraught with social implications, that one could argue (more convincingly than with the change to *country*) that Melville's change from *literal* to *liberal* was in fact a political matter, and therefore arguably *not* a candidate for change under the NN editorial principles.[6]

Not all of Melville's later revisions like *country* and *liberally* are accepted in the NN *Typee.* For instance, when Tommo says good-bye to Fayaway in chapter 34, Melville has Fayaway "sobbing indignantly" in the first British edition, but in the revised American edition she sobs "convulsively." The change to *convulsively* is clearly Melville's, but the NN editors have elected to retain the copy-text variant *indignantly.* Their assumption is that Melville's late intention to drop *indignantly* (which in context reveals Tommo's recognition of his betrayal of Fayaway, and is therefore more ironic) was influenced by some unspecified "politic reason" (*Typee,* 333). It is not clear here whether by "politic" the NN editors mean to refer to matters of politics or politesse. Chances are the change to *convulsively* (which essentially removes any hint of betrayal and gets Tommo off the hook) had more to do with private family matters than coercions from publishers or general readers. More specifically, at the time, Melville was courting his future wife, Elizabeth Shaw, whom he affianced around August 31, 1846, soon after sending his revisions to Wiley,[7] and the removal of *indignantly* may have been a small cover-up of Melville's island indiscretions for the sake of the feelings of his future wife and in-laws. The NN editors do not allow Melville this little cover-up, and perhaps with good reason. But what is lost in this refusal to grant Melville his final intention is the *fact* of his attempted cover-up, a fact that would affect our reading of Melville's conclusion and one that cannot be showcased in the clear reading text of the critical edition of *Typee.*

A final category of emendation is a change in text based solely upon the editors' sense of a need for change. In some cases a copy-text reading may make little or no sense, and editors may choose to emend the text even though no actual or intelligible variant of that text exists as a substitution in other print versions of the work. For instance, in the British copy-text for the NN *Typee,* we find the dubious phrase "Lacadaemonian nations" used in reference to the Polynesian style of mothering. In this case, the NN editors invented a new substitute phrasing as an emendation: they emended "Lacadaemonian nations" to "Lacadaemonian matrons." Although Wiley's American editions change the British plural *nations* to the singular *nation,* this option seems equally unlikely, as Melville's sentence calls for some maternal rather than political referent. Hence, the editors speculate that Melville intended *matrons.* In support of this invented option, and further speculating on how the erroneous *nations* ever came into being, they also argue that a copyist or printer may have (mis)read Melville's handwritten *matrons* as *nations.* Indeed, anyone familiar with Melville's handwriting can imagine such a mistake.

These examples indicate the nature of editorial emendation and the variety of critical judgments editors must make when they emend, from the choosing among actual variants to the invention of new wording. Some scholars and critics take umbrage at such editorial intervention, but their umbrage is largely unfounded. Editors have no choice but to make choices because texts are invariably variable for various reasons and with variant consequences. Textual fluidity is a fact, and it is the textual scholar's job to manage it. Critical editing, then, cannot will away textual fluidity; it can only describe it and, in the form of a critical edition, manage the display of it. Nor can editors confine or contain it. Indeed, editors' choices inevitably constitute yet another version of the fluid text they are editing. Thus, critical editing perpetuates textual fluidity.

Of course, we might question the edition's premise of focusing on

Melville's private or socially unencumbered intentions, or accepting that premise, we might argue, as one surely can with *liberally, indignantly,* or *matrons,* that an emendation may not fit the premise. But the fact that disagreements arise over particular judgments does not invalidate the critical edition as a genre. Indeed, a principal component of any critical edition is its announced presentation of arguments for copy-text and emendation in its notes and textual apparatus. And, generally speaking, the NN edition of *Typee* is a model in this regard.

But the materialist's complaint about eclectic critical editions such as this lies in part in the relation of the "clear reading text" to its editorial apparatus. In the NN *Typee* there are no footnotes to alert readers to the novel's many textual variants and emendations. As already noted, these fluidities are recorded in the back of the book. The concern is not that critical editions ignore textual fluidity but rather the smoothness of the clear reading text, a hallmark of critical editing, in effect denies us an immediate awareness of the actual roughness of the textual record, and textuality itself. Moreover, the relegation of the evidence of textual fluidity to appendices de-emphasizes the material reality of the processes of composing and publishing a literary work. As a social text, *Typee* needs to be displayed in all of its versions and editions, so that readers may have more immediate access to what Melville wrote and what was censored. It would be more instructive, McGann might say, to reissue British and American versions separately, or side by side, as an array of variant data. By displaying textual fluidity in the highly abstract form of the textual apparatus, and by showcasing the clear reading text, the eclectic critical edition unwittingly promotes among readers the naive assumption that the critical edition before them is "definitive" or "authorized" rather than the product of editorial intervention (which, of course, all editions, critical or documentary, must be). It encourages readers to assume that the Melville text before them is "Melville" derived unmediated from Melville.

Even readers who know the history of *Typee*'s composition and its different versions and who recognize the editors' emendations for the critical acts they are may nevertheless be lulled into the view that the edition before them is in fact what the writer intended, and not what it is: a highly educated speculation upon intentionality. The materialist's worry, then, is that readers may forget that the critical edition of *Typee* is a modern editorial construction aiming to approximate what the writer wanted before society and his contemporary editors forced changes

upon him. And this leads to a greater amnesia: that Melville actually succeeded in his time in overcoming the "practical considerations" of his
publishers and public.

It is with this anxiety over what an editor can and cannot do, and
what readers make of what editors do do, that materialists argue that the
eclectic critical edition actually subverts the historicity of a work. The
intentionalist would riposte that all the relevant textual history exists in
the textual apparatus for readers to inspect, and that it is not too much
to ask readers to flip to the back of the volume to make such inspection.
Moreover, the intentionalist notes that all historical construction is speculative, that critical judgments in editing are unavoidable, in fact desirable, and that the critical edition of *Typee* provides a vivid manifestation
of what scholars think the historical Melville probably wanted at a certain historical moment of creation. Seeking out a probable past is no
crime. Rather than subverting or transcending history, says the intentionalist, a critical edition is the best an editor can do to find the past and
engage a reader in it. It is, contrary to the materialist objection, the
essence of historicity.

To clarify the fundamental disagreement between intentionalist
and materialist over the historicity of a critical edition, we next need to
explore the strengths and limits of the variant historicisms of each camp.
At this juncture it is worth recalling that what we call history is not the
same as what we call the past. History is a writing up of the past, based
upon reports and primary artifacts that are themselves largely written
documents. Although it may appear to be a primary artifact, a critical
edition is essentially a history, or "write up" of the primary document in
question. The clear reading text is a crafted rendering of a past moment
of intentionality; the editorial notes and apparatus are a narrative of the
crafting. It goes without saying that such narrative constructs are necessarily subjective. Both Tanselle and McGann are aware that textual
scholarship is no more or less subjective an enterprise than any other historicist enterprise. And yet both see historical methodology as an exercise to reduce subjectivity or at least balance the desire to put ourselves
into the past (nostalgia) with the desire to acquire a distance between
ourselves and the past (analysis). For Tanselle, this process "teach[es] us
how to ask textual questions in a way that does justice to the capabilities
of mind" and in doing so "helps us see the process by which humanity
attempts, sometimes successfully, to step outside itself."[8] As a historicist,
McGann also recognizes the philosophical necessity of maintaining a

certain self-consciousness of one's subjectivity in trying to "step out-side"; however, in doing so he proposes a notion of history that comprises the present and future as well. In speaking of Pound, he writes that "the historical task is to attempt a reconstruction of that past [as seen in and through the present.] . . . But the Cantos reminds us that history includes the future and the historical task involves as well the construction of what shall be."[9]

Despite these measured stances, the two polarized historicisms of this textual debate have been characterized as exhibiting one kind of idealism or another. Tanselle may be called a Platonist seeking contact with lost moments of past creativity; McGann the presentist redefining past literary works as social events that operate now as then and onward to encompass a vision of futurity. But both have far more to offer. On the one hand, Tanselle grounds his attempt at the recuperation of past mental acts (or literary works) in a compelling ontology of textuality in order to heighten our awareness of human desire in certain acts of creation (*Rationale,* 76). On the other, McGann bases his historical recovery of the versions of works (or material documents) on a Marxian poetics that defines texts as events, which function to induce a sense of reality in readers through the representation or rather performance of the "incommensurate" nature of language and experience.[10] Neither approach denies the fluidity of texts, but finally neither provides a satisfactory strategy of editing that fully showcases revision, which is the driving force of textual fluidity. Nevertheless, both offer ideas that are crucial to the enterprise of editing the fluid text. And a closer look at Tanselle's ontology and McGann's poetics will enable us to fashion a more comprehensive approach to the fluid text and a fuller critical vocabulary for their analysis.

CHAPTER TWO

Work as Concept

Intentionalist Historicism
and the Ontology of Literary Work

Your thoughts dont have words every day
They come a single time
Like signal esoteric sips
Of the communion Wine

—Emily Dickinson, Poem 1476

Since textual fluidity is the product of revision, we cannot know revision until we have some sense of what we can and cannot know about intentions. Probably the most articulate spokesman for intentionalism in textual editing is G. Thomas Tanselle, who also offers an important framework of ideas for the better understanding of fluid texts.

Tanselle's perspective, as elaborated most concisely in his *Rationale of Textual Criticism,* begins with the understanding that language, apart from the act of writing, is intangible. This is indisputable when we consider that words first emerge in mind (not on paper) out of a struggle to give expression to feeling and thought before they are subvocalized, or uttered aloud in physical sound, or written down in some material form. The act of writing is the tangible extension of a complex process of mental acts that begins with vague gropings at ideas or expressions and invariably includes recursive sessions of preliminary scribbling, then more thinking based on the scribbling, then more writing, and so on until the literary work finally manifests itself in a material form that the writer might say is finished.[1] But even in this finished state, it may be

30

argued (and both Tanselle and McGann do) that the completed product (a document, or written text) does not put an end to the writer's
mental acts regarding that work, nor can it even be said that this particular written text is a fair approximation of what the writer would like to
say at that particular moment of so-called completion. The question
arises, then, where exactly does a literary work of art exist. On the page
or in the mind, in the written product or the mental process?

The answer, of course, is that it exists in both realms, and this may
be one source of literature's uncanny ability to use physical objects
(words) to move writer and reader toward a shared mental state and
transcendence of the physical. But more specifically this dual ontology,
according to Tanselle, is the reason that the analysis of intentions as a
historicist method is necessary for constructing literary works. To clarify,
we may follow Tanselle's familiar definitions of three literary states of
being: work, text, and document. A *work* is the set of intentions, desires,
and visions existing in the author's mind that together constitute the
author's conception of the literary work of art. As such, a work has no
tangible presence, but this is not to say that it is not real, nor that it is,
according to some detractors, some sort of Platonic ideal.[2] A Platonic
ideal is the preexistent form of an object or value that is a universalized
abstraction of that object or value. In Tanselle's view, the literary work
is not "ideal" in this specialized sense that it is the full and complete
abstract concept of a literary work. Rather, it is a mental version residing
in the particularly muddy quarters of a particular mind intended at a particular time. And it encompasses a full range of individualized intentionalities from the general and generic, "I want to write a romance about
whales" to the more specific, "My first line shall be 'Call me . . .' what?
Israel? no, *Ishmael?*"

The labeling of Tanselle's actually quite practical notion of the
intangibility of the work as mere Platonism has led to some serious misconceptions. Chief among them is the idea that the so-called work as
ideal is a transcendence of history. In grounding the work as a historically actual set of literary visions, Tanselle's aim is not to derive some
"perfect" or ideal literary work that transcends time, or the labor of
mental activity, but to approximate the work an author had strived for
in mind, or what Melville in one of his anxious letters to Evert Duyckinck called the "book in a man's brain" (*Correspondence*, 174). In
Tanselle's words, a writer's "desires have just as much historical reality as
do the texts that were finally published" (*Rationale*, 76), and it is the

text of this historically real but necessarily speculative and conceptualized work that the intentionalist textual scholar attempts to locate. Here, *text* denotes the projected *wording* not necessarily the actual *words* an author intends.

I use *wording* to indicate the ineffableness of the text of a work as opposed to concrete *words* found in the texts of a document. This distinction may be difficult to comprehend, but a famous textual fluidity in Poe's poetry may help. For the concluding line of "Annabel Lee," Poe originally wrote "In her tomb by the sounding sea." A later version revises the line to "in her tomb by the side of the sea." Taken together these two documentary texts indicate a conceptualized, word-less wording that encompasses sound, rhythm, image, thought, and certain lexical possibilities. This still-unformed wording occupies the space between mind and page; it can be talked about or around, or finally manifested through the specific approximations of actual words, as in Poe's two variant lines. Indeed, an important consequence of our perception of the material actuality of such a textual fluidity as this is to heighten our awareness of the intangible reality of the text of the work itself.

Because it is intentional, the text of a work is intangible, but we have a fair chance of knowing this text because it is physically manifested in *documents*. A document can be a single manuscript, a set of proofs, or a copy of a first or subsequent edition; it is any material form in which the text of a work appears. Tanselle's historicist approach is to approximate the wording of a work intended at some given time in the creative process by inspecting and selecting actual words from the material versions or texts of its documents. In turn the historicist editor assembles his or her own material version of the text of the work, which we know as a critical edition.

The necessity of this critical approach derives from the inherent unreliability of documentary texts. Obviously, the only way readers know of the existence of a literary work is through their experience with a document affixed with the title of that work (usually in print, not manuscript, often in a marketplace edition, less often in a scholarly critical edition). But like any physical object, documents are notoriously susceptible to corruptions and variations. I once opened an eagerly awaited copy of a colleague's new book of criticism only to find that the bookbinder had accidentally substituted the opening to *The Great Gatsby* for my colleague's first chapter. When I brought this to my colleague's attention, we marveled at how well his prose had improved since his last book, but we also called his publisher to ascertain in what warehouse the real text of his book might be found.

Publishing is rife with such documentary gaffes. But most are not so easily resolved, or even resolvable. Take, for instance, another seemingly obvious documentary error perpetuated through three versions of "The Town-Ho's Story" (chap. 54 of *Moby-Dick*) in which the entitled whaling craft cruises in the Pacific "eastward" of Lima. Surely, Melville intended to say "westward," and the NN editors of *Moby-Dick* have emended their text accordingly (243.17). Just as we know my colleague did not intend to plagiarize Fitzgerald and can use common sense to correct the "corruption," we can correct Melville.[3] Of course, Melville ("uncommon common sailor" that he was) may not have been using common sense when he wrote *Moby-Dick*. He may have intended a hidden meaning for *eastward;* perhaps, sailing in the Andes was his private metaphor for telling a tall tale.

Editors are obliged to make even the most obvious emendations with trepidation. In 1967, *Moby-Dick* editors Hayford and Parker were understandably baffled by the printed phrase "In thoughts of the visions of the night," which appears in all versions of "The Squeeze of the Hand" (chap. 94). The odd phrasing seemed to them to sound as though a copyist had inadvertently combined two alternative wordings ("In thoughts of the night" and "In visions of the night") one of which Melville had intended to cancel but did not, so that both options, not one or the other, were accidentally printed together. They thought the printed text was a documentary corruption, and they emended the odd phrase in their Norton edition to "In visions of the night." However, a reader wrote in to say that there is a biblical precedent for the oddity. Thus, in their 1988 NN edition they changed the phrasing back to "In thoughts of the visions of the night."[4] It might be argued that in both cases the NN editors would have been better off leaving "Melville's words" alone. But as a representative reader, a textual editor is obliged to ask what any reader would ask when confronted by apparent breakdowns in the text: are these the words Melville meant? And readers are sure to wonder at "In thoughts of the visions of the night." Editors may "blunder" (to use Hayford and Parker's unnecessarily self-derogatory term) in their editorial interventions, but if the textual fluidity is rightly managed, editors will apprise readers of the interventions they make, thus encouraging other readers to admire or complain. More to the point, editorial interventions (right or wrong) expose us to a deeper discourse upon the relation of "Melville's text" to documentary words and the gap they represent between intention and expression.

Documents, then, are the visible products that emerge out of an ongoing, largely invisible process, and the emergence of texts—whether they are manuscripts or books—can only hint at the processes that caused those texts. Each document is like a whale breaching from time to time at the surface of a dark sea that at all other times conceals the twists and turns of its submarine navigations. The actual causes of these breachings are (like the submarine navigations) invisible to us except as they are hinted at in the breaching text-objects themselves. Moreover, these breaching whales or documents are proximal; they are momentous but momentary emergences that can only partially reveal the writer's intended text. Thus, writing itself—either as it transmits texts from mind into manuscript, or from manuscript into print—is always a kind of *miswriting*. It matters not whether these miswritings, or textual fluidities, are possible errors *(eastward* for *westward)* or speculative editorial decodings (like *thoughts/visions*). Nor does the editor presume to "correct" the miswritings. Their value lies in their power to waken us to the problematic linkage between intention and document.

In the case of *Typee*, which has a more unstable textual history than *Moby-Dick*, the tangible documents—with indeterminacies like *peroration/promotion* and revisions like *savage/islander, literal/liberal,* and *indignant/convulsive* running throughout—vary more radically from each other and vary, too, one must assume, from the intended text of the work envisioned by the author. The existence of such textual fluidities underscores our twofold relation to the documents of works. On the one hand, we are dependent upon them as tangible, physical manifestations of the intangible work of art we wish to access. On the other hand, when the physical object does not adequately fulfill our expectations or when the different versions of a text emerge in other documents, we are caught between thoughts of textual corruption and authorial intention; and reading becomes a doubting. The mind of the reader automatically seeks additional and more immediate access to the mind of the writer if only to resolve this doubting.

To explore this problem of documents and mind, let's complicate my colleague's publishing problem a bit. What if the publisher not only substituted *Gatsby* for his opener, but had actually lost the only copy of my colleague's original opening, thus requiring him to recompose his first chapter for publication. And let's also suppose that in recomposing, my colleague could not help but revise. Thus, two documentary versions of the text—a lost original and a printed revision—would exist. And what if in the course of human events my colleague's fame reached the status of a Fitzgerald, and an editor wanting to publish a new edition of my colleague's book discovers behind some publisher's filing cabinet the lost original of his opening, how would that editor edit my colleague's work?

The printed recomposed (and beloved) version, it now seems, is a document that would not have existed without the production gaffe, and surely, the rediscovered original opening has merit; indeed it can be said to be closer to the writer's first intentions. But, the desperately written second version—printed and beloved—might contain expressions (second thoughts, better words) that hit the mark missed in the first, then-lost, now-rediscovered original. What is the ontological status of these two texts? Are they separate versions with separate intentions, or two expressions of the same intention? Which version is more desirable? With these two tangible documents before us, where, in fact, might the actual text of my colleague's work reside? Is it in the two variant documentary versions? or in the warehouse of the writer's mind?

To some extent the answer is both; but ultimately from Tanselle's perspective the answer is that getting at the text of a work means getting into "the minds in which works originate" (*Rationale,* 75). Of course, how one might venture into that mental territory is one of the more obvious problems confronted by intentionalism. And the problem is complicated by the equally obvious fact that the mind we wish to access is, for private and professional reasons, far more fluid than the texts it produces from time to time. Moreover, these evolving documentary texts (like snapshots of a moving object) invariably lag behind the writer's evolving mind. Surely, the solution to the problem of accessing fluid minds through fluid texts would be made simpler if the human mind, like a child, would only just stand still for one moment and say cheese. But it does not. Documents may give us a view of one changed mind and then another, but they only suggest evolution rather than represent it. How, then, do we access and edit a *changing* mind?

My colleague's case highlights another important problem for the intentionalist confronting a fluid text: While intentions surely shift—and it is the shifting we wish to grasp—not all intentional changes in a document indicate a shift in the conception of a work. What constitutes a significant change of mind? Did my colleague reconceptualize his work when he was forced to submit a new opening, or was this "new" opening (the one first printed) a rushed attempt to recollect and re-create word for word what he had failed to put on a backup disk? If, as in the first instance, my colleague did reconceptualize his opening, then the rediscovered original is significant evidence of his earlier thinking and supplies us with an important point of departure for his revised perspective. It helps define the gap between changing mind and changing text. But even if, as in the second instance, the printed revision and rediscovered original documents simply reflect two different attempts at a unitary, seemingly unchanged conception, readers with the assumption that no verbal change is without some degree of mental reconception will find significance in both documents, even if the two documents were (as in some Borgesian fantasy) the same, word for word. Thus, the document might reflect the beginnings of a transformation of thought, not fully comprehended by the writer as he wrote. Significance in this case lies in the fact of verbal change regardless of the degree of intention to change.

It is in the intentionalist's attempt to resolve such problems with a clear reading text, critical edition that the materialist parts company with the intentionalist. And at first one may be inclined to follow. The materialist would argue that my colleague's two openings constitute separate verbal events, and therefore each physical version should be edited separately. But, from the intentionalist perspective, this is only delaying the inevitable plunge into the writer's mind. To begin with, Tanselle would argue, each instance of this fluid text must be edited on its own terms, which is to say textual decisions requiring some cogitation of authorial intent at each moment of creation would have to be made. (For instance, the rediscovered typescript would have real and apparent typos like "eastward of Lima" or even confusing texts like "In thoughts of the vision of the night" that would have to be resolved.) Furthermore, readers would inevitably place these two separately edited texts side by side and, noticing variants, would inevitably ask the kinds of questions we have already begun to ask about the two documents, and these questions would necessarily plunge us back again into the writer's mind. From Tanselle's point of view, the question of origins cannot be obviated by separate editions, only delayed. Ultimately, the issue is not whether to talk about intentions, but how to do so sensibly and with sufficient complexity to manage the textual fluidity of a work as fully as possible.

This begs the question of how we might characterize this act of getting into "the minds in which works originate," or more precisely how do we access past mental events? The short answer is that we do not, but think we do. That is, we only simulate these events and call them editions. Let me explain.

We fantasize if we assume the act of simulating a literary work is a matter of *retrieval*. The past is not an object that can be reproduced; nor is it a series of events that can be relived. The past is not a bone one fetches; it cannot be retrieved. Nor is it possible to *restore* to some unitary original condition an object or text that is the product of a past process—neither a painting like *The Last Judgment* in the Sistine Chapel nor a text like the working draft manuscript of a novel—without erasing various intervening past conditions. Restorations invariably require defoliations. Nor, in fact, can we (to come finally to the term most commonly used) *reconstruct* the past because this implies that the past is some kind of physical construction like the firmaments of heaven, and all we need do is remake that construct from surviving artifacts. These misleading *re-* words—*retrieve, restore, reconstruct*—give us a false sense of our relation to the past. They give the impression that the past is a thing or object that editors and historians can get back to, pluck up, or *re*-create. The use or misuse of these words indicates, I think, our understandable tendency to confuse the tangible evidence that survives (fossil, painting, or documentary text) with the intangible processes that created them (evolution, politics, desire). However, their problematic nature does not dispel Tanselle's fundamental observation that past mental events, as impossible as they are to grasp, are nevertheless real— they happened—and seeking their reality, while speculative, is no fantasy. Intentionalist textual editing is an attempt to *construct* (not *re*-construct) or simulate an edifying version of a past mental event. The predicament posed by my colleague's case is not simply which version to use but how both may be used as tools for the simulation or *construction* of their "originating mind."

Ontology aside, the intentionalist agenda of finding the "originating mind" is to historicize the act of writing. The penetration through text-objects to irretrievable causes, the simulation of works, the construction of editions are the same kinds of problems that confront the historicist in contextualizing the past. But whereas a historian produces a critical explanation of past events, the editor inspects fluid texts and the various modes of intentionality they represent to produce a critical edition. As a reflection of the editor's conception of a writer's past intent, the critical edition is a historicist exercise in discovering a text that represents, in Tanselle's words, a "stage in the history of the work we wish to reconstruct" (*Rationale,* 70). To give shape to this wished-for stage, Tanselle asks us to consider two questions of agency and moment (73). Who (among a work's possible writers and editors) is the creator most worth knowing, and what "period of creativity" is most worth constructing? In posing these questions, Tanselle reveals broad possibilities for critical editing: Editors may focus on single writers or editors, at any moment of literary endeavor; they may construct texts that represent first, final, or intermediate intentions, as they emerge through any solo or collaborative configuration of agency. Contrary to the common belief (made plausible because of common practice, not theory) that critical editing "recovers" works conceived only at that stage in which writers are divorced from social constraints, the critical edition can also be used to display "social texts"—individual instances of a work appearing during moments of social collaboration—as long as the focus is on who intends to say what when. That is, we might envision an edition of *Typee* that emphasizes the editorial intentions in the mind of publisher John Murray, or of John Wiley, as opposed to an edition that represents Melville's mind before he ever met either editor. Thus, one of the more useful (and perhaps paradoxical) practical applications of intentionalist theory is that the study of intended texts helps us define social texts more clearly.

In important ways, Tanselle's theorizing has liberated textual criticism from ideologies of authority, canonization, and intentionality generally associated with his predecessors Greg and Bowers. In his rehabilitation of this line, the critical edition becomes a historicist methodology that can be deployed for the promotion of any editorial or interpretive agenda. This is not to say that the method is free of ideology either in its rationale or application. Once again, the NN *Typee* is a case in point.

Up until the postwar era, when the NN editors came to intellectual maturity, no carefully edited, standard edition of Melville had existed,[5] and most major Melville texts (including *Typee, Moby-Dick,* the tales, poems, and *Billy Budd*) reached readers in significantly varied versions, for a variety of reasons.[6] The entire NN critical edition project—entitled *The Writings of Herman Melville* and including editions of each published novel, tale, essay, review, lecture, and poem as well as all manuscript and unpublished materials—is to be heralded for its success in applying a much needed, uniform analysis to the textual record. Moreover, it is not likely to become outmoded, for despite the constructed stability of its clear reading texts, we can, with its apparatus, all the better gauge the historical fluidity of Melville's texts.

But like any historical construct, the NN edition is shaped by ineluctable ideologies that derive from the need for its existence. The prewar disarray of Melville texts was seen as the result of the mutilations and corruptions of time and society. And in creating a critical edition, its editors were able to account for and mend that mutilation. Moreover, these textual perturbations (such as the *Typee* expurgations) tended to conceal not only the "private Melville" laboring without concern for social reactions but a hotter, sexier, more politically radical Melville. Whether intended to do so or not, the clear reading text promotes a more uniformly liberal writer than what readers would perceive, if for instance, they read only the revised American *Typee* or the British *Whale*. This private, yet more politicized Melville may be the one we enjoy and desire the most; indeed, it is the one readers were and continue to be drawn to since the 1840s. But it is only one Melville that perforce overshadows many others, in particular the image of Melville as negotiator. Moreover, in the case of the NN *Typee,* this limitation forestalls any deeper analysis of the complexities of the expurgations, which, if pursued, would allow us to question the assumption that such a thing as the "private Melville" could exist in the first place.

As already noted, the combination of agency and moment that defines the "private Melville" (which the NN edition strives to simulate) is a Melville unrestrained by political pressures and considerations of the marketplace. If it were possible to imagine such an unencumbered mind, that mind might be worth simulating. And it is important to concede that such a mind can be imagined. But as Ishmael once said, "Nothing exists in itself," and we can only know this mind in the context of the countervening forces of social repression that did in fact alter Melville's text. That is, we cannot know the private Melville unless we know the various versions of the public Melville: the resistant victim of public pressure who would have just as soon avoided expurgation, or, for that matter, the negotiating Melville who consciously endorsed even promoted the expurgations. The problem is that like any mind, Melville's is a composite of interpenetrating, at times contradictory, mentalities, and we convert that complexity to a reductive singularity when we compartmentalize those mentalities, or attempt in some way to fix one mentality in one moment in time.

In search of the "private Melville," the NN editors come close to such temporalization of intentionality. Although they recognize, of course, that Melville played a role in creating the revised edition, adding to it material he wrote and wanted included, they also see this as a stage in the process that was imposed upon and largely unwanted by Melville. Thus, their editorial skill consists primarily in tweezing out and preserving the wanted revisions (intended texts) from the unwanted revisions (what would constitute a kind of social text) in the revised edition, and retaining all expurgations. The effect is to discount the possibility that some consideration of expurgation or self-censorship might have occurred to Melville in his earlier stages of composition. The reality of Melville's mind, I think it can be said, is not that his sense of artistic integrity was independent of social considerations, but that aesthetic and social concerns impinged upon his intentions throughout all periods of composition.

How much of a violation of Melville's artistic integrity were the expurgations? Even though Melville stated to Evert Duyckinck that *expurgated* was an "odious" term,[7] he also insisted in his July 15, 1846, letter to John Murray that the cuts allowed his narrative to move along more durectly. In fact, as manuscript evidence not available to the NN editors now indicates, Melville most certainly first conceived *Typee* as a personal narrative without the political and religious digressions that were eventually expurgated. Thus, a case can be made that the expurgations actually return *Typee* to its earliest and most personal, if not fullest, private condition. This idea gains some support in the fact that Melville strongly argued for his British editor John Murray's adoption of the American expurgations. In attempting to convince Murray to accept the revisions, he claimed that the expurgated passages offensive to the missionary cause were "altogether foreign to the adventure," that their removal "imparts a unity to the book which it wanted before," that they leave the "narrative parts . . . untouched," and that he is convinced that the "interest of the book" almost wholly consists in the "intrinsick merit of the narrative alone."[8] In other words, the socially forced expurgations may be seen as aesthetically justifiable.[9]

Of course, the NN editors' implicit view is that the arguments Melville is making for the artistic "integrity" of the expurgations are market-driven and economically self-serving. As Melville himself put it, the cut passages "possess a temporary interest *now,* to some" but they reduce the book's potential for "wide & permanent popularity" (56). It is no doubt true that Melville was hoping to enhance sales on both sides of the Atlantic by following Wiley's strategy of offending no one, but equally true is that Melville was aiming to convert his art, if not simply his first book, into something for the ages. In a later letter to Duyckinck, Melville articulates this problem in his familiar seriocomic vein. Speaking metaphorically of literary works as foods, he wrote "our dishes may be all venison & wild boar—yet how the deuce can we make them a century or two old?—My Dear Sir, the two great things yet to be discovered are these—The Art of rejuvenating old age in men, & oldageifying youth in books" (128). Part of Melville's unfolding aesthetic was fusing into his literary work something wild but also "old," something with a spice of youthful vigor but a spice that would last. *Typee* had been a good lesson in this regard. Melville's angry digressions had instantly dated his first book and detracted from "the narrative alone" whose "intrinsick merit" would, he hoped, outlast the controversies of 1846. By insisting upon the "odious" expurgations, he was most surely excluding a form of wildness in his text, but he was "oldageifying" *Typee* as well.

Obviously, by the time Melville tried to persuade Murray to adopt his cuts in July 1846, he was a different kind of writer from what he had been when he first published in February of that year, or from the still-tan, discharged seaman who composed the working draft manuscript a year before. As one may see in *Melville Unfolding,* this working draft shows evidence of Melville censoring himself early on, altering his text to appeal to an audience, and accepting his brother Gansevoort's suggested censorings of sexual passages later in the prepublication process. Each unfolding marks a different combination of a continuum of aesthetic and socialized intentionalities exhibited over a continuum of compositional moments. But the fate of any critical edition, it seems, is to focus on only one of these combinations of agent and moment and to model its text on the intentions associated with one authorial condition over another. Thus, an early but not necessarily the earliest Melville (a digressive, pugilistic writer alone in his study and for the moment unmindful of society's reaction) is preferred over the market-driven but narratological Melville (eager to make sales, write for the ages, and build a reputation). Such distinctions are worth making, but when we pin these complicated modes of intention to distinct stages in a writer's development and construct versions of texts to represent those stages (as the NN *Typee* does), we polarize the writer's mind, rigidifying its suppleness.

The problem with these static notions of agency and moment is that they cannot be combined to give an accurate depiction of the full fluidity of Melville's creative process. They are temporalizations of a phenomenon that notoriously resists such fixations. Creativity is both an aesthetic and rhetorical condition, and its solitary and social modalities exhibit their Yin Yang interdependency uniformly throughout shifting stages and times. To isolate these modalities in a given time period is to compartmentalize authorial intention, and make an abstraction out of the concrete realities of creation. It may be that such abstractions are a product of the inevitable limits of our historicist construction of past events. Knowing Melville can only mean knowing him in partial, mutually exclusive self-mirroring caricatures frozen at selected moments: private wild and young, older wiser and public. But the textual fluidities of *Typee* are links to the totality of intentions in the literary work. What we desire beyond the caricatures and textual variants is the moving picture of Melville, public and private, growing and unfolding; and the goal of the fluid-text editor is to simulate or construct that complexity.

Like any genre of textual scholarship, the eclectic critical edition has its limitations, but these limits do not invalidate the genre. It is not the only means of demonstrating textual fluidity, nor may it be the best conceivable, but it is at present the most sophisticated means of managing a fluid text. In chapter 7, I suggest some ways to adapt the genre for a fuller analysis of textual fluidity. Nor should we dismiss intentionalist ontology and methodology. As we have seen, documents are feeble representations of the texts envisioned by writers, but in reading we have no recourse but to depend upon this feeble documentary record to connect ourselves to the writer's mental vision and intended text. We can, in our frustrated attempts to grasp the elusive, lost particulars of the creative process, throw up our hands, dismiss the analysis of the creative moment, and turn our attention exclusively to the documentary words on the material page, saying, "This we can know and only this." But our inevitable discovery of textual fluidities—and all literary works have their fluidities—draws us automatically back to the "originating mind," or rather the writer's changing mind, and to the inevitable considerations of intentionality. And such considerations in turn sharpen our understanding not only of the intentions of the artist working solo, but of the artist working in a social context, represented by the intentions of collaborative editors. Thus, in order to discern one version of *Typee* from another, we must be able to distinguish the influences of one editor from another and those editors from Melville himself. To reiterate, we cannot fully comprehend a social text without understanding intended texts. With this in mind, let's turn to the materialist approach, and in particular McGann's poetics and editorial principles.

CHAPTER THREE

Work as Energy

Materialist Historicism
and the Poetics of Social Text

*Every society rewrites the past, every reader
rewrites its texts.*

—D. F. McKenzie

Broadly conceived, the intentionalist approach is grounded in an ontology of work, document, and text and deploys its methodologies to approximate the intentions of an agent or agents at a particular moment in the production of a literary work. The end product is the critical edition, which theoretically, can accommodate a multiplicity of intentionalities: the early, intermediate, and late desires of single writers or collaborative groups. In practice, however, the Greg-Bowers approach has generally been used to promote the *final* intentions of an *autonomous* author, and, not surprisingly critics, have come to assume that intentionalism means "final intentionalism." In several review essays, Tanselle has argued for the broader conception of intentionalism and more careful thinking about critical editions.[1] In doing so, he has helped rehabilitate the Greg-Bowers line into something better than it was. His road has not been easy, for, on the one hand, Bowers's at times imperious manner may have encouraged opposition to his views and, on the other hand, relevant complaints about the critical edition have themselves been peppered with misconceptions, even absurdities.

Bowers's enthusiasm for editing could reach levels of discomfiture in its somewhat ironic evangelism. Witness the serio-jocular conclusion to his famous essay "Some Principles for Scholarly Editions of Nine-teenth-Century American Authors" championing the eclectic edition: "Only this editorial process scrupulously carried out will produce editions of American classics that will stand the test of time and, heaven willing, need never be edited again from the ground up."[2] The impression one gets here, even after we account for a certain tongue-in-cheek tone, is that editors are doing God's work to stabilize (I would say freeze) literary works into an unsullied condition commensurate with their status as "classics." And once God's work is done; it is done (barring, I suppose, the occasional flood). Thirty years later in "Authorial Intention and Editorial Problems," Bowers's imperious manner had not diminished. In attacking the Norton critical edition's restoration of cuts made to Crane's *Red Badge of Courage,* he poses some angry rhetorical questions:

> [S]ince when is an earlier state of the same manuscript which has undergone a continuous process of reworking, since when can this rejected version be isolated as a true substantive text (to use McKerrow's phrase) on a par with the finally achieved intended form independent of any influence other than the author's own critical sense of what he wanted to achieve? Has not this red herring of a Norton edition made a travesty of authentic final intention?[3]

Bowers's inflamed "since when" rhetoric, although it is used to support a sensible position (that Crane, not his editors, wanted the cuts), nevertheless reveals the wooden assumption that our interest is in "authentic" texts only, by which he plainly means "author-entic." Early versions are seen as "rejected" hence invalid because they were not "finally achieved" or "true" or "authentic," that is, authorized. No consideration is given here for the idea that the earlier version represents something of critical importance that can also be the basis for a valid edition "on a par" with a "final intention" edition. And while Bowers certainly understood the critical relevance of authorial revision, his approach to the dilemma of works that exist in multiple versions of equivalent "finality," such as Beaumont and Fletcher's *Barnavelt* or William James's essay on Thomas

Davidson, is to create different editions for different kinds of readers: diplomatic versions for "scholars" and an eclectic version based on "some perhaps arbitrary principle" of selection for "general readers."[4]

One underlying assumption here is that general readers do not expect or need or want the kind of historicizing made available to scholars, but this condescension unnecessarily disempowers readers. Moreover, while an editor's adoption of an "arbitrary" principle of selection may be unavoidable, it will invariably lead to someone else's adopting another arbitrary view, and this would seem to give the lie to Bowers's prophesy that, "heaven willing," a well-edited classic "need never be edited again from the ground up." In Bowers's defense, one must say that his modifying phrase "from the ground up" implies a less positivistic stance than his words seems to suggest. By it, he means that editors shall perform the thorough collations that establish the full array of variants of a fluid text from which other subsequent editors can fashion their own variant editions. Bowers is not saying, or should not be saying, that works cannot be reedited, only that the textual materials upon which any edition may be grounded no longer need to be gathered; the spadework is done. However, few subscribed to this generous reading of Bowers's intent. Moreover, the idea that readers need only resort to the apparatus (Bowers's "ground") to gain the fuller picture of a compositional history, a standard defense made of the critical edition, is finally, as we shall see in chapter 6, highly problematic.

To be sure, Bowers's positivism has clouded as much as clarified the textual debate. Worse, it has provoked absurd counterattacks. One otherwise sensible scholar-critic has gone so far as to equate Bowers's putative scientism to Hitler and the prewar eugenics movement.[5] Fortunately, more measured counterresponses exist. In *Flawed Texts and Verbal Icons,* Hershel Parker observes that early versions of a text are often better than final versions because they more closely reflect a writer's originating creative process, and are by and large more aesthetically coherent. The assumption is that late revisions by editors and even authors themselves invariably involve localized changes that subvert the larger work of art. Scholarly editors need to intervene to help authors stay true to their original aesthetic goals.[6] Of course, Parker's assumption that early rather than late versions of a work have some sort of authorial authenticity worth retrieving is sensible only to the extent that the literary value of early versions is not made out to be exclusive of the later and intermediate versions. An exclusive focus on early versions only recapitulates in the opposite extreme the exclusionary focus on final versions. In fluid-text analysis, all versions are created equal.

James Thorpe, in his *Principles of Textual Criticism,* also attacks the Bowers line while maintaining a looser but equally informed intentionalist perspective. He acknowledges that a literary work is a "mingling of human intentions about which distinctions should be made."[7] It evolves "toward a collaborative status, and the task of the textual critic is always to recover and preserve its integrity at that point where the authorial intentions seem to have been fulfilled" (48). The editor's role is to help the writer achieve his or her desires, which may or may not be located in a "last version" of the work or in final intentions in general (46–47). Although Thorpe's language harmonizes with the objectives found in the NN critical edition of *Typee,* achieved through a Greg-Bowers approach, Thorpe concludes that the eclectic critical edition is "always dangerous" (190). In general, he does not reject the critical edition as a useful scholarly genre so much as he cautions against pretentious "scientific" methods of choosing copy-text (57–63) and excessive emendation (197).

Like others before him, Jerome J. McGann registers serious complaints about the use of final intentions as the only basis for shaping an edition, but grounds the complaint in a broader historicism and theory of the "social text," which severely delimits authorial intentionality, or more properly prepublication creative processes. In his *Critique of Modern Textual Criticism* (1983), McGann rightly discounts final intentions as the "ultimate measure" for editing, but this is a conclusion derived from the larger claim that the notion of the "autonomy of the isolated author" distorts our understanding of the inherently social rather than exclusively private nature of the literary work.[8] As a version of Romantic ideology,[9] the view that editors can approximate the desires of writers working in a socially unconstrained condition is to exalt what Jack Stillinger calls the "myth of solitary genius."[10] Writers cannot work in a social vacuum; thus, by necessity, "authority is a social nexus," according to McGann, "not a personal possession."[11] We do not, strictly speaking, own our intentions; they follow the structures of a culture. And with this Marxian perspective, McGann does not so much dismiss as delimit authorial intentions in the study of a text. They are relevant to a text's psychological history perhaps, "but a textual history is a psychic history only because it is first a social history."[12] The "sociology of texts" is primarily concerned, then, with the way poems function in a social context, or more appropriately, how extratextual, bibliographic structurings control meaning, not how poems originate before entering society.[13] More to the point concerning textual editing, authorial intentions become a kind of "subplot" to the larger social interactions a text engenders,[14] so that an editor's true focus is not on any reductive approximation of a writer's intended work but on the varied textual documents of a work that come down to us in a culture. McGann's historicism, then, seeks to establish the range of past reading experiences associated with the material or documentary versions in which a work appears.

If Tanselle grounds his intentionalism on an ontology of the literary work that turns our attention from text-objects to a conceptualized intended text, McGann grounds his historicism and materialist editorial agenda on a particular socialized poetics. On the surface, it may sound that McGann is taking the lower road, for while Tanselle's ontology seeks an inclusive sense of the being of texts and is rooted in an indisputable philosophical conception of the intangibility of language, McGann's use of a poetics may be seen to derive from an ideological agenda. But there is an ontology behind McGann's poetics.

For McGann, text is not the manifestation of a "conceived Work," but an "event."[15] That is, the reality of a text is located not in its status as a thing but as an action, or rather transaction, between words and readers. Moreover, poems do not simply transmit messages. Instead, as "forms of transmissive interaction" or "autopoiesis," they act as "self-generating feedback systems."[16] Texts are activated when readers read them, but once read and reread, they strike back at readers and transform them. Taking this poetics deeper in *Social Values and Poetic Acts,* McGann defines poems as a functional "set of social practices."[17] As a form of knowledge, they do not tell the truth; rather, they "induce reality and the truth" by engaging us in a self-conscious process of interaction with the "incommensurate" nature of experience itself. By this, McGann means that poetry, like any form of discourse, brings us to see gaps between ourselves and the past. Indeed, the language used to represent these ultimately alien or incommensurable forms of reality (idea and word, self and culture, past and present) is itself a mechanism of incommensurability in that words are arbitrary objects used as symbols of other objects. Poetry is particularly good at revealing such slippages because as a piece of language that always calls attention to itself, it is by its very nature a kind of embodiment of the incommensurate: "its special function is to display the eventuality of meaning through representations of the incommensurable."[18] By "eventuality," McGann is saying that meaning is an event; it is event-ual. The reality of a text, then, is not in its relation to intentions and the text-object "things" that come to us as representations of intention, but rather in its relation to the "eventness" of texts, or the social actions that the text-object induces in readers. The text, then, is "a residual form" of a social event, and the editor's function is to get to the event.

Once we begin to see that McGann's poetics involves its own ontology that defines textual being as a particular, conceived *process*, not as a conceptualized *work*, we quickly recognize the philosophical merit of his position. Whereas Tanselle edits texts with an eye to what the words are intended to be, McGann edits with an eye to what the words mean in differing events or moments of publication. His editorial theory follows directly from his poetics.

In *The Textual Condition*, McGann tentatively offers the notion of *autopoiesis* to encapsulate the socialized interactions about the "incommensurable" just discussed. As "autopoietic mechanisms," social texts take their reality from the "feedback processes" activated in part by "those who manipulate and use them."[19] Logically, the "manipulators" of texts are writers and audiences, however those entities may be defined. In Stillinger's words, "[I]t takes at least two people, a sender and a receiver, to constitute communication." But whether we call these manipulators writers and readers or senders and receivers, McGann and Stillinger stress (despite allowances for the sender's authorial intentions) the receptive end: "With a literary work, collaborative creative activity on the part of a reader is an absolute and unavoidable necessity."[20] These creative collaborators include publishers, copy-editors, book designers, illustrators, and printers, as well as readers (whose responses throughout the history of a work, as we know from *Typee,* can have palpable effects upon the materiality of a text). For McGann, the impact of these manipulators and users is manifested in a text's "bibliographical codes," that is, the material and rhetorical determinants that constitute the condition in which a text is displayed on the pages. This can range from anything as physically obvious as the illustrations and handscript Blake used to present his poems or the typography of a canto by Pound to matters less obvious but just as important, such as the ordering of poems in an anthology or their multiple appearances in certain magazines and books.

Essentially, McGann's most compelling argument for the social text is the recognition that the meaning of texts depends not only on the words themselves (or linguistic codes) but also upon the way the words are presented, so that the same text placed in different publication contexts will invariably have different effects. Each new physical context is a different "event." A materialist hermeneutics, then, locates meaning in the conjunction of a text's linguistic and bibliographical codes, which shapes the "social event" that makes a literary work what it is at a given moment.

But while the "textual condition" of literary works is always a combination of linguistic and bibliographical codes, McGann argues that the critical edition, especially the eclectic critical edition, favors linguistic codes (with its clear reading format) and is ill equipped (despite detailed apparatus) to display the variable bibliographical codes of a literary work.[21] In fact, the clear reading text of a critical edition erases the historical specificity of manifest bibliographical codes.

McGann's quarrel with the eclectic critical edition is rooted even more deeply in his wariness of the *narratorial* aspects of the genre. As a simulation of a past moment of intentionality, a critical edition is only as good as the arguments used to construct the simulation. In Tanselle's view such arguments must "satisfy the intellect by their effective marshaling of the apparently relevant evidence and by the harmony and coherence of their insights" (*Rationale*, 74–75). The problem with Tanselle's criteria of "harmony and coherence" is that they carry with them a rationalist ideology of smoothness that may not convey the aporetic roughness of the writing, publishing, and editorial processes. Tanselle would surely respond that harmonious and coherent arguments can be made about messy things and that editions, like histories, are not "just the facts" but what we may call "narratives of facts," which stand or fall on the basis of their ability to persuade "until new discoveries and more trenchant analyses render them no longer necessary or compelling" (75).

But it is precisely this *narratorial* aspect of the critical edition that bothers McGann. An edition, like any history, is both the editor's story of how a work came to be and the editor's version of the work itself. In *Social Values and Poetic Acts,* his most comprehensive treatment of social texts and the sociohistorical approach, McGann questions the validity of narrative as a mode of criticism, which he takes to be "a self-conscious response to certain social and historical factors" (149). Drawing upon Hayden White and criticizing the supreme critical fictions of Harold Bloom and J. Hillis Miller, he argues that narratives will always represent some ideology of continuity, and "if one is interested in *critical* knowledge, one has to be wary of this impulse to generate continuities" (132). Extrapolating this antinarratorial stance to include textual criticism, we recognize in McGann a distrust of the critical edition's tendency as a historical narrative to argue for the text of a work invariably on the basis of some ideological bent. This seems inevitable in any human discourse, even if the ideology is little more than one of "harmony and coherence." But even this fundamental rationalism blurs the line between historicist criticism and interpretation, for as McGann notes in a seemingly responsive echo to Tanselle, "Narrativity entails *order and completion,* so any details which would stand outside the (ideological) order cannot enter the discourse" (144; emphasis added).

Tanselle might respond that criticism cannot escape narrativity; it can only include strategies for containing or reducing subjectivity through the editor's self-conscious skepticism (as in the case of the editorial self-exposure over the "blunder" concerning "In thoughts of the vision of the night" found in the NN *Moby-Dick*). But McGann's fear is that such strategies can easily devolve into ideological "self-confirmation" (144). Better, he feels, that the historicist should follow some kind of "rhetoric of self-revelation" or "revisionary process that shows the mind in dialogue with itself," as did Montaigne. Of course, such Montaignean essaying is no less narratorial in a way than any other history. Better still, then, McGann concludes, the historicist should explore two nonnarrative modes to construct histories: the "array" of materials and the dialectic.

It is not clear, however, that the resort to array and dialectic can fully escape narrativity, for an array of documentary variants is only as good as its principle of selection, and is itself a kind of ordering of textual characters waiting in the wings to interact. And a dialectic within that array (or a dialogue among the documents) is fundamentally an argument or kind of plot. These devices seem only to be fragments of narrative, and no less susceptible to ideology for that fragmentation. To a certain degree, it can be argued the NN *Typee*'s lists of variants (an array) and "Discussions of Adopted Readings" (a discourse, if not dialectic, on emendations) not only coincide with McGann's expectations but also achieve an important element of (albeit passive) reader involvement. That is, evidence and rationales for judgment are displayed for readers' inspection. Nevertheless, McGann's preference for other editorial approaches—such as the diplomatic edition that renders the separate versions of a work in their specific documentary states or the genetic edition that offers a "continuous production text" of a work as it evolves through various stages of production—reflects his desire to minimize narrative in editing.[22]

McGann is not the first to favor diplomatic editing, although his arguments for it are new. However, in following the route McGann takes in transforming his poetics into editorial practice, we find two practical turns that are not necessary outgrowths of his theory but have become hallmarks of his approach nonetheless and which impede fluid-text analysis: he de-emphasizes the role of authorial intention in the shaping of a social text and seems to remove the crucial element of an individual writer's creativity from the shaping of bibliographic codes. In critiquing McGann's critique of modern textual editing, I want to address these two problems and demonstrate with an example from the manuscript and print versions of *Typee* that authorial intentions and something I call *revision codes* can be a proper controlling element of the social text.

Many of the shortcomings of McGann's delimitation (not rejection) of intentionality may reside in a too-severe employment of Marxian socialization. As already noted, intentions are psychological, and psychology, McGann flatly avers, is sociological. When it comes to bibliographical codes, "'author's intentions' rarely control the state or the transmission of the text," and given the "highly interactive" nature of textual transmission,[23] even the presumably autonomous activity of a writer writing in isolation is inevitably a matter of social interactivity. Texts represent, he continues to say, "the locus of complex networks of communicative exchanges." But McGann makes, it seems to me, a side step at this juncture (homologous to the problem we found in Tanselle) in going on to temporalize the process and pin it to one particular moment: "[T]he first of those [communicative] exchanges," he says, "is revealed at the time of a work's initial period of production" (62). It is not precisely clear what McGann means here by "production," but his subsequent discussion essentially precludes the writer's prepublication creative process from it. Apparently, production is the bringing of a text into publication, either the circulation of fair-copy manuscripts or the distribution and sale of print-texts. And authorial intentions are not a controlling factor in the creation of bibliographic codes or meaning at this point. Simply put, the writer has little to say in matters of house style, layout of pages, or even as with *Typee*, what portion of his text is reprinted.

No Social Text without Intention: Tommo Takes a Bath

While McGann's social text theory does not directly support or deny the implication that the creative process stops at the moment of production, his assignment of social texts to postproduction conditions suggests a needless compartmentalization of authorial intention. If the writer enters into play in his approach, it is primarily in negotiation with the makers, reviewers, and readers of books occupying a network of social spheres. The theory of social texts seems to offer no mechanisms for describing such autopoietic interactions as they may occur with a writer writing alone. McGann's notion of bibliographical codes is an efficient way of referencing the material reality of the extralinguistic features of a document, but it is less useful in describing those social negotiations occurring in the creative process that are materially evident in manuscript revisions, and that exist well before a writer submits his text to other readers.

Writers are never alone when they are alone. As I write these words, I feel the pressure of friends, scholars, and readers-to-come who shall vet, critique, edit, publish (I hope) and even (fantasy I know) favorably review my words. Don't think their presence is not already infecting the purity of my supreme thought. Of course, someone embarked upon a more imaginative writing project, say a novel, will work with similar constraints, but will also self-consciously strive to override or transcend the social. As Melville put it in his most social novel, *The Confidence-Man:* fiction "should present another world, and yet one to which we feel the tie."[24] Writing is a process of finding the canny within the uncanny and vice versa, of creating original other worlds that are finally familiar to us, of linking the personal and social to the universal and transcendent: it is a form of "oldageifying" a text, making it current but also for the ages. Writers may not, as Melville despaired, achieve pure originality, but they excel in seeking an authentic, or rather *author-entic,* relation to the problem of striving for it. The tension of that pursuit is as much a part of the social "event" of texts as any bibliographic code.

Initially, writers compose alone, generally removed from editors, and with some self-conscious distancing from social constraints, but they cannot avoid internalizing the problem of their socialized condition; thus, the "first" communicative exchange in writing occurs not at the moment of editorial production, but at the writing desk, and in the writer's mind. McGann's perspective does not seem to admit the relevancy of such individualized moments of social "eventuality."

In speaking of authorship, Raymond Williams argues from a broader Marxian view that the individual and societal are reciprocal, even though this reflexivity is often deformed into the view that individuals are merely conduits of social structure. "Indeed," Williams concludes, "any procedure which categorically excludes the specificity of all individuals and the formative relevance of all real relations, by whatever formula of assigned significance, is in the end reductive."[25] Literary production is a creative as well as receptive matter "in the material social sense of a specific practice of self-making, which is in this sense socially neutral, self-composition."[26] As anthropologist Clifford Geertz argues, rituals (and we may include writing as a rite) are an individual's performance of social functions.[27] Just as we cannot separate a particular performance from the musical score it follows, or a dancer from the dancing danced, we cannot remove the "specificity" and "the formative relevance of real relations" of solo authorship from our understanding of social texts. Otherwise, we risk a further recapitulation of the denial of the critical relevance of authorial intention in historicist thinking. McGann's notions of social text in theory and in editorial practice are too highly nuanced and useful to be leveled with the charge of Marxist reductionism. But with one scene of writing from *Typee* in mind we can, I think, see the critical need to expand his notion of the social text to more fully embrace intentionality and the larger range of fluid texts.

The scene in question involves Tommo's first attempt in chapter 12 at what becomes a daily bathing ritual at the river. Evolving through successive stages of what I call transcription, transformation, and translation (as more fully elaborated in *Melville Unfolding*), this fluid text (which appears in different versions in manuscript, first edition, and revised edition) is surely a social text, but one not adequately described by either linguistic or bibliographic codes alone. The rich interplay of authorial intentions and social pressures emerge only as we inspect the process of revision.

Tommo takes his bath, at first modestly and partially clothed, in the company of nude females. In time the ritual becomes a more ribald form of skinny-dipping, but in this initial scene Tommo must be goaded and teased into stripping. Melville revised this scene of his initial undressing at least three times. In manuscript, Melville's first inclination was simply to *transcribe* the memory of a feeling and an action.

> Somewhat embarrassed by the presence of the female portion of the company I removed my [shirt] frock & bending over washed my face in the stream. (MS 1)

Note Melville's restraint: Tommo is "somewhat embarrassed"; the women are an abstract "female portion." With this primal forest setting and fussy locution Melville aims, no doubt, at the Cooperesque, but by and large, his immediate goal is the simple recollection of a past event. These details are just the registration of a memory. The only revision in manuscript is the immediate decision to replace the refined word *shirt* with the more common *frock*. Though small, this change is consequential. As an act of spontaneous rethinking during initial composition, it reinforces Melville's first intention to recall the past more accurately. The sailor of 1842 would have worn his seaman's frock and not the more refined shirt the writer of 1845 was no doubt wearing as he wrote. But while Melville was simply transcribing a personal experience, he was also getting his character properly clothed, and worrying, it seems clear, about class (sailor versus gentleman) and the latent sexuality of his dishabille. In short, he was beginning to *transform* the remembered experience (his "rememory," as Toni Morrison might put it) to fit an internalized social negotiation, even as he was merely attempting to *transcribe* it along the lines of personal recollection. Because the revision of *shirt* to *frock* is materially present on the manuscript page, we can call it a bibliographic encoding of an authorially intended revision strategy, or a *revision code*. But as we shall see, not all revision codes are materially manifest in the transformations a writer makes.

By transformation, I mean a further stage of self-conscious revision to give words deeper meaning and effect. Indeed, later in the compositional process, Melville did just this by expanding his modest bathing scene considerably. Here is what he added:

> Somewhat embarrassed by the presence of the female portion of the company, *and feeling my cheeks burning with bashful timidity, I formed a primitive basin by joining my hands together, and cooled my blushes in the water it contained; then*

removing my frock, bent over and washed my*self down to my waist in the stream.*

No bibliographic or scribal hint of this expansion appears in the manuscript itself; we know it exists only because the passage appears transformed this way in the first British edition. Apparently, Melville expanded the text (for an editor would not presume to make such a passionate revision) in a later, now-lost draft either just before, during, or after his preparation of a fair-copy version, also presently lost. Placed beside the earlier extant manuscript version, this print-text revision reveals both psychological and rhetorical transformations.

Psychologically, Tommo remains in this revision "somewhat embarrassed." And yet at the same time Melville now gives him "burning cheeks," "bashful timidity," and hot "blushes." These blushes burn hotter than the tropics, and must be cooled; he now washes not just his face but his body "down to the waist." Obviously, Melville is reliving this previously transcribed experience more vividly; and most assuredly he is inventing it out of a mixture of memory and desire. It may be that the earlier and seemingly innocuous shift from *shirt* to *frock* actually triggered this deeper self-exploration, but whatever historical explanation we may construct, the fact of a revision pinpoints an actual moment of imaginative "unfolding" of what it feels like to inhabit a certain kind of passion. The sexualizing of the scene also has a rhetorical effect, for as Melville unfolds his sexual self-awareness, he also titillates his audience through his attempts to restrain arousal, to control the blushing. Tommo's display of modesty is for the reader's benefit; it assures us that our hero is neither prude nor sybarite but a reliable balance of innocence and desire; Tommo is the kind of young gentleman we can rely upon to keep a level head, even as he contemplates "going native."

Now, it is clear that a reader can come to this same rhetorical reading without knowing of the existence of the earlier manuscript version. What more do we learn, then, from an awareness that the print-text passage is the product of a certain moment of revision? To begin with, the variation affords us a new relation to the idea of intentionality. Granted, we need not fall into the trap of arguing that Melville intended the precise rhetorical effect we attribute to this passage, but the textual variation clearly indicates Melville's intention to change his language. The *fact* of any change necessarily implies Melville's intent to alter his relation to his audience, to transform not just himself but his audience. And it is this *shift* in intention and the *direction* of that shift that have both a personal artistic meaning for Melville as well as a larger cultural meaning for us. These are the dimensions of any revision code.

In terms of personal growth, Melville moves from an objective reporter to a self-exposing and yet self-valorizing (i.e., more credible) participant in a culture. As readers of Melville's fluid text, we, too, come closer to an experience of cross-cultural discourse; we witness more than a bath; we witness the mutual disrobing of alien cultures, a moment now of colonial first encounter in which we gaze sheepishly along with Tommo into the forbidden and, of course, alluring practices of the "savage mind." And the import of our reading of this scene is enhanced by our awareness of Melville's *intent to add* Tommo's blushes, which not only remind us of our own voyeurism at this point but our self-conscious shame over the colonial encounter. The textual fluidity of the passage reveals Melville's desire to transform us into participants in this act of wonder and self-critique; he wants us to become peeping Tommos, too. But more than this, our awareness of Melville's transformation of a moment of undressing into a moment of blushing and reliable restraint allows us to participate as well in the writer's "second thoughts" about his experience, second thoughts that reflect our own growing awareness of the sexual implications of cross-cultural encounter. Moreover, our added awareness that Melville is trying to restrain his sexuality in this expanded scene contributes to our sense that we are being manipulated to grasp a new cultural perspective. The reader responses derive solely from a contemplation of Melville's revision strategies.

Certainly there is nothing wrong with a blush; surely, it is the sign of purity of thought. But, like the word *virgin,* it implies as much desire as restraint. A blush is a sudden hot awareness that bids farewell to innocence, and when Melville's first readers and editors (unaware of Melville's earlier changes at this revision site) read his expanded passage in print, they insisted upon an expurgation. And Melville complied. Here is his third revision, found in the American revised edition:

> *I felt* somewhat embarrassed by the presence of the female portion of the company, *but nevertheless removed* my frock and washed myself down to my waist in the stream.

Even though the cuts in this revision are severe, they are not an exact return to Melville's original transcription stage. Notice that while the hot blushes are gone, Tommo's washing himself to the waist—a detail that did not appear in the earliest, most restrained version—remains. To recap the revisions: Tommo had, first, simply washed his face; then he blushed and cooled his body; now, the blushes are gone, but he still washes to the waist. Although this incomplete expurgation eliminates Melville's cagey rhetoric designed to balance self-expression, titillation, and reliability, the surviving language bears enough vestige of that hot transformation for us to see a significant growth beyond the first transcription stage.

This third-stage expurgation records a further social negotiation between writer and reader, or rather an actual *translation* from the hot but restrained language of a private but social moment to cooler language that his public would accept. Whereas in the first two versions of the passage we see Melville varying his rhetoric to meet the projected audience he hopes to engage, here we find Melville bargaining with an actual audience. He learns that blushes will simply not do and accedes to their demise. But what his censorious readers did not know is that the surviving "bare waist" offered a text still more lively than what Melville's earliest transcription had allowed. A bare waist in exchange for a blushing face was all the heat his audience would bear. If the expansion of the bathing scene passage to include hot blushes constitutes an authorially intended transformation, the removal of those blushes and retention of waist represent a further negotiation or kind of social *translation* of Melville's language and desire into a socially acceptable idiom, achieved through a collaboration of writer and editor.

Whether we are looking at Tommo's bath in its transcription, transformation, or translation versions, this fluid text is prima facie evidence of a complex set of revision codes involving authorial intent, social negotiation, and editorial coercion. We might argue (no doubt shall argue) over the rhetorical strategies and meanings derivable from these revisions, but we cannot deny the fact of revision manifest in this fluid text or the existence of intended revision strategies submerged within these fluidities or the critical and cultural relevance of these strategies.

Unfortunately, McGann's theory, which locates the beginnings of social text at the moment of publication (however broadly that may be defined), is not equipped to address the mixture of authorial intentions and social pressures found in the early transcription and transformation versions of Tommo's bathing scene. To be sure, McGann is not insensitive to revision; nevertheless, there are no bibliographic codes in his largely postpublication approach that can adequately describe the revision strategies rooted in a working draft such as the *Typee* manuscript. The NN *Typee* shares a similar editorial disregard for the working draft manuscript. Because it is an intermediate stage working draft and not a fair copy of Melville's intended text, it is finally "of little help" in constructing the critical edition (NN *Typee* 306). Although the editors do not use its variants to emend the copy-text, they acknowledge that the leaf offers "an opportunity . . . of learning something about Melville's process of composition" (365). Overall, the *Typee* working draft—a matchless specimen of textual fluidity in and of itself—finds little purchase in either the intentionalist or materialist camp. It seems too short and too inchoate to be a serviceable intended text, and too remote from the nexus of social interaction to be a social text. It is a textual idiot in search of an editorial theory that can address its idiosyncrasies and incorporate its revision codes into the ways we read a literary work.

Work as Energy: Toward an Editorial Synthesis

Although both intentionalist and materialist approaches acknowledge the fluid text as a reality and are in fact designed in their separate ways to manage the textual fluidity of a literary work, neither is particularly equipped to edit works in such a way as to make the authorial and social revisions equally accessible for our critical and cultural analyses of literary phenomenon. Some synthesis of the two approaches could be forged to serve the needs of fluid-text analysis, although not without some framework that overarches both. Let's briefly recount the theoretical strengths and limitations of the two approaches and then consider a frame.

Tanselle offers an ontological perspective on the literary work that typically places the construction of socially unimpeded authorial intentions at the center of its historicist agenda. This does not preclude the crafting of editions based on the intentions of editors or other collaborative "editors" effectively serving as emissaries of social power. In either case, the principal strength of this approach lies in its necessary endeavor to distinguish kinds of historical intentions (authorial vs. editorial) and support its judgments with coherent arguments. McGann endorses such traditional methodologies to the extent that they may be used to display multiple versions of a work. He offers as well a poetics of the documentary text as a social event and defines a literary work as the array of its versions, each of which may be experienced in its social context independently of the authorial intentions discoverable in the creative process associated with those versions. He also argues convincingly that our experience of a social text is shaped by its bibliographic codes.

To be sure, the chasm between Tanselle and McGann is not so large that we cannot bridge it. Granted, McGann sees a mighty gap in Tanselle's "unnecessarily restricted view of the processes of literary signification."[28] By this, I take him to mean that Tanselle's textual ontology is affiliated with a poetics of transmission exclusively through linguistic codes rather than one that interacts with readers through linguistic *and* bibliographic codes. But McGann does not propose to "discard any of the traditional concepts or tools of editing and textual criticism. [His theory of social texts] asks us, rather, to reconceive the framework governing the use of those tools and concepts" (62). Thus, social text theory redirects rather than rejects editorial processes, including the critical, if not eclectic, edition. For his part, Tanselle, who is not theoretically wedded to eclectic editions, does not reject the notion of social texts, and his critique of the Greg-Bowers line indicates his own reconceiving of the editorial framework. Rather, he has argued that since a social text must be achieved through the workings of nonauthorial collaborators (who as individuals must have intentions), those social text intentions (so to speak) can only be ascertained through textual analysis and rendered through emendation. Thus, critical editions (if not, again, the eclectic form of that genre) can accommodate social texts.[29] From a theoretical perspective we can and need to dispense with such terms as *intentionalist* and *materialist,* for materialists do not deny the relevance of intentions, and intentionalists ground their work in material objects.

But the two differ in their historicisms: the one seeking a private past, the other a public past. Both isolate crucial components of a culture: the inner workings of creative originating mind(s) to construct a text of the work; the interactions of texts and readers in a social sphere. But, as we have seen, both are limited by certain temporalizations inherent in each approach that deform our perception of the historical creative process. The intentionalist links authorial intention to a particular mode of mentality and moment in time; the materialist limits the socialization of texts to postpublication. As I have tried to show through textual problems posed by the *Typee* manuscript, these limitations detract from a fuller understanding of how writing and publishing operate in a continuum involving both individual and society. The fluid text is a way of conceiving of the entire process of writing so as to embrace intended texts and social texts, and this broader conception builds upon its own historicism, ontology, poetics, and rhetoric.

A fluid-text historicism focuses on the interpenetration of private and public pasts in order to make the evidence of literary versions, revision, and adaptation accessible to readers for critical and cultural analysis. The end product of this approach is a heuristic editorial construct (simply put, an edition) that exposes the logics and technologies of personal and cultural creation. The subject matter is not texts per se but *texts that can be shown to have changed;* and the analytical focus is on the construction and meaning of the forces of change; that is to say, revision.

Incumbent upon this historicist perspective is an underlying ontology of the literary phenomenon. The problem of the intentionalist and materialist textual ontologies lies in their mutually held concept of work as "thing." Tanselle's "work" is conceptual and therefore not strictly speaking an actual object, but it is nevertheless a concept conceived as a single thing. McGann's "work," despite his notion of text as event, is essentially an array of documentary text-objects. In both cases, the work is essentially a product or set of products, not a process. And this is not surprising since we generally perceive (erroneously perhaps) states of being as objects. An alternative to this is an ontology of process. In this view, a literary work is not a conceptual thing or actual set of things or even discrete events, but rather a flow of energy. That is, the phenomena that constitute a literary work are best conceived not as a produced work *(oeuvre)* but as work itself *(travaille)*, the power of people and culture to create a text. I choose this Einsteinian metaphor of energy as the substance of matter to stress the idea that a text is a physical manifestation of the alternating currents of individual and society over time. In this regard, *energy* encompasses but goes further than the author-bound idea of work as process currently offered by editorial theorists, for in this notion of work as energy we are free to consider the deepest psychological and cultural principles that trigger a particular process of literary creation, as well as the materialized pulses of combined private and public creativity that emerge as what we call texts or versions of a text.[30]

Perhaps the idea of work as energy is an abstraction that is just as, if not more, conceptual than Tanselle's notion of work as a conceived intention or McGann's concept of social interaction, for energy is invisible and intangible. But as a means of reorienting our focus on fluid, not static, texts, energy is a concrete and apt metaphor. It stresses a flowing of personal and cultural forces and urges us to follow that flow as it courses through and enlivens the full field of constituents—writer, collaborative editors, readers, material products, and social events—that make up the private and public labor invested in a literary phenomenon.

To some extent, this perspective shares the point of view of a third camp of editorial theorists, the geneticists, who see the literary phenomenon as a process of shifting but equally valid moments of authorized revision. But the fluid text encompasses more than the workings of a writer writing either alone or with collaborators. Since we are interested in the work *(travaille)* a culture invests in a work *(oeuvre),* we want our editing to make some accounting for adaptations of texts beyond the writer's authority or control. Such works as the Bible, Shakespeare's plays, *Frankenstein, Moby-Dick,* and *Uncle Tom's Cabin* (just to make a random selection) are the focal points for the work of a culture that extends beyond authorial genesis, editorial publication, and contemporary reception to the odd ways in which humans re-form and recast texts to suit their needs. Cultural adaptation of texts, then, is also a part of the energy of a literary work.

With this historicist and ontological reorientation in mind, we may gain a clearer sense of a poetics of the fluid text. Texts are manifestations of the work of a culture over time. They are the emergent physical embodiments of moments in that working, and their critical relevance, for our purposes here, is not, oddly enough, solely in the meaning of those individual textual embodiments, but in their *difference.* Indeed, we can go so far as to say that if a culture is defined by the work it performs, then the energy of that working can be measured by the distance traveled between the products of the working. To come to the point, the cultural meaning of a fluid text is in the pressure that results in changes made in one text to create another and the degree of difference, or the distance, between two texts. Thus, a poetics of the fluid text is a poetics of revision, whether that change is induced by an individual writer, a social demand, or as is often the case, a combination of the two.

What makes a fluid text fluid is its fluidity. This tautology is meant to stress an obvious point easily missed: When we read a fluid text, we are comparing the versions of a text, which is to say we are reading the differences between the versions, which is to say we are reading distance traveled, difference, and change. We are reading the energy of a culture that makes the change, an energy that has measurable meaning in our analysis of culture. It will be argued that since writers and societies combined do not necessarily intend for their revisions as revisions to have meaning, we cannot rightly say that there is a poetics to those revisions. To be sure, the design of a textual revision may not be consciously crafted, but the designs are there, and with them the impress of writers interacting with cultures. Where there is a design, there is strategy, and hence a rhetoric and poetics.

What, then, are the rhetorical and editorial implications of fluid texts for our understanding of authorial intentions, creative process, and social texts? In the chapters that follow, I want to address these matters in an attempt to establish a critical vocabulary for the study of textual fluidity and to propose guidelines for the editing of fluid texts. To do this, we need to focus on the forms of literary versions and the modes of literary revision that create versions. This will involve more editorial theory, including that of the geneticists, and, as before, the *Typee* manuscript will serve as a principal example.

CHAPTER FOUR

The Fluid Text Moment

Versions of the Version

Lord, when shall we be done changing?
—Melville to Hawthorne

Some years ago a colleague of mine had a fluid-text moment. Chances are such a moment has happened to you: an apparent slippage between your text of a literary work and someone else's text of the same work. The slippage may be small, but the effect can amount to textual satori, or a brief Zen-like glimpse into the true nature of textuality.

In her fluid-text moment, my colleague was teaching Richard Wright's *Native Son,* a familiar enough novel included in a course outside her field. In preparation, she had returned to her well-thumbed copy of Wright's controversial novel and, after some classroom preliminaries, was about to foment discussion, when a student asked what she made of the masturbation scene. My colleague was perturbed. She did not recall the scene, and being a citizen of the world, she was not likely to have missed such a scene. Asking her student to locate the passage in question, she discovered a number of things. First of all, even though everyone held the same book, the pagination in her copy of *Native Son* did not match her students'; and furthermore, they had the masturbation scene in their copies of *Native Son,* but she did not. In effect, two versions of *Native Son* were cohabiting the classroom.

Here's what caused this fluid-text moment. In his original version of *Native Son,* Richard Wright had had his black protagonist Bigger Thomas masturbate while a white couple makes love in the back seat of

64

a car he is chauffeuring. Later he kills the girl. But in order to get his novel accepted for publication in 1940 as a Book-of-the-Month Club selection, Wright had to agree to remove this scene. Reprints of that expurgated 1940 edition, and only that version, continued to be published for the next fifty years. However, in 1991, Arnold Rampersad constructed a new edition of *Native Son* for the two-volume Library of America collection of Richard Wright's works. He based this new edition on Wright's original typescript and in effect restored the expurgated masturbation scene. Now, my colleague is not so old that she ever saw the light of 1940, but that well-thumbed copy of *Native Son* from her less distant graduate school days was nevertheless a reprint of the 1940 BMC edition, and that is what she assumed the campus bookstore had supplied to her students. In fact, the publishing firm that had issued her old *Native Son* had come out with the new version of *Native Son,* a reprint of the 1991 LOA edition, and, none the wiser, the bookstore put the newer edition on the shelves.

Unanticipated fluid-text moments like this can lead to a wide range of useful reactions that call into question our otherwise unchallenged assumptions about what a book really is. Take, for example, the idea of an "edition." Most people assume that an edition of a literary work is any version of the work that is physically different in appearance to all other versions so as to call attention to itself in some way. Perhaps the book appears with a new introduction or a new binding, and these superficial changes may be seen as constituting an edition. But in fact they do not.

Technically speaking, an edition involves the actual resetting of the text in new type, and this different setting is usually based on a distinct publishing initiative, scholarly or commercial, with or without editorial principles, that may be announced or hidden. *Typee,* for instance, exists in several editions from 1846, each of which has marked differences in the text, and each corresponding to specific resettings or rearrangements of the lead type used in printing up the text. The first American edition is a new preparation of *Typee* based upon a single print-copy of the first British edition and is a thorough resetting of type. And while the subsequent American revised edition did not involve a completely new resetting of type, it did remove, reposition, add, and alter both text and type in pronounced ways so as to generate an entirely new version of the work. Thus, we have three physically different versions of *Typee* appearing in 1846.

Writers, their editors, and publishers are keenly aware of the defining elements of an edition because they make, promote, and sell editions. Readers, however—and this includes critics, teachers, and scholars—are often oblivious to what an edition is and can mean until a fluid-text moment hits them in the face. Of course, the publishing industry (which has an interest in proclaiming its texts "new" or "definitive" or "authoritative") has played fast and loose with the term. Usually with new classroom "editions" of a text, a publisher will simply issue the same text derived from the same plates or typesetting arranged in a slightly different format, and this often gives instructor and student alike the false impression that a "new edition" is nothing more than a reprint of a text with new introduction, pagination, and cover. This variation from one classroom text to another is only mildly disconcerting when one is trying to get a classroom of readers focused on the same page. But my colleague's moment derives from a clash of two "real" and altogether quite different editions of the same work and, as it happens, two quite different versions as well.

I introduce the term *version* here to pose a problem about editions. To what extent are different editions of a work relevant to the way we interpret, or even actually read, a text? How much difference in the physical edition makes a difference in our readings and reading? What is the critical mass of difference (to continue my "work as energy" metaphor of the previous chapter) that triggers in us a sense that the variant texts before us are actually different versions of the same work? Social text and intended text theorists would both agree that any difference is going to be critically relevant in some way, especially if we make it so. The different layout of print on the page is a sufficient alteration to create new meaning. But did the writer intend a significant shift in meaning by such alteration of bibliographic code? Is the writer's intention relevant to our reading of the sufficiently physically altered text? And so the textual debate between intentionalist and materialist goes on. As this chapter shows, the answer to these questions are not easy, but the questions are inevitable, for it is the nature of textuality that fluid-text moments inevitably occur; thus, the matter of editions, versions, and revision must be addressed.

Readers experiencing any fluid-text moment cannot refrain from asking basic aesthetic questions about the effect of the different texts upon the meaning of the work. They are drawn more deeply into the work by the textual fluidities they discover. The presence or absence of the masturbation scene in *Native Son* inevitably affects our interpretation of Bigger, his condition, his deeds. Even deeper, the comparison of the two versions of *Native Son* compels us to ask what social forces caused two versions to exist in the first place, and what the BMC expurgation means racially and sexually in 1940 as well as what the LOA restoration means for our time. An awareness of textual fluidities and versions automatically historicizes the reading experience.

But there are versions of a work, and then there are versions. Let me relate one of my own fluid-text moments.

Some years ago, I was well launched into a semester-long survey of American literature and was about to land upon Whitman. The text in question was "Out of the Cradle Endlessly Rocking" as found in the fifth edition of the *Norton Anthology*. Obsessively up-to-date, I was teaching from the third edition, which I prefer because it comes equipped with my various underlinings and venerable marginalia, the wisdom of my advanced age. I had just finished a powerful sermonette on Whitman prelusive to our discussion of "Cradle" and was reading out in resonant tones the poem's long opening sentence with its rhythmic repetition of prepositional phrases that somehow manage to hold themselves together in anticipation of the stanza's familiar culminating main clause: "I . . . a reminiscence sing." But as I read the final three words, a small chorus of students offered in unison: "No. It's 'a reminiscence *song*.'"

Interrupted in mid-culmination, I descended to the real world from my Whitman high in Emersonian consternation. Inspecting my students' texts I discovered that sure enough some of their fifth-edition copies of the *Norton Anthology of American Literature* printed the last word of the opening stanza of "Out of the Cradle" as the noun *song*, not the verb *sing*. Had the editor of the Whitman section of the anthology discovered a new version of "Cradle" different from the 1860 version they had used in their third edition? Or was *song* just a typo? Usually typos are "obvious" because, like my favorite typo a few words back, they do not make sense. But many typos are themselves real words (like *song* for *sing*) and carry enough meaning to make some sort of sense, if not the sense intended. Meaningful typos, once discovered, always force us to ask questions of intentionality. So I had to know: is *song* meaningful here; did Whitman intend it; is this a typo or what? The interpretive potential of the *song* variant (as opposed to the expected *sing*) were intriguing. "I . . . a reminiscence song" seems to create a tighter identity between the reminiscent chanter of the song-poem and the poem itself. The text seems to say, "I am a song of reminiscence," and in part that is precisely what "Cradle" is all about. This new textual version seems to out-Whitman Whitman. Of course, to make this reading work we have to presume the elision of the verb *am* from Whitman's syntax (so that the poem essentially gives us "I a song" not the expected "I am a song"), and this is a bit far-fetched, especially for Whitman, who is not shy of that verb. But at the end of his poem Whitman consciously drops a preposition in "The sea whispered me" so that we must read the sea doing two things at once: whispering to me and whispering "me." If Walt can drop a *to,* he might drop an *am.*

What to do? Rush to my library for a "definitive" edition of Whitman to set the record straight? I had a class in session. I did not panic. Coolly, I checked with other owners of the fifth edition in the classroom. What did their text say? *Sing* or *song?* You would expect them all to say *song.* Surprisingly (again), most did *not,* in fact, have *song* as their text; they had what my Norton Third recorded: "I . . . a reminiscence *sing.*" Only a few students had fifth editions with the line "I . . . a reminiscence *song.*"

As it turns out, *song* was just a typo. Here's what probably happened. In adding new texts to their fifth-edition canon, the Norton anthology production crew had to reshuffle and retype old texts, and in resetting the type a printer had inadvertently converted *sing* to *song.* And proofreaders missed it. The edition went to press with the error, but before too many copies of that printing had been made and distributed, someone (perhaps an editor pausing in the day's counting up of royalties) found the error and had it corrected in subsequent printings of the edition. This did not prevent a fluid-text moment from occurring, for the *song* typo in some plausible, if not perfectly grammatical way, "works," and readers in my class took notice of the difference, not initially as a typo but as an intelligible textual variant. Obviously, this fluid-text moment is not as bracing as my colleague's *Native Son* event. Her moment involved the conflict of intentions: a writer's and a publisher's. My moment involved a typographer's accident. Surely, this one typo does not constitute a new version of "Cradle."

Surely, it must take more than one variant to make a version. And surely, there is more to fluid-text analysis than the contemplation of isolated unintended errors. On the surface, we hasten to agree, but perhaps we hasten too hastily.

Consider some what-ifs. What if the *song* error had not been corrected, and the typo was perpetuated in this edition for a generation, or even a few years. Such has happened in the past; it is likely to happen again. And what if the typo were to become, perforce, the *familiar* wording of this text, so that in due course "I a reminiscence song" sounded "right," and "I a reminiscence sing" sounded offbeat. That can happen and has. Of course, one function of textual scholarship is to play custodian to our famous texts and prevent such gaffes, or correct them if they occur. But what if our excellent Whitman scholars were to nod in this function and just not *see* the typo. Not possible? Well, the Norton production staff and editors just didn't see it when they proofread. Readers depend a great deal upon the kindness of editors. Now, what if in the course of textual events one of my fine Long Island students took a liking to his Long Island forebear and became a poet inspired by Whitman and published a poem of his own making dedicated to Whitman entitled "A Reminiscence Song." Suddenly, the typo has, in this little fantasia of what-ifs, taken hold, had a critical effect, and become part of an intertextual discourse between poets old and new. Darwin tells us that species evolve in part through accident; culture is the same. But this textual fantasy tells us something more. It has the feel of reality about it. Like any other fluid-text moment, it gives us insight into the idiosyncratic nature of texts and the equally idiosyncratic transmission of culture.[1]

Without a doubt, textual versions have enormous critical potential. But the problem of what constitutes a version—major revisions or a single unintended variant—remains. And there are further complications. What the Wright and Whitman versions have in common is that they are both linked to, in fact coterminous with, specific physical print-text documents, and they are not imagined, or inferred from evidence external to those documents. What we have not mentioned is the kind of textual fluidity that might appear on a single physical document containing the remnants of multiple versions whose full existence can only be inferred. The working draft manuscript of *Typee* is such a document, and our "moment" with it (mine has lasted sixteen years so far) shall be intense and complicated. Here, the writer's revisions on the manuscript page indicate successive inferred versions of *Typee*. Furthermore, a comparison of the manuscript to the first edition demonstrates the likelihood of another version, a fair copy (now lost) different from those of the working draft manuscript and the first print edition. The versions of *Typee* inferred from this one manuscript document, once isolated, provide a rich bed for aesthetic and cultural analysis.

But our confidence in such analysis depends upon our ability to establish, from physical and inferred evidence, that the versions in question are indeed worthy of being called versions, that they are isolatable as a distinctive phase of creation and are not merely a handful of minor variants or accidents. Given our working definition of the literary work as the combined energies of private writers and public collaborators in a culture, we shall have considerable latitude in categorizing types of versions. But, our focus must go beyond product categories to the causal process.

The root cause of any version is revision. And the critical relevance of a version (however it may be formally categorized) is located in the nature of the revisions performed to achieve that version. Eventually, we shall look more closely at both authorial and nonauthorial revision and their practical modes. For now, let's see what formal properties of literary versions have emerged from the textual debate and especially that branch of critical editing known as geneticism.

Versions Physical and Inferred

Thus far, scholarly discussion of the theoretical and critical status of versions has been diffuse, ranging from brief pronouncements to more extended attempts at categorization. The two most important problems addressed throughout the discourse are

> What degree and manner of variation between two texts of the same work are required for us to label each a version of the work?

> What makes a version worthy of critical analysis, and hence editing?

Probably the earliest and most consistent definitional arguments in response to these problems come from that group of largely European textual scholars known as *geneticists*. Their position (as expressed in the works of Hans Zeller, Gunter Martens, Siegfried Scheibe, and others) has been known since the 1950s, but their impact has only recently been felt, most directly in Hans Walter Gabler's 1986 genetic edition of James Joyce's *Ulysses*. As we shall see in chapter 6, Gabler's synoptic approach mingles versions and hence lessens our sense of their separate identities even as it stresses the continuous processes of revision from one version to another. Finally, though, his genetic approach is an important step toward a full treatment of fluid texts.

The geneticists get their name from their basic assumption that a literary work is equivalent to the processes of genesis that create it and that a *genetic edition* of a work must display that process as it progresses through its various stages of composition and revision, in manuscript and print.[2] Because the emphasis is on displaying process and not a particular manifestation of the work in that process (beginning, middle, or end), geneticists reject the eclectic subgenre of the critical edition, which relegates all variants to the apparatus.[3] Rather than conflating the multiple versions of a work into one, or for that matter editing single versions of a work in facsimile, as we might find in the social text approach, they offer a "continuous production text" that displays all variants of a text so that the kind of critical edition they propose presents "text and apparatus [as] an integrated whole."[4] Gabler's *Ulysses,* now a flagship edition for geneticism, actually expands the approach. Like other geneticists, he uses an elaborate system of typographical codes to indicate the source of each variant (in manuscript or print) and its place in the sequence of the work's composition.[5] His innovation is to use this "continuous manuscript text" of *Ulysses* as copy-text for a standard reading text, and to display the two versions on side-by-side pages.[6] With all variants on display to the left, the user of this editorial integration, or "synoptic text"—something akin to the array of textual data McGann envisions—can acquire some sense of Joyce's work in process while reading the more conventional text to the right.

It goes without saying that the array of variants *(à gauche)* and the reading text *(à droite)* are two synergistic editorial versions of the various physical versions of *Ulysses* known to exist. By physical versions, we mean the actual typescripts and print editions of *Ulysses* presently available as well as documents no longer materially extant but that, by dint of corroborating evidence, had to have existed at some point in the creative process. Paying close attention to Gabler's heavily-encoded synoptic text, one may follow single sets of variants linked by codes to each of these physical versions, but there is little or no guidance in discerning patterns of revision and revision strategies from one physical version to the next, or in speculating upon modes of revision that might suggest multiple inferred versions contained within each physical version. While this is a provocative attempt to incorporate genetic processes into critical editing, Gabler's *Ulysses* provides only limited access to versions.

Even so, the geneticist approach offers the fullest discussion of versions to date. Hans Zeller argues that a version is "constituted by at least one variant." This is not to say, of course, that every variant itself constitutes a version for an entire work, but Zeller gives equal status to variant and version when he goes on to explain that "every variant or each new version may be regarded as the expression of a changed intention that is valid at a different point in time. The various versions are a diachronic sequence of distinct synchronic systems that together make up the history of the work."[7] But the problem is that while single variants may in theory achieve the status of a version, they may not have equivalent relevance to the creative process or equivalent impact upon readers. We have already entertained the possibility that the single variant of Whitman's *sing/song* could, in the course of time, constitute a cultural if not authorial version. But while unintended textual fluidities can grow into something meaningful, one wonders if any intentional one-word variation versions of a work actually exist in the real world, and not my imagination?

In speaking of the "social destiny" of a work as it evolves from *avant-texte* to its published version, Louis Hay (the articulate spokesman for France's *critique genetique* in France) tells of the shift of one word in the famous World War II poem "Liberté" by Paul Eluard. In manuscript the poet composed his poem for his girlfriend and inscribed her name throughout the text. But in print that name is changed to "Liberty," and it is this one-variant version of Eluard's resistance poem that gained great popularity during the Liberation.[8] Without doubt, this one word change creates in one stroke a significantly different version of Eluard's poem. Similar one-variant differences can be found in Melville. The already mentioned "L-word" in *Typee* (which gives us *liberally* and *literally* in separate British and American editions) thoroughly alters our reading of the concluding episode of a crucial chapter. It alone would constitute a reconception of the book. In the NN edition of *Moby-Dick* editors have added a set of quotation marks to the crucial "pondering repose of If" speech in chapter 114 ("The Gilder"), which effectively reassigns the speech from Ishmael to Ahab, thus altering the impact of the speech and entire chapter, the development of Melville's two characters, and, one might argue, the rest of the novel. This is not a one-word variant; it is a one-punctuation variant. These are compelling instances of how one variant might constitute a new version, but if one variant of a text makes a version of that text, as Zeller suggests, then any minor variation (intended or not) and every act of revision has equal weight as a version. Thus, the merely mechanical shiftings of *which* to *that* in the *Typee* manuscript, let's say, would constitute a version of *Typee* on par with the two "L-word" versions found in print. With this broad dispensation, we are left with little to indicate the relative importance of one set of variants from another. And to insist that these two categories of textual fluidity have equal relevance only tends to vitiate the enterprise of fluid-text analysis. Some critical distinctions are, therefore, in order.

In general, geneticism assumes that the creative process is a continuum of overlapping and interpenetrating actions flowing seamlessly from one to the next. And the idea of giving equivalency of variant and version is a natural outgrowth of this notion of continuous revision. But while this equivalency may have a certain philosophic appeal, the reality of the writing experience suggests that not all acts of revision occur seamlessly or with the same intensity or intent. There is ongoing tinkering, but there is also momentous reconceptualizing, or what Tanselle delineates as revision that merely refines versus revision that transforms or metamorphoses a work (*Rationale,* 81). An important challenge to our understanding of versions, then, is the problem of finding certain telling seams in the creative process that allow us to denominate some sets of variants as versions and others not, whether that set is one variant or many, intentional or not. While geneticists may not address this matter directly, we can find their sense of a solution tangentially referenced in their discussion of intentionality and "authorization."

Obviously, authorial intention is one natural measuring stick for versions. That is, groupings of variants can be distinguished as versions if editors can demonstrate the writer's intention to use those groups to alter the literary work. But to sustain the critical validity of each version, some of which may be derived through collaboration with editors, the geneticist is reluctant to use authorial intentionality as a validation of one version over the other. Their approach to this problem is linked to their notion of *authorization.* Along with the materialist camp, geneticists hold that, while each authorial variant is logically the product of some kind of authorial intention, the exact nature of that intent is, according to Zeller, "not only impossible to determine . . . but also impossible to isolate . . . as a separate entity within the history of the work."[9] Gabler, it should be noted, moderates this view. For him "authorial intention . . . is a textual force to be studied," and his edition is "designed precisely to lay open the records reflecting the operation of the author's intentions in the making of the text."[10] Obviously, intentionality plays more of a role in Gabler's version of geneticism. Even so, Zeller's sense of the impossibility of discriminating one intention from another, in effect, gives all such intentional acts equal authority, and each therefore has an equal right to be included in a genetic edition of a work.[11] Given the practice of geneticism to valorize no one particular version or manifestation of intentionality, but to valorize all from first to final, editors need at the very least some criterion for distinguishing authorial versions from others that are external to the writer's creative process (let's say an expurgated edition). Significantly, this is not to say that geneticism seeks to exclude such unauthorized collaborative endeavor from this process. Here, "genesis" is rightly seen to extend into the realm of social text. Thus, rather than depending upon authorial intentionality as the basis for editing a text, Zeller proposes the concept of "authorization of the version as the guiding editorial principle."[12]

In "Theoretical Problems of the Authorization and Constitution of Texts," Siegfried Scheibe expands on Zeller's notion of "authorization" to state that what legitimates a version as a version is that its text in some way "corresponds to the author's will and decision."[13] Outsiders may participate in the creation of a version, but a version is no longer a version if the author no longer plays an active or even passive decision-making role. In Scheibe's words: "The authorization given by the will of the author ends with his or her future inability to make a new decision about the text" (183). With the notion of authorization Scheibe turns to further discriminations of versions and concludes with an important, critical distillation. In general, he considers early versions that reveal the original conception of a work or a decisive change in a work to be more relevant than later versions that tend to involve fine-tunings of already conceived texts. His focus here is on what he calls the "turning points [that] determine the production of a work and the textual versions in which these turning points first become recognizable" (190).

The metaphor of "turning points" provides a useful critical device for classifying otherwise undiscriminated sets of variants as relevant versions, for it seems to correspond to the writing process itself, which may evolve in a gradualistic manner until a certain cataclysmic "turning" occurs in which the work suddenly (whether through solitary authorial or collaborative editorial interventions) becomes something other than what it was before: hence, a new version. Louis Hay is getting at this process when he notes "that writing tends alternately (and sometimes simultaneously) towards communicating and holding back."[14] We have already seen such fluctuations with Melville's exposition, expansion, and then reduction of Tommo's bathing scene. Each involves a distinct "turning point" or "irruption" (to use John Wenke's term) of creativity,[15] and each is quite possibly the touchstone for a distinct version of *Typee*.

If the analysis of fluid texts requires a more sophisticated treatment of versions than we have heretofore witnessed, there is no doubt that geneticism makes a significant contribution. Its emphasis upon creative process as well as social text presupposes the notion of work as the collocation of authorial and cultural energies. Moreover, the focus on "turning points" gives more shape to Tanselle's notion of metamorphosing revision. Still, the equal valorization of variant and version in geneticism tends to reduce all versions to an indiscriminate continuum of intentionality that impedes rather than furthers the study of versions. To my mind, more rather than less delineation of the modes of revision is needed. Moreover, such modes of revision require a forthright acknowledgment, not dismissal, of intentionality. It is not clear, for instance, how an editor looking for "authorization" in a version is to discern an author's "will" or "decision" from that of a collaborative editor; nor for that matter is it clear how the author's "will" is much different from "intentionality" (which, to repeat Zeller, presumably cannot be "isolate[d] . . . as a separate entity within the history of the work"). It may be that the limitations we find in geneticism are due in part to the contrarian pose geneticists have had to assume in the face of the dominant Greg-Bowers tradition of intentionalism. In order to make an editorial stance *against* eclectic editions and *for* creative process, geneticism has adopted a hyper-objectivization of textual fluidity that unnecessarily discounts the role of intentionality and simply renames it *authorization* or *will*. The result is a failure to distinguish versions even as geneticism clearly tries to showcase them. Moreover, the limiting of versions to authorized versions only narrows the scope of social texts permitted in its purview, for as I argue throughout, a text's full fluidity extends into numerous kinds of cultural revision, beyond the writer's death and "will." Thus, from a fluid-text perspective, genesis can be both authorized and nonauthorized. Although Zeller's linking of versions to "turning points" will prove to be useful, geneticism is, finally, only partially fit for the task of fluid-text editing.

The strength of geneticism lies in its devotion to the deeply textured display of an individual's creative process. This is a needed complement to social text theory that focuses primarily on the impact of cultural collaboration on textuality. But rather than defining versions from the level of the single variant on up to turning points, the social text approach poses another problem in its tendency to equate versions with physical documents only. This raises the larger question of whether a version is coterminous with documents or exists conceptually, like Tanselle's notion of text.

The most comprehensive spokesman for the former view is Jack Stillinger, who in 1994 followed up his impressive 1991 study of *Multiple Authorship* with a much needed but decidedly problematic study of multiple versions entitled *Coleridge and Textual Instability*. In a concluding chapter providing "A Practical Theory of Versions," Stillinger deftly recounts, and distances himself from, positions taken by geneticists and such intentionalists or supporters of "ideal" texts (to use his term) as Tanselle and Peter Shillingsburg. He adopts a form of "textual pluralism" that argues that "each version of a work embodies a separate authorial intention that is not necessarily the same as the authorial intention in any other version of the same work."[16] Here I take Stillinger's notion of pluralism to mean that no one version of a work (earliest or final) has priority over another, and that editing a literary work means editing a plurality of versions. In this regard Stillinger echoes Donald Reiman's earlier pronouncement that the future of scholarly editing lies in "versioning," that is, the editing of significant variant documents rather than the conflation of documentary variants in a single eclectic edition. In his essay on the matter, Reiman usefully argues that the measuring stick for determining a version worthy of its own edition is that it must "exhibit . . . ideologies, aesthetic perspectives, or rhetorical strategies" that are "quite distinct" from other versions.[17] Stillinger, however, provides no such criteria for discrimination. In fact, his pluralism devolves (almost, it seems, out of exhaustion) into a dissatisfying relativism in which all versions have equal weight and each will somehow rise in the democratic hurly-burly of free and open discourse to its own level, which would be all well and good if such a thing as freedom in the marketplace really existed.

But Stillinger's editorial conclusions (and hopes for the democracy) are not as important right now as his definition of versions. Taking a strictly materialist line, Stillinger defines a version as a "physical embodiment of the work."[18] This is to say that each variant document constitutes a separate version, and presumably each version is located on its own separate document or set of documents. Such strict identification of version and document works for many aspects of the textual condition. Texts appearing in unaltered fair copy and proofs are single versions embodied in singular documents, although the occasions for these documents—the readying of materials for publication—are likely to represent distinct, late stages of composition (usually the refinements of a conception rather than turning-point transformations).

But other textual circumstances—working draft manuscripts and revised editions—do not fit, for such documents may (in fact often do) contain evidence of multiple, reconceived versions. In the case of working draft manuscripts, this evidence may be often partial and broadly dispersed throughout the document. That is, one rarely finds two versions of a poem neatly inscribed side by side. Rather, we see layers of revision upon revision, and the remnants of versions interspersed here, there, and often elsewhere. The *Frankenstein* manuscript, for instance, reveals evidence of revisions by Percy as well as Mary Shelley, which surely indicate in places variant but interpenetrated conceptions of the novel. In more complicated manuscripts, such as the *Typee* working draft, the versions invariably lie one over the other in what appears to be a wilderness of cancellations, insertions, and transpositions. Each revision site may bear the traces of distinctly different conceptions linked to different versions. Moreover, the archaeology of the revision site is such that one may not be able to discern the exact sequencing of the revisions within the revision site. (Typically, a site may register several changes, and the precise ordering, or sequence, of each step in the revision process is always a matter of speculation.) Some revisions clearly trigger others, but some may also appear to be utterly independent.

Finally, and most significantly, versions not to be found on any extant document might be inferred through evidence found in a working draft manuscript. Such inferred versions will have no full presence on any physical document even though their existence is real and meaningful. For instance, in the *Typee* manuscript Melville's chapter numbers do not match those in the first edition. The only inference to draw from this is that Melville made major insertions after composing his first draft but before creating his fair copy; however, no document containing those insertions survives. The precise text of this inferred version does not exist, although the version itself had to have existed, and traces of it can be found, somewhere, in the first eleven chapters of the first print edition. In a working draft manuscript one can put a finger on a single, physical revision site and call it a turning point in the composition of the work that effectively delimits variant versions of the work in process, but finding full texts of the two versions that revolve around that turning point may be impossible. Even so, those versions are real and demand our attention.

Stillinger forthrightly acknowledges this problem but simply moves on: "In the face of such difficulties, the more nearly certain procedure is to take each manuscript as a discrete version, and all its cancellations and revisions as being part of that single version."[19] This determination becomes a theme throughout Stillinger's "practical theory." The assumption seems to be that metaphysics or some ontological analysis of the status of versions or the role of intentions in discerning versions cannot help us resolve this issue, so our only recourse is to arbitrary distinctions. He writes, "[T]he degree of textual difference necessary to distinguish one version from another is entirely arbitrary" (132). And the authority of a particular version also "lies . . . in someone's arbitrary definition" of authority. With this pragmatist approach, Stillinger notes that the case one makes for one version's relevance over another's will depend upon "the criteria used to define authority . . . and interpretation of the evidence in each case" (132). But the jacobinical result of such pragmatic pluralism, Stillinger concludes, is that in assessing versions "[w]e are going to have to make and defend our specific choices on an ad hoc basis, hoping that someone else likes them or is moved to accept them. In theory, everybody can be right in such matters, and the one who is rightest will be the one who musters the best rhetoric to argue in favor of an actual, particular version of a work—even if it turns out that it was chosen simply because it was the version that the editor or critic liked best" (140).

Stillinger's pluralism is, I believe, intended to encourage healthy discourse on the validity of versions in a fluid text, but his willingness to see reasoned argumentation devolve into any rhetoric that might win the day muddles rather than sharpens the discourse on textual fluidity. Stillinger's conclusion seems more of a desperate relativism occasioned by the frustration of trying to contain what he calls the "ubiquity of versions." Let me risk inching out onto a positivist limb and suggest that a more fluid rather than arbitrary set of criteria for discerning versions might actually serve the cause of Stillinger's pragmatism better than his surrender to determinations based simply upon what one "likes best."

To begin with, if our goal is to establish ways of determining what a version is and which versions are worth discussing, we need to distinguish what was worthy as a version in the historical development of a work from what may be critically worthy for certain readers at certain times. Of course, what is historically worthy is always critically worthy, but in distinguishing the historical from the critical at this juncture, I mean to remind ourselves that even though many versions are undeniably attached physically to documents, documents can also reveal multiple *inferred versions* that are nevertheless historically real even though they can only be speculated upon and constructed out of partial evidence found in the document. These historically constructed versions have a reality, even if they are only partially represented or inferred in the document. They are worth grasping *at*, and are only perceived (or rather apperceived) through discourse. Secondly, there is little utility, it seems to me, in basing arguments for versions on arbitrary assertions of, let's say, personal aesthetics or ideology, even if one exposes those biases forthrightly and warns readers of one's bias, for such candid admissions only wave a flag of subjectivity that ultimately flies higher than one's obligation to try to contain one's subjectivity, or to balance it against that of others in the field. The "best rhetoric" is that which is grounded upon the reliability of the critical editor, and reliability is established through the editor's forthright discourse upon his or her struggle with the problematics of the "ubiquity of versions" that conglomerate into a work.

Stillinger's identification of version and document is a fairly standard (although not necessary) hallmark of social text theorizing. And its inadequacy for treating working draft manuscripts, which are crucial to the analysis of creative process, only underscores the need to extend social text theory more broadly to include prepublication or precirculation documents.[20] Peter Shillingsburg, who proposes a more Aristotelian pluralism reminiscent of the Chicago school, offers a conceptual definition of versions that, at the very least, affords us certain "unities" in determining categories of versions.

Shillingsburg's brand of pluralism differs from Stillinger's free-for-all of versions in that it aims to coordinate a plurality of editorial approaches: documentary, aesthetic, authorial (i.e., Greg-Bowers), sociological (social text), and bibliographic. Editors need to be aware of the equal validity of these five approaches, and they need to consider the kinds of knowledge and information each approach can provide before deciding which approach is best suited to solve their own individual editorial problems. A work like William Wells Brown's *Clotelle* (our first African-American novel, appearing in at least four versions preceding, spanning, and following the Civil War), might best be edited in a documentary or sociological fashion, whereas Melville's *Pierre* (appearing in only one version) might best be edited with an authorial or bibliographic approach. While his own preference is to edit a work so as to "foreground rather than submerge the evidence for Versions"—a position that would seem to place him in the materialist or sociological camp—Shillingsburg also grounds his approach in an intentionalist ontology.[21] For him, a version (like Tanselle's notion of the literary work) is primarily a concept. That is, it exists as "one specific form of the work . . . intended at some particular moment in time."[22] By "form," he means essentially a mental or conceptualized condition of the text. As such, Shillingsburg's conceptual version is not fully manifested in any physical form but may exist in mind as incipient ideas or be "embodied" in developmental stages involving notes, jottings, or perhaps even "essayed" inscriptions.[23] We cannot be sure how many mental versions of a work may have transpired in the author's mind, but we can infer some of those versions from surviving documentary evidence.

Shillingsburg's notion of versions as conceptualized stages of composition reaffirms Tanselle's fundamental point that literary works, in any form, are intangible. This allows us to see that while documents consist of tangible inscriptions of word in ink on the page, the revision of those inscriptions implies various stages of development, and this in turn allows us to identify intangible but inferable and very real versions of the work. One small case in point from the *Typee* manuscript occurs in a passage in which Melville labors to describe the number and arrangement of buildings found on the sacred "Hoolah-Hoolah ground" (NN *Typee*, 91). It is clear from the revisions that he began by thinking that he would describe two buildings, but as he inscribed the word *verandah,* he stops himself midcomposition, remembers that there were actually three buildings to describe, and revises the passage accordingly. At the same time as he clarifies the physical ground, Melville records a clearer sense of the tribe's class system of priests in one building and chiefs in another. In this instance, Melville's memory of the sacred ground appears archaeologically in the stratified cancellations and insertions on the manuscript page. The mental picture of a three-building compound with its more precise articulation of class sits atop a discarded mental picture of a classless, two-building compound. Each depiction is inextricably linked to the other, and each may be taken as a conceptual version of the scene.

Perhaps a more critical example of what Shillingsburg might call "developing" or "essayed" versions occurs when Melville contemplates in manuscript how he will render Tommo's friend Toby's recitation of his near-fatal attempt to escape the valley. Because, as he relates it in manuscript, he (or rather Tommo) cannot remember Toby's exact words, he proposes, "for the sake of unity," to make up words and speak them as if he were Toby. Further inferred revisions of Toby's subsequent speeches, not found in the manuscript but appearing in the first edition, indicate that Melville continued to modify Toby's language in this direction. The document shows not only this tactical revision, but that in the process of writing, Melville was altering his narratorial relation toward his characters. He was becoming more of a dramatizer than a personal narrativist. Now, in Stillinger's dispensation equating version and document, we can only say that these two inferred, early conceptions of *Typee* are merely "stages" of composition. But with Shillingsburg's conceptual definition of versions allowing multiple versions to exist on one document, we can come closer to a more complex view of the energy Melville put into his "working" to create *Typee*. That is, the manuscript reveals a major shift in Melville's conception of his book from a travel account to something more dramatic, something resembling a romance.

In wrestling with the problem of what degree of variation constitutes a version, Shillingsburg offers four analytical "unities" that allow us to measure variation in one version and another. They are content, time, function, and material.[24] Content, time, and material are obvious enough. One version will differ from another because its literary content (words) varies, because these variants are written necessarily at different times, and because they may appear in different material formats (manuscript, magazine, book). But probably the most crucial of the four is that one version may be distinguished from others because it functions differently either aesthetically, rhetorically, or socially. This functional "unity," it seems to me, has more utility as a measuring stick than the others, for while a piece of writing may appear with small content changes at different times and in different formats, it may have no appreciably different impact to make it appear as a different version. Mere variation in linguistic or bibliographic codes does not constitute a version unless those differences can arguably be said to have a significantly different function. McGann rightly notes that any reappearance of a text in a different bibliographic form, even if that reappearing text is, like his example of Matthew Arnold's "Empedocles on Etna," unchanged, will constitute a new version because the bibliographic recodings from one appearance of Arnold's poem to the other will have a different impact on readers.[25] And this, it seems to me, is an unassailable condition of textuality and rhetoric. Packaging affects meaning. However, a version that repackages the same text *is* a distinct version not because the bibliographic codes are different but because repackaging (made manifest through the variant bibliographic codes) implies a different rhetorical function. Thus, a set of variants in a work is most convincingly categorized as a version if it can be demonstrated that they perform a significantly different function.

It should come as no surprise that the problem of determining what constitutes a version is a qualitative (functional) rather than quantitative (content, time, material) matter. We have already discussed from the geneticist's view how even one variant can be a functional turning point that allows us to delineate successive versions. But we can also address this problem from the other end and ask whether a version can contain so much variation that it is no longer a version but a separate work. While this is an important question to ask, if only because others consistently ask it, we shall find that it is finally a red herring.

The intentionalist James McLaverty in his essay on "Issues of Identity and Utterance" introduces the problem of determining when a version might become a new work by offering the philosopher's fable of Theseus's ship. This parable (like others used to explain textuality such as the *Mona Lisa/Hamlet* puzzle) has a certain charm, but minimal utility.[26] The parable is this: In its long sailing, Theseus's ship undergoes such thoroughgoing repairs that no original materials, from masthead to keel, survive. Under these circumstances, is the returning ship the same ship as the ship that first sailed?[27] Applied to the case of textual versions, the question would be if every word in the text of a work were revised, would the revised text constitute the same thing as the original work?

Texts are intangible language manifested through tangible words that by their nature can be inscribed differently (in different hands or fonts) and still be called the same text. As I write this sentence, I am inserting it in ink down the margin of a typed page. It now appears in neat print before you as you read this book, and looks quite different from my revised typescript, but it is the same string of words or text that appears in my handwriting. Ships, however, are made of perishable materials that are strictly speaking irretrievable when they perish. A decayed mast can be replaced by a new one, but not by the same mast. But, the word *mast* does not perish; in fact, it can appear in different shapes or bibliographic codes—*mast* or *MAST* or *mAst*—and remain the same word or linguistic code. In short, literary works are not ships; or at least they are not material in the same ways for this parabolic analogy to be effective in explaining literary versions, or the drifting of versions into independent works.

Nevertheless, let's follow McLaverty's navigation of Theseus's ship in the admittedly murky waters of textual versions. McLaverty argues that the ship in its different manifestations may still be the same ship (and hence a version of the Ship) if there is some "continuity, from one stage to the next, of matter, structure, and function" (137). So far so good. The idea of continuity or linkage will be an important feature in our further discussion of versions. And McLaverty's use of "function" resonates nicely with Shillingsburg. But McLaverty adopts a narrow view of functionality when he then goes on to imagine a possible scenario involving a textual infantilization of *Gulliver's Travels*. What if Swift, he asks, had prepared a children's version of his famous satire, without the satiric scenes? Would the resultant "fairy tale" be *Gulliver*? McLaverty concludes that because the function of the children's work would be different, it could not be identified as *Gulliver* (138). Essentially, McLaverty is tacking the problematic ship parable in the wrong direction away from the nature of versions and toward a reaffirmation of the identity of a work to its original. Aside from the fact that it is, in fact, impossible to separate fairy tale from satire in Swift's work, the children's text he imagines cannot fail to be a version of Swift's classic rather than a uniquely different work, for though its text is radically modified for a different audience, its new "function" does not make it any less inextricably linked to the parent text. Continuity, not functionality, is the real issue in the parable of Theseus's ship. Presumably Theseus's hand upon the tiller, or his deed of purchase—that is, his authorial presence manifested in his revision strategy—is enough to establish the continuity of the different versions of his craft. From a fluid-text perspective, Theseus's refitted ship will always be a version of the original as long as some history of a link to the original can be remembered or constructed.

In due course, McLaverty denies that he can ever make any sense of such histories (141) and jumps Theseus's ship for his own more useful but still problematic notion of "utterance." Unfortunately for our purposes here, this approach, for all its merits, takes us further away from any resolution of what constitutes a version. Drawing upon speech act theory, McLaverty argues that versions are "actions of the author" (141) that are definable by speaker (writer), text, and audience. Happily, this essentially rhetorical view allows us to define versions not only as their texts are meant to be voiced by the writer, but also as they are voiced with the listener in mind. But McLaverty restricts the "meaning" of an utterance to the realm of publication, for while prepublication utterances may exist (in manuscript, let's say), the writer did not intend the *history* of such variant speech acts to have meaning (144). It is no doubt true that writers are too busy writing to worry about the meaning of the history of their revisions, but the fact is that such prepublication compositional histories do have meaning the moment we decide to construct such histories, and it is only when we make such a construct that we can then begin to wonder if that construct might not, in fact, correspond to authorial motivations unrecognized by the too-busy writer at the time of composition. Writers revise and make versions; readers make the histories of revision. McLaverty wants, it seems, to place an arbitrary boundary between prepublication and postpublication utterances, and thus restricts the notion of versions severely. The history of Henry James's famous postpublication revisions is clearly meaningful, in part because James says as much in his introductions to the revised editions. But more, that history is meaningful primarily because the revisions exist for readers to compare and read. It is equally clear that writers intend their prepublication revisions, and if those revisions and versions become available to readers, the history of those utterances have equal validity as readable, interpretable utterances. They also have meaning as an expression of the writer because as a kind of "essaying" of ideas and feelings, they reveal the direction a thought might have taken and the potential substance a word might have assumed before the published words were finally fixed in print.

In McLaverty's speech act approach, with its performative aspect, this notion of essaying is substituted by something akin to "rehearsal."

That is, a text is taken as a kind of performance of a script (i.e., the conceptual intended work), and in such a dispensation, prepublication draftings are like a rehearsing of the script to get it right, or getting it to the point at which the text becomes the right performance of the script.[28] As such, these rehearsals are discardable. But the problem is that McLaverty's performance analogy is misapplied, for as any actor, director, or playwright will tell you (sometimes begrudgingly), the text of an utterance will evolve during and because of rehearsal. But a deeper problem is that writers are not actors following a script; they are making up the script as they work. Their draftings are inventions not rehearsals. As such, prepublication essayings, revisions, or versions must have meaning as utterances.

But if, in the view I am proposing, the range of versions is so wide as to include pre- and postpublication utterances and such nonauthorial and nonauthorized versions as censorings, translations, and bowdlerizations, then when, we continue to ask, does a version exhibit so much variation as to become an independent work? The answer, from a fluid-text perspective, is "Never." This is so because logically speaking a text derived from another text will always be a version of that text. A version can never be revised into a different work because by its nature, revision begins with an original to which it cannot be unlinked unless through some form of amnesia we forget the continuities that link it to its parent. Put another way, a descendant is always a descendant, and no amount of material erasure can remove the chromosomal link.

In his *Rationale of Copy Text,* Tanselle approaches the problem from the perspective of an editor deciding which version of a work upon which to base an edition. In doing so, he provides some important insights into the kinds of versions most worth studying. Even so, he does not address the logical impossibility of a version becoming a "different work." Tanselle makes a useful distinction between what he calls "horizontal" and "vertical" revision. The former seems "to refine the expression of a passage without changing the drift or general effect of the whole, whereas others (not necessarily more extensive) seem to metamorphose a work into what one can only call a different work" (81). Horizontal revision may also be seen as "preparatory to more climactic versions," which, as the product of vertical revision, are in themselves a "transform[ation]" constituting "what may be thought of as a new work." Thus, we might consider Wordsworth's 1850 version of the *Prelude* to be a different work altogether from its earliest and much shorter 1805 precursor. A story made eventually into a novel, such as was the case with Hemingway's *For Whom the Bell Tolls,* or an author's adaptation of a novel into a play into a movie script suggests even more likely examples of major textual "metamorphosis" of one work into another. But to call these versions independent works, when they have some degree of interdependent overlapping text and are obviously the products of lifelong creative projects, is highly problematic.

To some degree, this is a problem of semantics and the inadequacy of current usage of *work* and *version* to bear the full complexity of textual fluidity. *Work,* as it is used here, is a conceptualized notion of an intended literary creation, and as a conception it denotes a thing in its full and independent form. Of course, our only concrete sense of this concept is derived from the sum total of extant physical and inferred versions. *Version* denotes text that bears some proximal relation to the work either as a fragment or as a thing complete in and of itself. The slippages in these definitions take us to the heart of the problem of why a version of a work cannot be or become a separate and independent work. A version, like any text of a work, is effectively an approximation of or attempt at achieving the work; and accordingly, there is an implied teleological relation between version and work in that a version in manuscript (but also in print) may be taken as a step toward a full manifestation of the work, or telos. In this view a version is inextricably linked to the end at which it is aimed, no matter what separate state of completion it seems to have achieved, no matter how different it appears to be from its precursors or from a "final" version to be achieved later on down the line. With this in mind it is definitionally impossible for even the most heavily revised version to be taken as a "thoroughly different" work. The revision might appear to be thoroughly different, but this does not negate its genealogy. If a version were to be a work separate and independent of its related versions, it would have to have its origin in a completely different conceptualized work, in which case it would not be conceivable to call it a version in the first place. It would be a work in its own right.

The paradox may be derived from Tanselle's overreaching use of "metamorphosis." Think of a frog, and the versions of frog that we know from our pond-watching days. Egg, tadpole, frog. Now, one might argue that these versions of frog are separate works, but they are clearly moments in a process. Even the most familiar and graspable frog is just one version that produces egg versions, that become tadpole versions, that become frogs. Of course, a book is not a frog; it is composed in a linear temporal frame until the writer gives up on it or dies or publishes, whereas frogs (like any reproductive species) are self-perpetuating. But the point of the analogy is that if a literary work is "conceptual and intended," it exists as such only as an inference based on our inspection of the cumulative concrete versions that survive in some way in the textual record. And since versions are linked and derive from one another or from a shared source, we can only see the literary work as "work in process." To return to the problem of a version being taken as a separate work, this work process may evolve from version to version, but one of its versions (the frog) cannot leave the process and become another work (a prince). In such cases of radical revision, the so-called new work is not new but simply a version of a process that involves radical revision. If frogs do become princes, it is only because there is that of frog in every prince, and a prince is just a version of frog.

So putting the two words *version* and *new work* in a sentence with the hope of articulating some interrelationship invariably leads to paradox. A version may be taken as a separate work when it was never a "version" to begin with. That is, if a version of a work can be called independent of the parent, then it was not a version of the parent in the first place. Dickens's decision to offer readers a more optimistic conclusion to *Great Expectations* constitutes a radical reconception of the book; and, surely, the change evokes a radically different reader response. But we shall continue to refer to the two texts of *Great Expectations* as versions, not separate works, for the simple reason that we cannot comprehend the optimism of the one without knowing the pessimism of the other. These qualitatively different endings gain their meaning in part from each other, and our awareness that Dickens radically revised them. Therefore, they are versions of each other, not separate works resulting from separate creative projects. In fact, no matter how radically different any version of any work becomes in the course of time and revision, it will remain a version because its inception began with the first version in the project and its link to all previous versions makes it always a version.

All this may seem a mere semantic exercise, but the consequences for fluid-text editing, to be discussed in chapter 7, are crucial, for to edit a version of a work necessarily means to edit, in some way, all versions of the work. In the following chapter, I want to clarify a fluid-text definition of the version but do so primarily as a step toward further understanding the root cause of all versions: revision.

CHAPTER FIVE

Readers and Revision

> . . . *but then authors, they say, never read*
> *their own books; writing them, being*
> *enough in all conscience.*
>
> —Herman Melville, *Redburn*

If we define work, not as product, but as energy, then we must view versions accordingly. As determined in chapter 3, literary *work* is the collective energies put into the creation of a piece of writing by a writer, editors, and the culture. To push the metaphor, *versions* are pulsings of that collective energy that register themselves partially or fully in packets of matter (physical documents) or whose registrations may be inferred from such documents. The proper study of versions, then, lies in the discovery of meaning in the process of the transformation of energy into matter, which, as we shall soon see, is a matter of both genesis and revision.

Why and how a version emerges as a materialization of authorial and cultural pressures is the primary focus of fluid-text analysis, and to further clarify the nature of versions, we can affirm the following eight determinants of a version.

1. *Versions are physical but not always available.* This is to say that versions of work may be attached to and coterminous with physical documents or drawn from inferences found in physical documents. Any single document may constitute a single version, and evidence of multiple versions, fragmentary or full, can be found on a single document. Versions, therefore, may be both *physical* and *inferred*.

2. *No version is entire of itself.* The defining feature of a version is that physical or inferential evidence shows it to be *linked* to another version. In this regard a version cannot, logically, be revised into a separate work because the fact of revision establishes the linkage to its predecessor.

3. *Versions are revisions.* Versions are always the result of some textual alteration either authorially intended and/or editorially coerced, or culturally induced, or accidental. Revisions may be initiated by or on behalf of the writer; they may be prompted by editors; they may be demanded by readers; thus creating in each case a version. Accidental revision is relevant if the unintended error (an undetected but meaningful typo, a dropped passage or switched chapter) becomes familiarized by a particular readership.

4. Thus, *versions are not authorizations.* Since not all revision is made by or even sanctioned by the writer or the writer's agents, we cannot necessarily link version to authority. Editors, adapters, and readers in the culture and beyond the writer's control alter texts to create their own versions of a work. It is, of course, vital to the study of fluid texts that we be prepared to distinguish authorial from nonauthorial revision by a close analysis of intentions, but we are not required to study only authorial versions. Versions, whether authorized in some way or not authorized, are equally valid and have relative significance depending upon the critical ends for which they may be used.

5. *Versions are different.* One version's link to another is manifested by its similar workings; however, a version must be defined by its *degree* of difference not similarity. While it is true that all revision has meaning, a version's revision results in substantial differences in the nature and impact of the text. Thus, *macroscopic* revision creating substantial rearrangements or substitutions of text may suggest a version, whereas *microscopic* revision or the fine-tuning of a text may not. A version always makes us aware of the distance between itself and its linked partners.

6. *A version must be more than the sum of its variants.* This is to say that versions are defined not only by the degree of revision (or difference, or distance) but also by the *direction* of the

revisions. The comparison of sequential versions will always reveal a *strategic* pattern of revision evincing some *reconception of the function of the work* itself. (Not all macro revisions may be strategic; and micro tinkering, if shown to follow a new aesthetic design, can perforce be seen as strategic.)

7. *Versions have audiences.* That is, one version distinguishes itself from another by its attempt to manipulate a readership differently, or by its embracing of new readerships. Moreover, specific historical readerships may be attached to specific historical versions. Thus, a version has a definable *rhetorical impact*, and a test of its relevance is that it will necessarily alter our reading of a work.

8. Accordingly, *versions are critical constructs.* Although a version must have some (if only minimal) physical grounding and hence some kind of survivable physical embodiment, its presence is established through historical and editorial, hence critical, construction. Thus, the existence of a version is always arguable, and our sense of its variant impact upon our reading is only as good as the arguments in support of the variant readings.[1]

Modes of Production of the Version

With the literary version defined as in the preceding list of determinants, we can also categorize specific instances of the version. Here I try to account for physical and (as they may occur) inferred versions throughout three modes of production: creation, publication, and adaptation.

Creation

In this mode of production, writers think, scribble, write, and rewrite, creating from time to time various documents that may themselves constitute physical versions of a work in progress or bear evidence of inferable versions.

Journals and letters. Writers may articulate ideas for literary works in journals for themselves or in letters for others. Each instance may be taken as an inferred version of a work. Unlike such writers as Emerson, Hawthorne, and James, who maintained journals methodically, Melville kept only three very sketchy journals, each associated with a specific period of touring and none related to his early years at sea or the creation of *Typee*. But his letters to editors, such as his defense of the American expurgations to his British publisher Murray, indicate his conception of *Typee* as it had evolved from one version to the next. (This and other matters concerning *Typee* in this section are discussed more fully in *Melville Unfolding*.)

Notes and rehearsals. Writers may scribble out ideas in typical "prewriting" fashion in order to get ideas started and juices flowing. We may infer certain early versions of a work from such scribbling. Once again, we have little evidence of Melville's having performed such outlining for *Typee*. We do know that during his maritime years and upon his return home from sea, Melville regaled sailors, friends, and family with yarns and that these oratorical rehearsals surely served to hone the language he used to relate certain anecdotes in *Typee*. Also, on the inside of the cover folder containing his manuscript for *Typee*, Melville doodled different versions of the character's name *Marheyo*, indicating his desire to modify his Polynesian spelling into something more accessible for Western readers. This in conjunction with other evidence reveals a possible "turning point" between two inferred versions of *Typee:* the travel narrative and the romance.

Working drafts. Once writers find themselves actually composing, not just scribbling or jotting notes (if they engage in such preliminaries), they have embarked upon a working or rough draft, which as likely as not survives as a set of papers, some showing heavy revision, others (probably the cleaner rewritten pages of earlier, now discarded sheets) less. The *Typee* manuscript is a three-chapter fragment of a working draft that was significantly shorter than the first published version and bears evidence of at least three versions of the work.

Circulating drafts. Writers may copy their work for others to read and help edit. A classic instance of this is Eliot's sharing of his *Waste Land* typescript with Ezra Pound, who removed large chunks of the text, creating something close to the version with which we are now familiar. Similar evidence on the *Typee* manuscript suggests that Melville passed his working draft on to his brother Gansevoort, who suggested several changes and one or two major excisions. But unlike the *Waste Land* circulating draft that bears two full versions of the poem in one document, Melville's fragment only hints at his brother Gansevoort's complicity in creating a separate version of Melville's evolving work.

Fair copies or typescripts. Documents prepared for publishers may vary significantly from working drafts that precede them and print versions that follow. We can be certain that Melville prepared a fair copy of *Typee* and that its text must have been different from the working draft text because chapter numbering on the draft does not match the print numbering. Moreover, the fair-copy text did not resemble the first-edition text because evidence in letters reveals that Melville added material and his brother edited proofs before publication.

Publication

Well before publishing, a writer has inflected his work to fit his or her internalized notions of audience and culture. Such negotiations are unavoidable and not necessarily undesired. But the moment of publication is a fabled turning point in the creative process, for when a work is submitted for reproduction and circulation to a broader public, a writer must surrender certain elements of control, and new versions immediately emerge. Publication may occur in manuscript or through mechanical means.

Manuscript publication. In the days before presses, books were reproduced in manuscript with considerable variation occurring from one document to the next. *Piers Plowman,* to name only one of many examples, exists in several radically different nonauthorized manuscript versions circulated among radically different audiences. But even after Gutenberg, poets from Donne to Dickinson have prepared and distributed their works in manuscript rather than print form. There is little evidence that Melville engaged in the practice of circulating manuscripts to readers other than editors and publishers for the purposes of print publication. *Billy Budd,* which was never published in Melville's lifetime and existed for thirty years in its not entirely finished state, was surely intended for print publication rather than manuscript circulation.

Print publication. Physical documents emerging from the first phases of print reproduction—copy-editing, galleys, and page proofs; magazine issues, first editions, and corrected copies of editions—are likely to reveal numerous micro revisions and some macro revision that may constitute a version of a work. *Typee*'s first British and American editions vary substantially from the manuscript and from each other. The likelihood of significant new versions due to censorship and other reader pressures occurs in a second phase of print publishing that includes revised, expurgated, bowdlerized, and abridged editions of a work. As we know, the revised American edition of *Typee* is famously expurgated. Illustrated and scholarly editions may attempt to be more respectful of authorial intentions, although not necessarily. And this third phase of publishing also eventuates in more physical versions. *Typee* has been heavily illustrated, as one might expect given its vivid description and lurid scenes, but not in Melville's lifetime. And it has been edited by scholars at least three times (Stedman, Weaver, and the NN editors).

Adaptation

At some point, works of enduring popularity are likely to be transformed into a different format or genre. These acts of cultural revision are an extension of the creative processes initiated by the writer, but are generally performed without any authorial participation. Translation extends access to a work but only by rendering it entirely into a new text; without doubt it is the most thorough of revisions and is necessarily an act of critical construction, and as such a translation is undeniably a physical version of the work. Other transformations involve adaptations of text into different genres: comic books, stage and radio productions, films, operas, recordings, and the visual arts. *Typee* has appeared in two comic book versions and two films.

But while we may conclude this segment of our inquiry into the nature of versions with the happy assumption that our eight-point definition and three-tiered categorization will have some utility in establishing critical boundaries for fluid-text analysis, we must also admit (to paraphrase one writer paraphrasing another) that these categories are only a Versionology full of Leviathanisms, but signifying nothing. Nothing, that is, unless we dig down to the cause of all versions, which is revision, and to the deeper structures of change.

Revision Codes

The problem with categorizing types of versions, as my allusion to Melville's attack on systematic classification in the "Cetology" chapter of *Moby-Dick* implies, is that it attempts to know the literary phenomenon by classifying the things constituting it (versions), rather than the processes and forces (revision) that eventuate in the things. Things (documents, whales) have substance and are real, but the phantom forces that generate these objects are more real, even though grasping the phantom is tough to do. Ishmael wants to know the phantom; Ahab wants to kill it. Let's follow Ishmael.

The focus on text-objects (things), especially for bibliographers and editors, is understandable, given the assumption that no two objects occupy the same space, and there is an undeniable comfort in seeking out a unitary object to edit or analyze rather than a hydra. In editing, we invariably seek to construct one version of a text. To a large extent, this is a response to that book publishing convention which generally insists upon printing one and only one text per book, and this convention is itself a response to the limits of readers, who are conditioned to read one text at a time only. But fluid-text editing, that is, the editing of a process or the energy of a work, not simply its text-objects, requires us to edit multiple versions at once. It begins with the assumption that two texts need to and *can* occupy one space. Indeed, in working draft documents they *do* occupy one space: revisions are piled on top of revisions. For fluid-text editing to make process rather than object manifest, it must struggle against the accepted conventions of publishing and the habits of readers. It must manage and display the hydra of revision.

From a fluid-text perspective, the important feature of a version, then, is not so much What It Is (object) but How It Got To Be What It Is (process). Thus, before we can begin to explore what meaning revision might have, we need to ask questions about the *work of revision (travaille)*. For instance: How does revision differ from genesis, or the work of origination? And: What is revision's relation to intentionality? Accordingly: What function does revision play in the act of writing? More specifically: What *triggers* revision? And what role does audience play in triggering revision? Ultimately we are asking: Who is doing what with whom? These inquiries concerning what I have called *revision codes* will help us read and edit the fluid text.

Genesis and Revision

The study of the intentions and forces behind textual fluidity has little to do with genesis and everything to do with revision. What can one say about genesis except that it is everything and yet nothing to speak of? Words happen. They seem to come from nowhere. *Ab nihilo*. Boom. What can you say?

To be sure, a good deal of thought and feeling precedes the formation of words in the mind well before the tentative jotting down of notes or test phrasings. But these thoughts and jots come out of a consciousness that is always veiled from us, the readers of the words, and even for that matter from the writers of the words themselves. Words happen, and the most we can say is that the writer participated consciously in some way in this leap out of darkness. Writers, when asked, "Where do you get your ideas," will speak of this process of genesis either darkly, or defensively, or joyously, or with mixed wonder and despair, but rarely with any kind of specificity that engenders further critical discussion. Critics are understandably frustrated in trying to derive much meaning out of the intentions and forces that drive genesis. It is a brick wall or white whale, and our only critical resort is to generalized speculation about the possible mental conditions that might have accompanied the moment of genesis. Words just happen.

Let's say we have discovered the working draft manuscript of *Moby-Dick,* and at the top of the first leaf we see the words "Call me Ishmael" clearly inscribed. Melville wrote it; he intended to write it; there it is. We can interpret the meaning of these three words, but their presence in manuscript tells us little about how they got there, or about Melville's intention to write those words and not some other words. Whatever thinking, feeling, and mental word formations occurred in Melville's mind before he inscribed the words are lost to us. In effect, the *genesis* of "Call me Ishmael" in this imagined scenario is meaningless. But revision is a different matter.

Let's now say that our imagined working draft of *Moby-Dick*—and remember, I am just making this up—showed the following:

>   hm
> Call me Is⫶ael.
>   ^

Orthographically, such a revision—the substitution of the letters *hm* for the letter *r* in "Israel" to render "Ishmael"—is small, but would have enormous implications for the study of the novel and, suddenly, Melville's intentions. Even though this example is imagined, the historical possibility of "Call me *Israel*" is not far-fetched. Melville was considering writing up the story of a beggar named Israel in 1849–50 just before he landed the idea of *Moby-Dick.* (Later he did that write-up as the 1855 novel *Israel Potter.*) Moreover, Jacob/Israel figures throughout Melville's writings and is a central image in his late poem "Art." Biographically and rhetorically, the playing upon the biblical Israel would have made as much sense for Melville, at that point in his life, as his use of Ishmael. (Imagine the psycho-semiotic field day before us: Melville would have had to substitute his own initials—HM—for the r in *Israel* to render *Ishmael.*) And needless to say, the idea that Melville might have written "Call me Israel" not "Ishmael" is enough to alter anyone's reading of the entire book: Melville's greatest speaker might have been the clever bounder Jacob rather than the outcast wanderer Ishmael.

Interpretive potentials aside, the point of this imagined revision is to dramatize a simple human fact: we gravitate toward revision in ways different from our gravitation toward genesis. This is true because revision always reveals *an intention to change meaning,* and we sense that a text with a history of revision is always more deeply interpretable than if that same text were known to us only as an act of genesis. Moreover, critical and cultural meanings can be derived from the distance and direction charted by the end points of the intended revision.

We do not have to invent an example in order to show that a revised text bears more evidence of intentions than unrevised products of genesis, for real examples abound. And the power of revised texts to excite a critical response in readers should tell us something about the importance of revision, not simply in the study of the personal and societal forces that may have caused the revision, but also in the way we read.

Emily Dickinson's line "Sleep the meek members of the resurrection" in her most famous fluid text, "Safe in their Alabaster Chambers" (no. 216), has meaning enough concerning the idea of death as a sleep awaiting a reawakening. But students become far more deeply engaged with the line when they read the revision: "*Lie* the meek members of the resurrection." First, there is the discussion of how *lie* implies finality in death, but then the discussion grows to include the problem of *why* Dickinson made this change, and what the change suggests about Dickinson's tone and rhetorical strategies in both versions of the poem. In a poem that mocks those who feel assured of resurrection, *sleep* implies some validation of their false assurance; the idea of shifting to *lie* is to make the dead seem deader.

Of course, we can come to this conclusion about *lie* without knowing it had once been *sleep.* The inertia of *lie* is connoted in the word alone, not in the fact of its having been revised from the less inert *sleep.* Why bother with textual fluidity? But this objection can be countered in two ways. First, our sense of the meaning of the word *lie* necessarily alters when we see it paired with its predecessor *sleep.* As a textual fluidity, the meaning of *lie* takes on the special light of its having evolved from some other word. The word has a genealogy. Taken as an initial act of genesis, *lie* would be nothing more than the denotative, dictionary *lie.* But taken

as an element in the process of revision, the word has its own new con-
notation that takes the flavor of "not *sleep* but rather *lie*." The word
requires a new kind of spelling to express its meaning; it needs to be
encoded in some new way, either as *sleep/lie,* perhaps, or *sleep* → *lie.*

But a second and more important response to the objection that we
can arrive at the full meaning of Dickinson's word choice without knowing its genealogy is that *the fact of the shifting* of the words (not just the
shifted words themselves) has meaning. In this regard, our understanding that the revision code *sleep* → *lie* should read not simply "*sleep* was
intentionally changed to *lie*" but also something like this: "You readers
think these meek members simply *sleep,* and that they, like you, will find
resurrection, but in fact they *lie,* for what is dead is dead, and neither
you nor they shall rise again." Here, the shift from sleep to lie is fraught
with the tension of a more insistent rhetorical engagement, one that
involves authorial intent and reader response.

The working draft of the *Typee* manuscript is rife with such revised
texts, or what I call *revision sites.* Perhaps the simplest but most intriguing site or set of sites has already been mentioned: Melville's play with
savage and *islander.* What is interesting here is that Melville often revises
savage and *native* to *islander;* however, on rare occasions he also alters
islander to *savage.* In this case, the revision code *savage* → *islander* does
not quite suffice in signaling the complexity of the revision. Something
like *savage* ↔ *islander* might be better, or, to borrow the mathemati-
cian's delta sign for omnidirectional change, we might designate the
revised word as Δ*savage(islander).* (This symbol has the benefit of
flagging words that have a revision history without unduly interfering
with our ability to read the word; thus, this device for revision coding
may have, as we shall see in chapter 6, an editorial as well as critical utility.) This curious but useful designation is enough to signal a textual
fluidity and to encourage questions about the degree of change implied,
but the fact of revision as it impinges on the creation of a version is also
a matter of the *direction* a pattern of revision takes the text, from one
intended conception of that text to another. In this regard *sleep* → *lie*
indicates a small degree of change designed to realize more fully an
existing intention. It is a tactical or micro revision. But Δ*savage
(islander)* indicates a more strategic pattern of revision throughout the
working draft that signals a reconception of the writer's use of a culturally loaded term, and one that is central to the print version of *Typee.*
Δ*Savage,* then, may stand for a turning point in Melville's creative

process, or even as the *trigger* of a new version of *Typee,* one that is more socially aware than its predecessor.

Obviously, not all revision sites have a "delta function" that can afford them sufficiently strategic distance or direction to warrant their rising to the status of a version. But of those sites that do have this quality, we can ask further questions about the nature of revision. How do these "triggering" sites come about, what causes them, what is the function of their Δfunction? Less gnomically, what purpose does such "macro" revision serve? Because revisions are rhetorical and therefore involve a writer seeking to unite with a reader in new ways or with a new reader altogether, we may attack this problem from two rhetorical angles: who performs the revision and with whom in mind. Let's look first at the kinds of readers involved.

Audience: Three Kinds of Readers

Revision is a ritual of self-fashioning and cultural negotiation. A step beyond the inscrutable moment of genesis, the more scrutable act of revision first requires that the writer become a reader. Revision is the writer-as-reader's rewriting. It is also a writer's dance performed with other readers in mind. But beyond the authorial realm, we also know that these other readers also revise a writer's text, insisting upon changes, cuts, new endings, sequels, and more. These rituals of revision—authorial, editorial, and reader induced—are fundamentally social events and hence rhetorical, and our revision codes must always reflect this basic fact. But who are the audiences of a fluid text?

Literary critics posit a general reader; literary historians seek out a writer's actual or historical readership among contemporaries and reviewers. But the fluid-text analyst looks to readers more intimately connected to the creative process itself. In this case, writers and editors are themselves readers; they are readers empowered to alter the text. It is assumed that collaborators are merely cowriters; fundamentally, they are also "first readers," and their revisionary cowriting is a function of their reading. To distinguish the work of one such "revising reader" from another, we must be willing to discriminate intentions. Crucial to our grasp of the rhetoric of revision, then, is the constructable intent of writers and collaborative editors who initiate revision. Rather than discounting intentionality, to use McGann's echo of Keats, as an elusive "unheard melody,"[2] we need ways to pin it down and measure it. This is not because we may have a lingering nostalgia for the vanquished notion of authorial autonomy but rather because we have a simple need to clarify the role of "editors" as early readers and participants in the creative process of social texts. The rhetorical impact of collaboration cannot be understood unless we know the extent of each collaborative editor's creative participation in the rhetorical conditions of the revision process. With this in mind we can discern at least three kinds of readers.

We begin with the understanding that writers are social beings shaped not simply by social pressures, but by their self-conscious attempts to find a relation to those external pressures. Their "autonomy" if it exists at all is in their resistance to the elements that give them shape: their language, family or associates, and cultural ideologies. Production begins when, writing alone and comparatively isolated from professional editors, writers give individual expression to words, feelings, and thoughts that necessarily embody internalized social constraints. Thus, some degree of social collaboration first occurs intellectually at the moment of genesis.

We generally think that when writers are alone, they are alone. But they are not. Two people sit at the writing desk: the writer writing and the writer reading. Writers are their own *first readers*. And whomever they project into that readership during the moment of genesis—a supreme reflection of their perfect being, a dissatisfied spouse, mother, father, older sibling, a god of some sort—is the embodiment of the first level of prepublication collaboration.

A *second reader* emerges as a writer begins to revise. There is above all the writer as self-editor, who plays with language to get words to convey thoughts, memories, and images more effectively; and there is the censoring self-editor, reflecting an internalized sense of decorum, politics, marketplace, and larger audience concerns. There is the proofreading self-editor, who usually in some finalizing stage not only corrects but suddenly remembers more and adds more. To use McGann's term, "autopoiesis" begins with the creative process, for the constant revision and recursive re-creation of texts is a process of self-collaborative feedback. To the extent that these stages of revision can be discerned in the material text itself, they are deeply fundamental evidence of intentionality, not merely, as McGann puts it, a "subplot" to the real story of further social interactions.

Revision and the creative process continue beyond the writer's sensorium when *third readers,* that is, the first external revisers, enter the dance. These are nonprofessionals who edit a writer's work, suggest changes, demand revision, plead, coerce, and cajole. Pound was one such third reader for Eliot. His effusive/devastating marginal scrawls and excisions in pencil on Eliot's typescript of *The Waste Land* are clear evidence of two sets of intentions interacting creatively. What is important to note here is that our understanding of the Pound-Eliot collaboration exists only to the degree that we can discern one set of intentions from the other: the intentions of the writers in his or her capacities as first and second readers from the intentions of a collaborator, or *fabbro* (to use Eliot's word for his editorial bro, Ezra Pound) as a third-reader editor.

Professional editors and book-makers may be added to the list of third readers. They make their presence known by demanding expansions and excisions of text but also by dictating matters of house style, book design, and distribution. Without a doubt, these individuals take control of a writing project, and as with Gordon Lish on Raymond Carver; or Maxwell Perkins on Faulkner, Thomas Wolfe, and Marjorie Kinnan Rawlings; or Murray and Wiley on Melville, they are for the most part the first line of collaborators in the social text as initially conceived by textual sociologists. But here as with preproduction editors, we cannot understand the nature of the collaboration without separating the collaborator's intentions from those of the writer and his or her other second and third readerships.

The list of fluid-text readers goes on, and the story is the same. Reviewers, as in the case of *Typee,* were powerful enough to force Melville's third reader Wiley to demand expurgations from first and second reader Herman Melville. Illustrators and adapters constitute a later set of nonauthorial collaborative readers, whose work can modify the writer's text. Reprinters, bowdlerizers, and *Reader's Digest*–izers (whose commercial intent is paramount) and the scholarly editor (whose usually posthumous interventions cannot escape ideology or intention) are emissaries of a culture and modifying readers as well.[3] The general reader also plays a role in revising texts. They put down their money, read what they see, make of it what they will, take their thoughts to bed or school, and shape their response, in writing or in mind, to their own willful intentions. At times, they grow angry with or idolatrous of a text. They fight back in school board hearings and in libraries or courts to censor or remove texts; or out of love for a text, they become adapters or illustrators or translators themselves and change the text to create a new vision. These readers revise on behalf of themselves and in some sense as agents of a culture. They are destroyers and preservers, whose intentions, like them or not, have a profound effect upon what we read.

There may be more readers than these, but they represent a full range of interconnected collaborations, feedbacks, and intentions in the history of a fluid text, which is necessarily a history of intention, revision, and rhetorical response. Rather than delimiting the role of intentionality in the wide-ranging fields of creative process, book production, and reader response, we need to learn how to make distinctions, as Thorpe puts it, about the "mingling[s] of human intentions" (37) manifested in the many kinds of readers who manipulate a text. These readers are revisers, and what they desire and do shapes the fluid text.

Revisers

To distinguish the kinds of readers who, throughout the entire literary phenomenon, play a role in revision and the creation of versions, we need to delineate more clearly the interpenetrations of intended texts and social texts and the ways in which readers who revise texts actually revise. This inquiry requires a three-pronged response related to the three categories of version we have already established. Just as versions may be classified in terms of creation, publication, and adaptation, revision can be an authorial, editorial, or cultural process.

Authorial Revision: Getting It

Writers are often asked how they do what they do. As already noted the question is usually framed in such a way as to focus on genesis: Where do you get your ideas? Since genesis is essentially an automatic (and inscrutable) rather than reflective process, this kind of interrogation often puts interrogated writers either on the defensive or in a jocularly deceptive mood, and their responses are frequently brick walls for criticism. How did E. L. Doctorow compose *Ragtime?* It began with his staring in the middistance between typewriter and the wall of his study and envisioning a car breaking down. The rest grew out of that image. Critics are bound to be frustrated by such anecdotes, and this natural frustration has led critics to discount the creative process in general as a valid arena for critical analysis. But it may be we are asking writers the wrong question. The focus should not be on genesis but revision. Why did you change this word? How did you get from here to there? From *sleep* to *lie* or *savage* to *islander*? In the broadest of terms, revision at the authorial level is change in its most elemental degree. It is also performed in isolation. Let me clarify.

Authorial revision is an elemental process of "getting it." I refrain from saying that writers revise in order to "get it *right*" or "get it *straight*" because this implies some finality to a process that is by nature fluid, continuous, and often "finalized" merely by the accidents of time and publication. Nor is the "it" that writers are trying to "get" merely a single block of language that most nearly approximates an object of desire—an image, symbol, character, action, idea, and so on—although, of course, such ends are part of the "it" to be got. Rather, the "it" achieved is a *moment of satisfaction in the writer's attempt to realize a relationship between self and thing desired.* I write to discover what I want to say, but the saying is always an essaying of thoughts and feelings. If no attempt can finally achieve an ideal connection, then the real object of revision is not so much an end product as it is some coming to terms with the very problem of connecting words and "felt thoughts." This is not to say that writers (as their own first and second readers) revise for the sake and pleasure of revision (although that is not far from true). Rather, the "getting" at the "it of revision" comes closer to revealing a writer's historical meanings than any single word or passage that finally "gets got" into print. This is true because the analysis of a revision process can yield historically constructable strategies and tactics of the getting of words to approach thought, whereas the analysis of words and passages divorced from the context of their revision process cannot.

Writers invariably work at first in isolation. This may seem in contradiction to our earlier premise that because we are never free of social constraints, "no one is alone when they are alone." But even in public spaces, café or bar, a writer gathers herself up into a state of concentrated self-absorption that establishes a mental barrier to all else. The writing process happens when the writer finds himself "somewhere else." This isolation or creative alienation is not only a verifiable psychic state; it is also symbolic. It symbolizes the writer's desire (if not actual realization) to achieve an autonomous, independent "me" in relation to the external shaping forces of a culture that are "not me." A writer may write in affirmation or rejection of his culture, either consciously or unconsciously fulfilling its dictates, or consciously denying them. Arguably, "a political unconsciousness" suffusing the culture also shapes one's denial of that culture, thus making an act of denial just a form of hierarchical affirmation. But while the writer's act of isolation may be culturally determined, it is in fact a symbolic declaration of cultural independence, and one's independently engendered revisions on the page manifest a conscious attempt to position oneself vis-à-vis a culture. This is true even when the revisions are clearly self-censorious, for they suggest a willful retreat based on a constructable strategy of self-definition. The independence of revision is not an act of total denial or "negative freedom"; it is achieved by degree and through negotiation in relation to the language and a culture. It is in a very real sense what one can "get" at a particular moment. In short, then, authorial revision is the getting of words in closer approximation to felt thoughts, performed in isolation, to achieve a more clearly defined relationship between self and culture. Melville's "dance" with *savage, islander,* and *native* is the writer's private attempt to establish both his departure from and identity with the ideologies of his culture. Somewhat paradoxically, then, authorial revision sites may be seen as independently engendered social texts.

But the fundamental question remains: what degree of authorial revision may result in a separate version of a text rather than just the refinement of an existent version? The answer can only be derived individually for individual cases, and each answer will be debatable. But the terms of analysis for this manner of revision seem clearer now. It is not enough simply to say that the revisions must realize a reconception of the work. We need to clarify the nature of reconception. As we have been defining it, authorial revision involves a "getting" of self and thought, and a "repositioning" of one's self and thought to language and culture. It is also a rhetorical manipulation of words to achieve an entirely *new* distancing from and an affirmation of both self and audience. If such gettings and repositionings in a writer's revisions can be linked to *a new and distinct rhetorical strategy,* then the revisions may be said to be a reconception of the work and thus constitute a version.

The *Typee* manuscript provides a range of authorial revisions, some *re*-conceptual, others not. The largely methodical rearranging of antecedents and pronouns appearing from time to time, such as the shuffling about of the words *Toby, my companion, his,* and *he* on one leaf, is at best a minor realignment of Melville's sense of self with language and the character or real person Toby. The rhetorical shift, to me, is decidedly tactical and relatively inconsequential. And it will remain inconsequential in my mind until, of course, someone constructs an argument making its rhetorical strategizing consequential. Melville's revision of his description of the buildings on the Hoolah-Hoolah ground to conform to his memory and sense of social class is more of a reconception. However, Melville's announced rethinking of his method of conveying Toby's speech to the natives not only amounts to a recharacterization of Toby but is also a strategic redistancing of himself from both the individual and character, as well as a new way of thinking of himself as a writer. Here the getting at self and language and the shifting relation of self to culture combine to argue for a strategic reconception. Such authorial revision implies a version.

Editorial Revision: Doing It "Better"

When writers break their isolation (as we have defined it) and submit their writing to *third readers,* they initiate a phase of collaboration that we may call editorial revision. In this process, an editor may be a friend or relative suggesting revision or a copy-editor requiring house styling, or professional editors and publishers making changes either before, during, or after publication. Publishers not in negotiation with writers can make editorial revision without the writer's consent, and such revision and the imposition of bibliographic codes upon a linguistic text are also a matter of editorial revision. This mode of revision is not so much the elemental matter of *getting it* that we find in authorial revision as it is the presumption of *doing it "better."*

Generally speaking, the separate vision of an editor is one of betterment, however that may be defined. Thus, by "doing it better," the editor attempts to bring the text closer in line with his or her notion of the writer's goal with his/her own personal agenda as a reader, or the agenda of the publisher or of a readership the editor presumes to represent. The likelihood of a patterned set of editorial revisions being taken as a separate version depends upon the distance between the writer's own revision process and the editor's "betterment," regardless of the writer's complicity or lack thereof in the editorial reconfigurations. That is, an editorial version may or may not be "authorized."

The *Typee* manuscript is written almost entirely in Melville's hand. The few but patterned instances of his brother Gansevoort's editorial interventions may be used primarily to substantiate more fully Melville's own independent performance of tactical and strategic revisions beforehand. In this regard, Melville seems to have followed almost all of the two dozen, predominately grammatical suggestions. Only a couple of changes, whose furious penciled swirls seek to tone down sexual references, are substantial enough to change the original text's rhetorical impact. They more clearly reflect Gansevoort's variant sensibility or his conception of the audience's variant (i.e., more conventional sexual) sensibility. The case that these revisions may be part of a separate, let's call it "cleaner," version of *Typee* is enhanced when they are linked to further changes Gansevoort might have made later on and on Herman's behalf in the British proofs, the removal required by Murray of a salacious dance scene, and additional cuts made by American editor John Wiley in the first American edition, not to mention cuts of a sexual nature Melville himself probably made in the revised American edition. Gansevoort's manuscript revisions seem to be the vanguard of this inferred, "cleaner" version (spread out over various stages of composition as evident in various physical documents) meant to "better" his brother's text. The record suggests that Melville took his brother's advice, and that of others, and even added to this particular pattern of revision. And since these editorial incursions have a recognizable rhetorical strategy, they readily combine to make a version. Moreover, even if Melville had rejected each suggestion and maintained each sexy text, the ignored editorial suggestions would constitute an inferred version, for the suggestions, insofar as they are recorded, reveal a consistent, desexualized, editorial reconception of the work.

Melville's complicity in these and other editorial revisions—most obviously his arguments to Murray in favor of the Wiley expurgations—raises an important problem of collaboration and intentionality: how does one distinguish authorial from editorial revision. The problem seems easily resolvable if, as in the case of Gansevoort's interventions in manuscript, all editorial hands can be distinguished from the writer's. Indeed, the revision codes for Gansevoort's most significant suggested revisions are layered for us in manuscript like archaeological stratifications. Melville's saucy harem reference to Macheath of Gay's *Beggar's Opera* (manuscript p. 31) appears in Melville's hand like the lowest foundations of a lost city.

> With Captain Macheath in the opera I could have sung "Thus
> I lay like a Turk with my doxies around"

Gansevoort's pencilings loop over this three-line passage in manuscript as if to scribble it away; and Melville's subsequent cancellation—three lines of ink over his brother's penciled loops—accepts the manuscript expurgation. This linguistic coming and two goings visually stratified on the manuscript page represent a complex phase of complicit editorial revision. The revision codes at this revision site are also materially symbolic of Melville's passing, at this one point, from the condition of a solo writer to that of an editor. We also see here the layerings of progressive intentions: Melville's expression, Gansevoort's negation, and Melville's acceptance of the negation.

Here the separate then merging roles are clearly delineated, but such is not the case when we consider subsequent revisions, not appearing in manuscript. A collation of the reading text of the manuscript with the print-text of the first British edition reveals hundreds more revisions in Melville's text performed possibly by Melville (as a revising writer), Gansevoort, Melville's sister Augusta, who may have fair-copied *Typee,* publisher John Murray, his copy-editor Henry Milton, and Melville again (as a revising editor). Moreover, some of these revisions may have occurred as Melville prepared his fair copy of *Typee* from the working draft or during the regular preparations of that fair copy for publication. A case in point is the two uncanceled sentences that follow Melville's above-quoted, deleted Macheath reference:

> Never certainly was effeminate ottoman in the innermost shrine of his serglio attended by lovlier houris with more excess of devotion. Sardanapalus might have experienced such sensations but I dout whether any of the sultans ever did.

These lines do not appear in any print version of *Typee.* They may have been clipped wholesale by any of the individuals mentioned above at any time. Or they may have been authorially revised by Melville in various stages. Or they may have been editorially revised by editors, including Melville as compliant editor, also in various stages, until the entire passage was in effect whittled away altogether. There is simply no material evidence, aside from the absence of the lines, to help clarify who did how much when.

The conundrum is this: we know the consequences of multiple hands clapping on this text, but how many versions are dancing on this space between manuscript and print? Can we by inspecting these distant manuscript and print variations alone discern patterns of revision that suggest rhetorical strategies? Can we assign separate strategies, hence separate versions, to separate editors? Speculation on such matters can be a useful exercise in sorting out what is at stake in the editorial process.

Surely, Henry Milton would have corrected the misspellings of *seraglio, lovelier,* and *doubt,* unless Augusta had already caught them and revised them in fair copy. Both might have snipped off "with more excess of devotion" in order to let "lovelier houris" stand alone. And Melville might have accepted the snip. But if that phrase had been retained, Murray might have thought such an arabesque from an alleged sailor, no matter how toned down, would undermine credibility, and he might have thus cut the whole first sentence. The second sentence reference to the murderous Sardanapalus, slayer of wives, might have been something Gansevoort, while reading proofs, might have removed as he had earlier removed Macheath in manuscript. But Melville himself might have made the cut, in some moment of uxorious regret, even at the last minute, thinking of the married ladies in his family or of his future fiancée. Or maybe Murray put the kibosh on Sardanapalus. Many cooks make their cuts for various reasons: house style, family concerns, private bias, public taste, and so on. But how high are the stakes in these revisions? Does any one possible configuration of revisions alter the work to such a degree that we may say it has effected a significant reconceptualization; or do the revisions merely fulfill what the writer himself, as his own first and second readers, would have embraced? As such, these speculative revisions might constitute a "stage" of development toward the actualization of a version. And this, of course, only prompts us to ask what kind of revision in a developmental stage might trigger a new version. Naturally enough, it seems to me, we recognize that changes in spelling are not as relevant here as matters pertaining to sexuality, and that any set of revisions or stage of development in the editorial process that probes deeply into the writer's presentation of self vis-à-vis an audience necessarily argues for a version.

Without concrete information concerning an individual editor's revision strategies, we cannot satisfactorily conclude anything concrete about editorial versions. One recourse to the paucity of information is to lump all revisions together and attribute them to some sort of transcendent editorial collective that in attempting to "do the text better" represents the invisible hand of culture. The appeal of the transcendent editorial collective is undeniable. It obviates laborious scrutinizing of revision sites for evidence of more specified strategies and perilous speculations on intentionality. It accentuates the probability that the combined editors (Melville included) shared a single desire to get *Typee* quickly to market and accepted by a large reading public. And no doubt this kind of shared editorial desire existed. We can, with *Typee*, go even further: it is quite reasonable to assume that upon seeing the Sardanapalus reference, various editors would have independently and without conferring called for its removal. This kind of editorial agreement implies a certain degree of cultural imperative in the processes of revision, and it is an easy step to presume that an editorial collective transcends the idiosyncrasies of individual editors. However, the imperatives of marketplace and decorum, while obviously influential, are not performed upon a text without intermediaries. People as well as forces make a culture, texts, and revisions. And there is finally a lessening of critical impact when we argue for an editorial collective as the source of a version.

Understanding once again that the peculiarities of the composition history of any literary work will dictate their own particular solution to the problems of identifying editorial revisions and versions, we can nevertheless advise ourselves in all cases to forestall leaping to the idea of editors acting as the collective unconsciousness of a culture, even if that idea may become, in the course of scholarly investigation, a critical inevitability. The best first course of action, it seems to me, is to take each identifiable editor for what he or she is textually, that is, a set of strategies constructed out of patterns of revision. If patterns of revision are even remotely discernible and assignable, we can infer possible versions from those patterns and thus become better situated to articulate, as finally we must, the varied colors of their presumed cultural collectivity.

Cultural Revision: Making It Like Us

Having warned against the often inevitable but highly problematic critical gambit (one hesitates to call it a fallacy) of the editorial collective, I am sure to open myself to derision by suggesting that there is, beyond the editorial arena, something called cultural revision. The idea that a culture can, like the invisible hand of economy, revise a text is itself highly problematic, and therefore exciting as it relates to current approaches to cultural analysis. The problem is one of adaptation.

Once a text leaves the control of its originating writer and editors, once it enters not simply the "public domain" of copyright law but the public consciousness as a symbol or icon of cultural identity, that text will be transmogrified in various ways. *Frankenstein* became a theatrical and musical spectacle shortly after its publication in 1818 and well before Mary Shelley's own revision of 1831, well before John Balderston's 1928 play, and well before James Whale's 1930 film and its scores of twentieth-century knockoffs, including the parodic *Young Frankenstein* and brilliant *Gods and Monsters*. The remarkable fluidity of Stowe's text of *Uncle Tom's Cabin* is evident in a similar, long-standing proliferation of performance or cultural versions known as "Tom Shows" appearing on stage and in films from Civil War to Great War. *Moby-Dick*—not the whale, not the book, but the cultural icon—did not fully enter the American collective consciousness until the 1920s, not because of the academic revival of Melville but because of the two Barrymore film versions (one silent, one sound). Sometimes this kind of cultural revision occurs even before the writer and editors have their final say. *Billy Budd* became a play (1949), an opera (1951), and a film (1962) before the text of that work, surviving in unfinished manuscript form, was reliably established by Hayford and Sealts in 1962.

Although Melville's hoped-for illustrated edition of *Typee* never materialized in his lifetime, that text's images of island sensuality, especially Fayaway's dramatic unfurling of her tappa dress to make a sail for Tommo and herself in their canoe, were so visual that they seemed to stick on readers' retinas with a persistence of vision lasting into the twentieth century, when several illustrated editions finally emerged. As with any text that in some way takes on a life in the culture beyond that of the original text, *Typee* has a discernible iconic value. Even so, because our focus is on the working draft and because cultural revision is an arena so broad as to require a future book of its own, I shall not explore the cultural versions of *Typee* found in modern illustration, comic book, and film. However, cultural revision is a crucial extension of the fluid text, and it provokes important questions. How does the nature of cultural revision differ from authorial and editorial revision? Who are the agents of adaptation and for whom do they speak? How can adaptation be used to measure a culture?

Granted, *cultural revision* is a convenient misnomer. The term is misapplied because nothing so abstract as "culture" can be said actually to compose the adapted text. As with editorial revision, that task is always performed by individuals, usually in groups and often in true, shoulder-to-shoulder collaboration. Stage and film adaptations are intensely collaborative not only in the development of the new text, but also in the performance and production of the text. With so many variants, it would be a Herculean labor to assign creators to the performance versions within each text version of an adapted work. Our recourse though is not to mystify the efforts of the many collaborators by attributing production to a collective or political unconsciousness. Our recourse is to become Hercules: to particularize and historicize. The film version of Ahab circa 1956 is not the image of Cold War; it is John Huston, Ray Bradbury, and Gregory Peck in dialog about Ahab during the Cold War.

But though cultural revision is a misnomer, it is a useful misnomer, for as much as we recognize that people, not a cultural abstraction, are the revisers of popular versions of literary works, those revisers, in taking on the burden of adaptation, are, nevertheless, taking on a significantly larger project than that of even the writer and editor. They must position themselves vis-à-vis the original text and hence presume in some way to "speak for" the author; they speak, too, for themselves, and to and for new markets and/or different audiences. This complex positioning once again recalls Geertz's notion of ritual as a private *performance* of a public culture. Here, the enactment of a particularized "ethos" out of a universalized "worldview" is like a group of adapters working together to realize a version of the world that a given text represents. Thus, misnomer or not, cultural revision or adaptation is a culture's revision of a text even as it is a creation by specific idiosyncratic revisers. Whereas authorial revision is a matter of "getting it," and editorial revision is "doing it 'better,'" cultural revision is "making it like us," a process of refashioning the work to resemble the audience insofar as "us" includes the "me" of individual adaptive artists who do the refashioning.

It goes without saying that any cultural revision is sufficiently distant from its original as to constitute a version. And like translation, which is clearly the most textual of cultural adaptations, such cultural versions are inherently critical acts designed to bring the original text more in line with either the expectations or current needs of a culture. The measure of a culture lies in the distance between the original's rhetorical strategies and those that emerge in these adaptive remakings of a text in our own image.

All texts are fluid. They only appear to be stable because the accidents of human action, time and economy have conspired to freeze the energy they represent into fixed packets of language. Some understanding of the hidden private and public processes that engender a literary work can be achieved through the study of the revision codes and strategies that link one physical or inferred version of a text to another. We have investigated here the kinds of versions and modes of revision that constitute the fluid text. But how may the totality of this literary phenomenon be edited to accentuate revision, and how may such editions be made to serve both critical and pedagogical ends?

CHAPTER SIX

The Pleasures of
the Fluid Text

I desire the writer. I need his figure.

—Barthes

It may be bad enough that in chapter 4 I have defined literary work metaphorically as "energy," but, worse, the metaphor is also a pun that plays on the received notion of "work" as a thing *(oeuvre)* against the notion of work as process or labor *(travaille)*. Puns have a way of being dismissed even more quickly than metaphors, so I return to this idea of work as energy in apologetic tones because I think it is more solid than the punning might suggest, and I have yet to concoct a trope that can more succinctly convey the point.

A literary work is more than the sum of its texts; it is the combined energies of individual and social forces which through the processes of authorial, editorial, and cultural revision evolve from one version to the next and emerge from time to time as documents to be read by readers. Quite simply, certain agents of change "labor" in order to write; these writers and editors then "labor" to revise; still others "labor" to make the writing over in their own image; and readers "labor" to read and revise again. Perhaps more than any other object in a culture, a literary work is the locus of private and public energies.[1] So, the idea of work as energy has philosophical impact, and as I endeavored to show in chapters 4 and 5, we can begin to clarify the energy that constitutes a fluid text by learning to look more critically at versions and revision. In the concluding chapters, I want to consider how our critical "narratives of revision" (our labor histories of textual fluidity) can be used to shape the way we edit fluid texts. Theoretically, this goal is all well and good, but there are practical problems, both editorial and pedagogical, that complicate the analysis of textual fluidity. How do you edit energy? How do you teach it? How might these efforts extend reader access to the pleasures of textual fluidity?

Modern editing, literary theory, criticism, and classroom instruction have an understandable fixation on single texts, if only to address the simple need among theorists, critics, teachers, and students to locate the same words on the same page at the same time. Pinning fluid texts down to a fixed, single version most assuredly facilitates unified reading experiences and intellectual discourse of a certain kind, but a single reading text is at best only a benevolent despot to those interested in a discourse upon textual fluidity. The tyranny of the single reading text necessarily eliminates reflection upon the energies that drive texts from version to version.[2] Worse, by masking the energies of revision, it reduces our ability to historicize our reading and, in turn, disempowers the citizen reader from gaining a fuller experience of the necessary elements of change that drive a democratic culture.

I hope to show in this chapter that such historicizing is not just an option to "aesthetic" reading, nor is it merely a kind of "time line" contextualizing of a text, but is itself elemental to the reading process.[3] Reading is an idiosyncratic actualization of a document from the past; it animates through the present reader's consciousness and in our present tense the thoughts and creations of an earlier, other consciousness, world, and time; it enables us to become the self-aware conduit that connects then and now. In reflecting upon the shared "realistic historicism" of Hegel, Balzac, and Tocqueville, Hayden White states that history can "sensitize [us] to the *dynamic* elements in every achieved present, teach the inevitability of change, and thereby contributes to the release of that present to the past without ire or resentment."[4] Any literary work (when presented in its full, or even partial) textual fluidity, necessarily partakes of the historicizing experience White describes. While this sensitizing is not a certain assurance against "ire and resentment," such historicizing necessarily heightens a reader's awareness of the instability (fluidity) of democratic life and thereby sharpens one's intellectual survival skills in such a culture. Similarly, the reading of fluid texts accentuates the submerged but always present fact that a literary work is textually dynamic, that by itself it represents a history of change, that it is the embodiment of a confluence of desire and power.

Indeed, if the fluid text requires this kind of historicist reading—and not simply the juggling of multiple texts side by side, but the acquiring of a capacity to read the interval between any two versions—then this kind of reading requires in turn new strategies of book editing, designed for pedagogical as well as critical use. Inevitably, our discussion will turn (in chapter 7) to matters of apparatus, our ability to render and map the revision codes of a fluid text, and the efficacy of books in the age of hypertext. But as prelude to all this, we need to revisit the genre of the critical edition, or what I shall begin now to call the *edition imaginaire*, for no fluid-text edition can be any thing other than a critical construct of both mind and culture. Accordingly, we need to consider what a critical edition can and should do to encourage fluid-text reading. Eventually, I will apply this more fluid notion of critical editing to *Typee*. For now, to illustrate what I mean by the *edition imaginaire*, let's turn to Hershel Parker's problematic "Kraken edition" of Melville's problematic novel *Pierre*.

*P*ierre Imaginaire *and the Limits of the Critical Edition*

Calling the critical edition an *edition imaginaire* is no derogation.[5] By *imaginaire* I do not mean to suggest that the historical construct we call an edition is a mere flight of fancy in the editor's imagination. As stated earlier, editions, like histories, are not "made up"; they are, however, "made." And to the extent that this made thing reflects the mind-set of its maker, and to the extent that the maker is shaped either by or in conflict with an ideological superstructure of a culture, a critical edition is most certainly an embodiment of what an editor imagines a particular moment in the creation of a literary work to be. An *edition imaginaire* is not irrationally derived; rather, it reflects the editor's "image" of the writer's originating condition, a condition that cannot be known but only speculated upon, or imagined. Without doubt, an editor's speculations are colored by the literary theories and politics that suffuse the editor's culture, despite any announced editorial policy to reduce such subjectivities.[6] Thus, for this reason good editions display their data in a textual apparatus that explains their emendations. That is, editors select from an array of variants (or create new variants themselves) the ones they imagine most likely approximate the intentions they imagine the writer had in mind. A critical edition is a highly complex, presumably well argued "what-if," a supposing of what might have been. And this is no more so the case than it is with any history, which is inherently supposititious and also *imaginaire*.

You may be thinking, "There is really little new in the substance behind the wordplay on *imaginaire;* it's just more punning." But what is at stake here is the added view that critical *editions imaginaires* function in two concurrent modes, rhetorically and heuristically, and that an edition of this kind increases its effectiveness when it uses heuristic strategies to lessen the rhetoric.

A critical edition is by nature rhetorical in that, as a single-text embodiment of an imagined moment of creation, it becomes a matter of debate regarding copy-text and emendation; it is something that must be "argued for," and debate and argumentation are fundamentally matters of rhetoric. This "polemical" aspect, to borrow from Shillingsburg, of the *edition imaginaire* is unavoidable in the critical edition that showcases or foregrounds a single text only; nor is it desirable to attempt to eradicate the polemics. Indeed, the best critical editions display opposing arguments in debatable matters forthrightly along with the apparatus. Few, however, make an attempt to use the edition heuristically; that is, to foreground variants, to confront readers with the fact of textual fluidity as they read, and, most importantly, to engage them in the process of historicist judgment. Such strategies of confrontation are heuristic because, by participating in the construction of the text as one reads, the reader must learn new reading skills and a new sense of text and history. Readers must also be aware *that* they are learning as they learn. The best *editions imaginaires* are resolutely self-conscious.

Hershel Parker's Kraken edition of *Pierre* has been attacked, but largely for the wrong reasons. The general objection has been that rather than offering a text based on Melville's final intentions, Parker offers one that represents his "imagined" sense of Melville's original conception of the novel. But there is nothing wrong in this; Parker's bold focus on Melville's originating intentions does not violate the fundamental principles of critical editing. The problem with the Kraken edition is that it does not adequately direct the reader's reading of the text. If this provocative *Pierre imaginaire* errs, it does so because it is highly rhetorical and hardly heuristic.

Despite the ironies and instabilities implied in its subtitle, *Pierre; or,*

The Ambiguities (1852) is Melville's most stable text. Unlike *Typee*, *Moby-Dick*, many of the tales and poems, *Billy Budd* in manuscript, or even the limited-run *Clarel*, this novel is virtually devoid of textual variation. Melville did not leave a manuscript or proof sheets; the British "edition" of *Pierre* is little more than a limited binding up of the American sheets; and no revised edition exists (NN *Pierre* 329, 415). Poorly reviewed, the book's one edition sold poorly. In general, the print runs of Melville's other books managed to trickle out of existence throughout the century. Not so *Pierre*; seventy-nine copies remained "in print" or rather in storage just before the writer's death (NN 393). The only subsequent editions have been posthumous, largely academic publications (Robert S. Forsyth's Knopf edition, Henry Murray's Hendricks House, and the 1971 NN edition), and since these make mostly perfunctory emendations, we would be hard-pressed to classify any of the modern editions of *Pierre* as a separate version.

Given the virtually invariant condition of the documentary record of *Pierre; or, The Ambiguities*, we are tempted to say, without ambiguity, that this work is *not* a fluid text. But then, no text is not fluid, and nothing exists without ambiguity.

We know that the documentary record of a literary work—its manuscripts and editions—is simply the surviving physical remnant of now irretrievable developmental stages, the energies of which have been long since expended and lost in the creative and editorial processes. While we can be certain that each literary work *(oeuvre)* is the product of a working *(travaille)* that involves textual fluidities (versions), we also know that the evidence of the working (the versions themselves) may no longer exist in material form, so that a given published text may appear stable when, like all others, it is in reality fluid. The one unambiguous statement I am willing to make is that all works *are* fluid texts, although some reveal their fluidities more or less fully than others. *Pierre* is a case in point.

For Hershel Parker, Melville's text—a mix of gothic romance and psychological novel—is far more fluid than it appears. Since the mid-1970s he has promoted what we may here call a "two-*Pierre*" thesis that is as problematic biographically, aesthetically, and editorially as it is compelling.[7] On the basis of Melville's contract with Harper's, two letters (one redated in light of Parker's thesis), and some cagey guesswork involving Melville's deteriorating relations with Evert Duyckinck,[8] Parker argues that the writer was so angered by negative reviews of

Moby-Dick (including Duyckinck's ambivalent critique) and the insulting royalty terms proposed for *Pierre* that he derailed his work-in-progress by inserting into it a satiric but aesthetically ruinous attack on the literary establishment. To integrate this digression effectively, Melville also abruptly converted his main character from the naive scion of the American aristocracy into a more worldly writer of popular poems. But the digression itself flowed, like the "endless winding way" of a river, into something that became the very flesh and sinews of the remainder of the novel: in the novel's final section Pierre in turn converts from poetaster into a writer of dark fiction, a hunter not of Leviathan but, as Melville told Hawthorne, of "Krakens," an emblem (like the armless Titan Enceladus in Pierre's dreams) of the futilely defiant artist, and a portrait of Melville himself. Thus, the *Pierre* we know is a lengthy, anger-engendered, and, according to Parker, largely incoherent diversion from an original, shorter, more coherently conceived psychological novel.

Parker's two-*Pierre* thesis involves another conversion; it recasts what we have always thought to be a fixed text into a theoretical fluid text. Lamentably, the material textual evidence of this fluidity is nonexistent. We know from an addendum to the Harper's contract that Melville's royalties were boosted a bit to accommodate a significant increase in the length of the novel from the 360 pages originally stipulated. But no manuscript, which would surely bear palpable witness to the kinds of insertions and expansions (or inferred version) Parker speculates upon—the kinds of revision we do see in the *Typee* manuscript—survives. Parker's thesis, then, is a good "guess," one that feels right in some intuitive sense, and one that exceeds other theories of composition in complexity, but one that must remain a guess pending more solid evidence. Although one or two critics have challenged Parker's thesis,[9] the debate has not engendered much heat: Current criticism seems largely indifferent to modes of analysis based on compositional history or what Parker calls "the New Scholarship."[10] But in 1995 the stakes were suddenly raised when Parker issued his "Kraken" version of *Pierre,* and as a consequence, a theoretical fluid text became, irrevocably, an actual fluid text. The riverrun from theory to actuality in this case is not so "endless" but it is somewhat "winding," and merits a sentence or two.

For decades Maurice Sendak, the well-known artist and writer of such children's classics as *In the Night Kitchen,* had been a Melville enthusiast, had even written his own *Pierre* (about an angry lad who does not care), and had contemplated but rejected the idea of illustrating a Melville work. Urged by the editor of the Melville Society to reconsider and nudged by him to attend the 1991 Melville Centennial conference in Pittsfield, Sendak responded at a special showing of a play version of *Moby-Dick* to a suggestion by Joyce Deveau Kennedy that he should illustrate *Pierre*. A light in the night kitchen came on, and the artist later arranged with his publisher HarperCollins, the very company that had angered Melville 150 years earlier, to issue its Kraken Edition of *Pierre*, with thirty or so color pictures by Sendak conjoined to a text edited by Parker. Although Sendak's sexualized renderings of textual moments are themselves a controversial critical revisioning of Melville's novel and hence a new version of that work in their own right, it is Parker's editorial excisions—his presumption in cutting Melville's words to fit his theory of composition—that have made the Kraken version of *Pierre* editorially controversial and made Melville's *Pierre* fluid. Some would say Parker has willed the invariant, stony text of *Pierre* into this condition of fluidity; Parker states, however, that he is in fact "reclaiming the original *Pierre*," or rather, supplying a version of what the novel might have looked like in its earliest form.

Parker's "reclamation"—it is not, of course, but rather a construction of his imagined version of the original *Pierre*—requires the removal of the satirical, antiestablishment section consisting of Books 17 and 18 (to follow Melville's nomenclature), as well as Book 22, in which Melville's teasing and sardonic narrator looks over Pierre's shoulder as he writes, or rather fails to write. Because the manifest content of these chapters (about thirty pages of the NN text) digresses upon the writing process and profession, their removal can be performed with little or no damage to the plot. Parker also removes other, smaller, more problematic chunks of text that allude to Pierre's writing career and that cannot be so easily extracted from surrounding text. By my count, the Kraken *Pierre* is minus about 15 percent of Melville's published text.

Of course, Parker's Kraken text should not be confused with any physical document containing the actual, "original" text of Melville's *Pierre*—that manuscript item is, in fact, physically irretrievable. Parker's text is, like any critical edition, an approximation of the editor's conception of a theorized original. This may seem like a far cry from material reality, and it is, but the function of Parker's Kraken is that it should stand beside Melville's actual published version so that readers may gauge the distances, travail, and energies Melville managed in bringing his work into being. On the other hand, the excised materials include memorable passages on writing and publishing as well as Pierre's momentous dream of Enceladus. As we shall see, these kinds of losses force us to see that dividing *Pierre* into two versions—Melville's first intention (as approximated in Parker's Kraken text) and his final intention (as approximated in the NN edition)—is too severe; there are intermediate stages in the creation of *Pierre*, and no manner of excision (the only editorial tool for Parker in this project) can reliably convey those versions.

My critique of the Kraken edition has less to do with its testing of the limits of the critical edition than with its highly rhetorical rather than heuristic approach to the newly imagined fluid text it attempts to render. The edition's inability to treat the intermediate stages just mentioned shall be discussed in due course. For now it is enough to point out the edition's structural problems. To begin with, the volume is designed primarily to showcase Sendak's brilliant illustrations and not to explain Parker's excisions. With an elegant font and generous spacing, the four hundred or so pages (measuring only six by eight inches) are devoid of footnotes or editorial apparatus. Apart from Parker's largely biocritical introduction and his half-page "Note on the Text," there is no discussion or even display of any of the excised texts. The only indication of an excision is the use of three asterisks in brackets: [***]. Readers who have not read the novel before, who are not aware of the edition's mission, or who have not read Parker's introductory material are just as likely to overlook the asterisks as they are to ponder their function as they read. If a heuristic edition is designed to make readers more conscious of fluidities than they normally would be through a reading strategy of self-conscious textual interruption, the Kraken edition is about as far from heuristic as any other commercial market publication. The worst that might be said of its paucity of editorial discussion is that it is designed to promote Parker's two-*Pierre* thesis rather than engage readers in a discourse upon the likelihood of it. What can be said in its favor, however, is that Parker's bold editorial presumption all the more urges us toward finding a better way of editing a fluid text.

A heuristic discourse is necessary because once Parker alerts us to the possibility of two *Pierres*, we begin to imagine others. There is, for instance, at least one other intermediate *Pierre* that grew out of Parker's supposed original and toward the final published version. The likelihood of such a stage of production is high because Melville had not actually completed *Pierre* when he was (presumably) angered into adding his satiric attack and transforming Pierre into a writer. Thus, he must have had a Pierre-as-non-writer conclusion to his novel in mind, although not on paper. If Parker's anger thesis is correct, Melville then proceeded to write a new Pierre-as-writer ending, which is the ending published in 1852. Parker's Kraken project proposes that one can approximate Melville's originally conceived but never composed ending by simply cutting away any writerly references we may find in the ending Melville finally published. This might work if Melville had already written his originally conceived nonwriterly ending and then revised it through insertions of writerly material. But according to Parker, Melville never did write his *originally conceived* ending; and he therefore could not have revised what he had not already composed. Another possible version of Parker's thesis, then, is that the first sixteen or so sections (before the digressive Books 17 and 18) constitute an unfinished fragment of Melville's "original" conception, that the digressions represent a momentary intermediate stage of anger, and that the remainder of the novel as it now exists in print, roughly from the digressive books to the end, constitutes a second intermediate stage of creation (between first intentions and final printing) with a newly conceived conclusion in mind. This inferred version of the novel's finale approximates a point in Melville's writing after his angry insertion of Books 17 and 18 but just as his anger over the literary establishment subsides and he begins to incorporate the new Pierre-as-writer character into his final chapters. A fourth stage of composition would be the pulling together and polishing of the three fragments into what was finally printed by Harper's.

Looking at Parker's actual excisions illustrates what I mean by the two intermediary stages. In general, his emendations are surgical. The digressive and satiric Books 17 and 18 are discernible units of aesthetically disruptive anger that can, in fact, be clipped as one might perform an appendectomy, that is, with relatively little trauma to the narrative. But in removing the later, more effectively interwoven references to Pierre as a writer, Parker's surgery becomes more risky, like slicing cancers from healthy organs. As Melville continued writing his new ending to *Pierre,* he cooled, eventually incorporating his anger more effectively into the tissues of his narrative. Thus, he was able to transform his rage into a problematic critique of how writing, itself, might become a future cure of Pierre's former woe: his adolescent inability to speak out his being. When, for instance, in Book 19 Pierre catechizes Isabel on the "indifference" of virtue and vice, he begins by rejecting his old writings for something grander: "I will gospelize the world anew. . . . I will write it; I will write it." This new direction in his life grows out of the voiceless, "prewriterly" Pierre who in the early sections of the book cannot effectively express his unutterable adolescent ire. In this case, the idea of Pierre as angry writer is not a narratorial cancer to be excised but a philosophical and aesthetic transformation integral to Pierre's psychological growth. But, because his formula of excising all references to Pierre as a writer demands it, Parker cuts this "gospelizing" line, taking with it healthy tissue, and, worse, bringing us no closer to Melville's presumed original ending. What Parker's surgery does, unfortunately, is remove material that derives not from an original stage of composition, which the Kraken edition valorizes, nor from a final stage that the NN edition valorizes, but from an intermediate phase in Melville's creativity as he begins to become reconciled to the anger Parker imputes to him and before he fully incorporates that anger into his narrative, a stage that includes the richly allegorical dream of Enceladus, also removed in Parker's edition.

Interestingly enough, the problem with Parker's *Pierre Imaginaire* is not that it cuts the good Melville "gospelizing the world anew" along with the "bad" Melville of the more expendable satiric Books 17 and 18—any critical edition might in theory propose to do as much—the real problem is that the edition makes little or no attempt to argue for each cut and thereby engage readers in the logic of the cuts. The edition is far more rhetorical than heuristic and therefore suffers in credibility. To be sure, by focusing on "original" rather than final intentions, Parker effectively challenges the limits of the Gregian tradition, but in valorizing original over all other intentions, he merely replaces one temporalized conception of Melville's "work" *(oeuvre)* with another. The total "energy" of Melville's labor is lost.

In earlier days, Parker once called upon critics to "analyze [Melville's] dual or multiple intentions that shifted as a result of the blows dealt him by his publisher and by the reviewers of *Moby-Dick* and as a result of other, perhaps still identifiable, forces in his life."[11] Unfortunately, Parker's highly rhetorical *Pierre Imaginaire* does not follow through on this early jeremiad on multiplicity. Without any kind of apparatus to map Melville's shifting intentions, the Kraken edition fails to realize its heuristic potential to showcase Melville's "shifting," as distinguished from one particular thing he shifted to or from. Although it gives us a new fluid text, the Kraken *Pierre* is a frozen fluidity.

How might one envision a more heuristic *Pierre Imaginaire?* In a book format, Parker's excisions could at the very least be included on the page, but bracketed, or reduced in point size and leading, or set off in blocks or sidebar boxes, with notes giving a rationale for the excision. In an electronic format, all versions of *Pierre* could be placed side by side, so that the first American edition, the NN edition, the Kraken version, and any inferred intermediaries could be witnessed, individually or in couplings assembled on the screen at the user's discretion. Thus, the editorial emendations of texts composed early, intermediate, and late could be examined and discussed. While hypertext enthusiasts will insist upon the inevitable dominance of electronics, and surely electronic archives and editions do facilitate fluid-text analysis, I will argue later in chapter 7 that what is needed is an editorial strategy that combines both book and electronic technologies.

Much of what any fluid-text edition entails, however, must be concerned with the problem of how to combine reading text and editorial apparatus in ways that heighten the reader's awareness of textual fluidity and versions but does not seriously disrupt the pleasures of reading. The problem is that the complexity of fluid texts often requires a highly interruptive apparatus that invariably spells the death of "easy" reading, and even patient scholarship. The Kraken *Pierre* offers a minimalist apparatus—little more than a set of asterisks indicating cuts—that is unobtrusive and that allows for a smooth read, but the engagement with the fluid text is nonexistent by virtue of that smoothness. Solutions to the problem of apparatus must focus on encouraging new ways of reading so that users of a fluid-text edition may effectively turn their attention to the historicism and aesthetics (if you will) of "reading fluidity." As we shall see next, this is a seemingly insurmountable task that textual scholars and critics are only just beginning to address.

The Tyranny of the Single Reading Text and the Case of the Disappearing Apparatus

Typically, textual scholars are content to showcase the clear reading text they have labored to produce, relegating the textual apparatus, which contains the evidence of textual fluidity, to a secondary position for readers to inspect, if they desire. Thus, learning about the text is optional, and this is (perhaps) acceptable, if all you want to do is read a single, fixed text. But in reading a fluid text, learning about the text (that is, its variants) is not optional. Not only must the reader read self-consciously but the editor must make the edition aware of itself, and readably so. The apparatus must be more visible, and enticing. It must teach readers how to read what they are reading.

The more heuristic an *edition imaginaire,* the more reliable it will be. Teaching textual fluidity as we edit a fluid text requires us to display the fullest range of variants and versions and even go so far as to help readers find pleasure in reading the display. Discovering such pleasure begins with the understanding that readers can take comfort in being guided through new and deeper ways of reading. They also recognize that an edition that teaches and explains also empowers them to discern and interpret fluidities in their own lives. Thus, readers stand to grow in unexpected ways as they engage a fluid-text edition, and to the extent this is so, the fluid-text edition will grow in reliability, and in pleasure despite the formidable barriers of textual fluidity. Because of this heuristic factor, a textual apparatus that actively teaches is everything in a fluid-text edition.

On the surface, this may sound like a remarkable inversion of editorial aims, for we often presume that an editor's primary mission is to present a clear reading text, whether that is the text of an intended work, a unique document in facsimile, or an inferred or intermediate version. An editor's textual apparatus is typically rendered in heavily coded and abbreviated form and, with the important exception of the genetic approach, placed somewhere on the periphery of the clear reading text, either as footnotes or back matter. In such a configuration the apparatus often becomes an option many readers, critics, even historicists do not take. The mission of the fluid-text editor, however, is not to showcase single, clear reading texts but to use the apparatus to expose readers to the *distances between* multiple versions. Accordingly, the editor's primary obligation is to map out the variation, chart paths from one version to another, and enable users to lead themselves along those paths. This is a highly involved way of saying that a fluid-text edition promotes the act of "reading historically," and the engine of that promotion is its textual apparatus.

The challenge, then, is to make the textual apparatus more prominent and yet more readable, and this requires us to look more closely at how a textual apparatus functions as a "history" (so to speak) and to inquire into what it can and cannot do. In the past two decades of textual debate, French and German geneticists have taken the lead in developing ways of presenting both text and apparatus in order to emphasize textual fluidity, but not in ways that are fully satisfactory, and not, of course, without responses from intentionalists and materialists.

As already noted in chapter 4, the geneticists' focus on authorial revision indicates their affinity for the fluid text. They build upon at least two historicist assumptions. From a hermeneutical perspective, a textual fluidity is not simply an indication of authorial intent, it is, in Gunter Martens words, a "communicative sign referring to an historical substratum of meaning";[12] it is a symbol of social, political, as well as personal change. When readers are made aware of a textual fluidity as they read, the effect of this sign of the "text's historicity" is to reduce the reader's subjectivity as an interpreter. That is, readers will no longer take the text as "timeless" and hence allow it to become merely a reflection of their immediate, idiosyncratic sensibility; rather, they will begin to see the mutable aesthetic object as a function of a past that is both alien to and yet potentially inclusive of themselves. This automatic distancing between text and reader heightens the historicity of the reading experience.

In moving from hermeneutics to editorial principles, geneticists also assume that a fluid text must be edited in such a way as to facilitate the reader's awareness of textual historicity and to encourage them to read historically. Just as the reading of a textual fluidity necessarily decenters the text and historicizes the reader, editing must also decenter both text and reader. Accordingly, for pioneer geneticist Hans Zeller, critical editing must be an act of self-conscious historicism. Of course, this view is no different in kind from the conventional view of textual criticism as a rigorous, self-doubting discipline; however, it does differ in the degree of editorial decentering. Zeller stresses the need for editors always to undercut their own authority by

> endeavoring to make essential interpretative decisions recognizable and verifiable by also supplying certain questions to be answered differently than the editor has answered them, but also would allow answers to be found to questions which the editor did not answer, did not yet pose, and could not foresee.[13]

Rather than attempting to achieve editorial invisibility, editors must make their presence known as they display textual fluidities by posing problems about the unknown, and by stimulating readers to surpass the mutual editorial agenda. Thus, the editor adopts a decentering role to augment the decentering nature of fluid texts, all with the aim of increasing the reader's obligation to read historically.

The best way to achieve reader awareness of textual fluidity is to alter the conventional layout of a page and interrupt the "easy" reading of a clear reading text by bringing the apparatus onto the reading page or even inserting it into the reading text itself so that text and apparatus become "an integrated whole." For Zeller, it is enough to spread the apparatus out in a series of notes at the foot of each page. Hans Gabler goes further. For him, the apparatus should not be a "textual or typographical adjunct," and he proposes an "integral apparatus [as] a mode of text presentation incorporating variance into invariant context."[14]

As already noted in chapter 4, Gabler's "continuous manuscript text" is an "integral apparatus" that inserts the textual variants of the physical versions associated with Joyce's *Ulysses* (the manuscripts, typescripts, and early print pieces) within a running text of the work. The inserts are made typographically through a set of brackets and symbols indicating the source and sequencing of each variant. This "synoptic text," which appears on the verso of each page, serves as the copy-text for Gabler's clear reading text, which appears on facing rectos. In other words, with Gabler's edition open before us, we find a full set of variants displayed linearly in the continuous manuscript text on the left-hand page, and an emended, clear reading version that settles on one set only of variants on the right.

At first, and perhaps always, the apparatus to the left is a severe challenge to our normal practice of linear reading. One must always pause in virtually every line to weigh each variant crammed within brackets and festooned with odd symbols. The reading experience is a bit like hiccuping. Inevitably the reader resorts to the smoother reading text to the right if only to keep track of Joyce's narrative. Thus, to the hiccuping in each line, one adds the darting of eyes from left page to right. Fluid texts can be painful. If you can keep in mind the complex compositional history of Joyce's various typescripts as you internalize the many codes for those stages of composition, and if you can retain one set of coded variants long enough to compare it to those that follow and come before, you have a fair chance of figuring out one or two localized patterns of revision on a single page, before sunset. Despite these problems, the clear reading text to the right is more guide than supplement to the cumbersome left-hand synoptic text. If rightly used, the reading text is made to serve the apparatus, rather than vice versa, and this inversion of functions is an editorial strategy worth emulating for fluid-text editing. But the energy put into reading the synopsis of variants inevitably out-matches the reader's patience, and the eye ineluctably gravitates to the easier clear reading text to the right. Thus, and again, the tyranny of the single reading text prevails.

For McGann, this inverted reading experience is all the richer for the arduous and alien aspect of the apparatus. In his laudatory review of Gabler's *Ulysses,* he argues that Gabler offers us "an imagination of Joyce's work," an "imagined" text that "completely overhauls the way we think about the text as a whole."[15] Gabler's *edition imaginaire* is in fact a postmodern work—"a self-deconstructing and unstable text" whose "procedures make the structure of fluidity—its finite limits—very clear." As with the postmodern aesthetics of L-A-N-G-U-A-G-E poetry, its "style is impersonal and maintained in a surface mode ('languaged'); it is intertextual and self-referencing; the form of order is stochastic" (188–89). The overwhelming impact of this "languaged" and seemingly arbitrary and random artifice is to embody the full fluidity of *Ulysses,* and in doing so to "remove forever that illusion of fixity and permanence we normally take from literary works" (182). It is, to use Martens's term, a "communicative sign" of fluidity.

But McGann's inclination to aestheticize this sign, while fully con-sistent perhaps with his own poetics of text as social event, signals a retreat from historicism. To begin with, the claim that Gabler's "diacrit-ics . . . are a grammar of an artificial language" gives undue linguistic sta-tus to mere code work. Granted, the codes may be seen to employ a grammar of some sort, but in the long run they are just an abbreviation of normal syntax denoting the historical sequencing of variants. The artifice is a convenience (although a highly interruptive one), not a lan-guage.[16] Nevertheless, McGann reads the surface of Gabler's apparatus as postmodern poem, and while nothing should prevent him from doing so, his doing so may give the unintended impression that the primary reason for the apparatus is that it functions as a poem. Whereas its real function is that it should be read as a map: a map of revision.

As with any editorial act, Gabler's edition creates a new line of fluidity even as it attempts (somewhat paradoxically perhaps) to record and contain previous fluidities. The synopsis is a version in its own right and may be read, as McGann seems to show, poetically as an emblem of fluidity. The single reading text is yet another version, and one may read both synopsis and reading text together, synergistically, in an equally poetic fashion as an even more complex emblem of the interaction of reader and text, but in both cases, it seems to me, such poeticized readings exploit only the apparently "stochastic" surface features of textual fluidity, assessing perhaps a writer's word choices as "events" impinging upon the reader's corresponding event of reading, but not penetrating to the historical event of revision that effected the variations. What seems lacking in such postmodern poeticizing is the exercising of our potential to read the text historically. Granted, McGann is sensitive to the historicizing potential of Gabler's edition when he explains the compositional conditions of the two instances of textual fluidity he selects for discussion in his review. But he does not endeavor to guide readers in how to fashion "narratives of revision" out of Gabler's abstract mapping of Joyce's variations. While fluid-text editing must surely involve new ways of reading, it must also help readers to clarify the difference between reading the apparatus as a languaged surface and using it to construct past language events and to map Joyce's not at all stochastic, shifting intentions. Ultimately, a poeticizing of Gabler's apparatus undermines its historicist function and diverts attention away from new critical readings based on such historicized reading.

For Tanselle, Gabler's synopsis, however it may be read, is not so innovative.[17] Critical editing has always grounded its texts on a study of compositional history, creative process, and textual fluidity. And for that matter the Gregian tradition (well in advance of Gabler's *Ulysses*) has produced admirable, apparently ignored "genetic" texts such as Bowers's edition of Whitman's 1860 *Leaves of Grass* and Hayford and Sealts's 1962 Chicago edition of *Billy Budd*. Gabler's synopsis differs from Hayford and Sealts's genetic text in that the former is a conflation of variants from different sources, whereas the latter records the revisions found on a single set of manuscripts. Even so, both genetic texts display variants in what Tanselle calls an "inclusive" format that incorporates coded data and variants within a running text, as opposed to an "appended" format that places that data in footnotes or endnotes. Elsewhere, Tanselle elaborates on the two modes, arguing that an editor's choice of the *kind* of edition to be constructed (critical or diplomatic) is "fundamentally independent" of the more practical decision of what *form* of apparatus (appended or inclusive) to use.[18] For while critical editions have in practice typically used appended apparatuses, there is no principle that dictates this. In the particular case of editing a text with multiple, sequential versions, the decision to use an inclusive or appended apparatus is simply a matter of what is more "convenient for the reader" (589). That is, a reader can just as effectively reconstruct the editor's sense of the sequence of revision whether that information is displayed within the running text (à la *Billy Budd* and *Ulysses*) or in an appendix (à la the NN *Typee*).

While Tanselle's relegation of the choice of apparatus to matters of convenience is quite sensible, something in it seems awry. Reasoned choices in the making of books are always based on principles, either announced, hidden, or unacknowledged, and no choice is without an impact on readers. Ease of reading is not a matter of convenience; it is a matter of access, and modes of access reflect editorial priorities, hence principles. An apparatus that is too severely encoded or too marginalized—and most are both—sends a clear message that the reading of the single reading text is more important than the reading of the apparatus and for that matter of textual fluidity. I want, then, to argue that there is more than convenience at stake in the construction of an apparatus.

In his comparison of the genetic texts of *Billy Budd* and *Ulysses,* Tanselle makes an important point about the difficulty factor in all apparatuses, which, despite his view, implies an elevation of the merely practical issue of ease and access to a matter of principle. Both editions employ, he says, a complex set of symbols that encodes the processes of revision and/or variation throughout various sources. By any estimation, it takes "time to master" these codes, and once mastered they give only a rudimentary mental abstraction of the textual fluidity the editor wishes to convey. In the *Billy Budd* edition, the inclusive apparatus is a typographic rendering of the false starts, cancellations, and insertions that appear on the manuscript page. Occasionally, when the revisions pile up, the editors supply abbreviated explanations of the sequence of readings. "The difficulty of reading the transcription," Tanselle remarks, "is a reflection of the difficulty of reading the original."[19] However, since Gabler's inclusive apparatus conflates the variants found in all the transcript versions of *Ulysses,* its measure of difficulty does not reflect the difficulty of reading any single or combination of sources, "it is merely the difficulty of an apparatus" (590). The implication is that the difficulty of Gabler's cluttered continuous manuscript text bears no correlation to the difficulty of working through the compositional history of *Ulysses*, and that if its integrated apparatus could be more easily assembled in an appendix or footnotes, Gabler should have done so. But in stating that the difficulty of an apparatus *may reflect* the difficulty of the manuscript it is intended to embody, Tanselle does not mean to say that the sweat one endures in reading an apparatus *should* in some way be commensurate to the sweat in reading the revisions in manuscript themselves. He is simply articulating the fact that a transcription of the words on a working draft document (such as any given leaf of the *Billy Budd* manuscript) will be difficult to read because the oddly placed or canceled or inserted pencilings on the document transcribed are difficult to read. But if this is the case—if a textual apparatus will always be difficult and perhaps more difficult than the original upon which it is based—it is a damning testimony of the ineffectuality of an apparatus to clarify textual fluidity.

Of course, the idea of a transcription and its apparatus is to make the text of manuscript and print variation *easier* to read. Canceled words or obscured and otherwise illegible words are rendered clearly in uniform print type; and the reader has better access to those written words. But beyond this, a transcription of a working draft manuscript does not help in conveying the probable sequencings of revision that occurred in the writing process. Often the codes designed to denote sequencing are, to begin with, too hieroglyphic to entice readers into a pursuit of revision steps, and finally too simplistic to render the complex operations and interconnections that typically occur during a revision process. The fact is that the reading of a transcription's apparatus, whether inclusive or appended, is often more difficult than the reading of the revisions on the original artifact. Indeed, it is a different kind of reading so alien to most readers as to send them packing, leaving only those few academics with "a need to know" to fend for themselves. Once fending, even the most resolute decoders know not to trust their decodings without comparing them to the original. The better editions of manuscript material place photoreproductions of manuscript originals and transcriptions of the manuscript side by side, and the best of these dispense with codes altogether and attempt to mimic typographically the spatial arrangement of cancellations and insertions on the page with various colored inks, different fonts, or point sizes.[20] But even here, what is rarely, if ever, attempted in any apparatus is an explanation or narrativization of the sequencing and strategies of revision. Rather than reflecting the difficulty of reading an original, a textual apparatus is not only difficult in different ways; it also tends to convey only a portion of the kinds of knowledge required for fluid-text analysis.[21]

A textual apparatus is a necessary inconvenience that is bound to interrupt the conventional pleasure of the text. It is a surprise to no one that single reading texts tyrannize our attention and pull us away from the historical complexity of textual fluidity. Moreover, in the due course of publishing, as scholarly editions perform their function in providing texts for cheaper, less cumbersome, commercial and classroom editions, textual matters become even more severely marginalized, or they simply vanish. Thus, in addition to the tyranny of the single reading text, we must contend with the fate of an apparatus, simply to disappear. Witness *Billy Budd*. The previously mentioned Hayford and Sealts edition, unique for its time, carefully combines (although not side by side) both genetic text and clear reading text so that readers can in one volume explore Melville's manuscript revisions in each transcribed leaf and also read a critically edited version of the complete manuscript. It is by any estimation an exemplary heuristic edition. Access to it, however, has been severely diminished by the marketplace, for though the reading text half of the edition is now the standard for reprints, the edition containing the genetic text is out of print.

Even Chicago's paperback of this edition, which reprints the Hayford and Sealts reading text with extensive explanatory notes and a small sample of manuscript leaves, includes none of the Hayford-Sealts genetic text. The 1984 Library of America edition of Melville's works reprints the reading text with minimal notes and only brief mention of the compositional history. Of course, such matters of fluidity are not within the scope of the LOA project, but that is precisely my point. When further distribution of a critically edited text is achieved, the text is invariably separated from its apparatus, in which are located all the features (textual notes and lists of variants and emendations) that legitimize the critical edition's critical status and engage readers in textual history. Years of editorial work go into the creation of a critical edition, and the apparatus (beyond its actual utility) is the concrete sign of that work, a passport, if you will, of the reading text's reliability, historicity, and authenticity. But when this work is passed along to the larger reading public, it crosses the border without papers. Its passport apparatus is exchanged for misleading labels like "definitive" or "authoritative," which mystify the editorial process altogether.

Textually scrupulous, nonprofit projects like LOA tell readers where they can go to find the disappeared apparatus. (In the case of *Billy Budd,* however, you must have access to a research or excellent college library, or search the internet book dealers, in order to find a copy of the full Hayford-Sealts edition.) The message to readers is that matters of revision and variation are not, and need not be, of immediate interest in the reading of a literary work. More commercially minded publishers (which is to say all of them) have no obligation to preserve any part or even any allusion to the textual apparatus that grounds the text they publish. Happily some classroom text publishers, such as Norton Critical Editions and Penguin Classics, make serious efforts to provide detailed textual analysis. The Norton *Moby-Dick* (1967), the precursor to the 1988 NN edition, gives a reasonably decipherable textual apparatus, including most of the substantive British and American variants.

Unfortunately, in an unsettling instance of the Disappearing Apparatus, the recently revised Norton *Moby-Dick* (2001) dropped its textual apparatus entirely, thus making its claim to be a "critical edition" somewhat misleading. Currently, the Penguin *Moby-Dick* (1992), which reprints the 1988 NN text, is now the only college text of the novel to supply a list of textual emendations. However, the list is so hieroglyphically rendered as to be incomprehensible to Moses, let alone your typical college reader. Take a look at the following entry, which represents a major textual alteration:

CHAPTER 114: (535:8) ""Oh"" NN for "ₐ≈"; (535:26) "it."" NN for "≈.ₐ".

The story behind this coded enigma is this: In neither the British nor American first editions of *Moby-Dick* do we find quotation marks around the "Oh, grassy glades" speech in "The Gilder" (chap. 114). However, in the NN text (used by Penguin), the editors have inserted quotation marks. The Penguin encryption somehow records this emendation, but it cannot tell readers what this editorial change means, that it effectively reassigns the famous speech from Ishmael to Ahab. Convincing arguments for this emendation can and have been made (NN *Moby-Dick* 901), but not in this hyperabbreviated form, understandable to maybe twelve people in the universe.

My own experience in putting together the Penguin *Typee* (1996) opened my eyes to the difficulty of creating an effective textual apparatus. It was understood that I would use the reading text of the 1968 NN critical edition of *Typee* as the text for this reprint, and I was happy to oblige. But in order to convey to readers that Melville's text had been expurgated, I had hoped to insert brackets into the reading text around each expurgated passage. In doing this, I was emulating NN editor Harrison Hayford's own inclusive apparatus strategy in his earlier 1964 Signet edition of *Typee,* the precursor to his 1968 NN edition. Penguin did not allow me to follow Hayford's 1964 Signet strategy because, it was argued, the 1968 NN reading text was "definitive" (as they would put it on the back cover of my edition, over my protest) and therefore should not be altered. Wanting my readers to be aware of the fluidities of Melville's text, I consequently prepared as back matter to the Penguin edition a table of expurgations, drawn from the NN edition's encoded data, which instead provided complete first and last sentences of each expurgated passage so that users would have a more immediate sense of what was censored, whether the expurgation may have been based on personal, political, religious, or sexual matters, and where in the reading text to find the full passage. A similar, but partial list of substantive emendations and a reading text version drawn from my transcription of the *Typee* manuscript were also added to this appended apparatus. The entire back matter goes a good deal further than any other edition to enlighten readers willing to flip back and forth between text and appendices about the various stages of textual fluidity to be found in *Typee.* Various instructors have reported success in the classroom with this volume, and I am gratified to hear it, even though the disallowed inclusive apparatus of simply bracketing the expurgated texts as they appear in the reading text would have been far less cumbersome, only slightly interruptive, and more readily instructive.

What I learned in 1996 was that the uphill battle to promote the analysis of fluid texts requires the support of publishers, who with an eye on the bottom line and a focus on "definitive" single reading texts are disinclined to explore innovative ways of reading. However, what I learned in 2001 is that not all publishers are alike. In my edition of Melville's *Tales, Poems, and Other Writings* (2001), Random House provided generous support for creating innovative ways of presenting manuscript variants for *Typee, Billy Budd,* and the poems "Art" and "Camoens" in pleasurably readable formats. The traditional apparatus has not so much disappeared in this edition as it has been transformed. But instances of commercial fluid-text editions like this are rare.

For many textual scholars—intentionalists, materialists, and geneticists alike—the problems of the tyranny of single reading texts and of the disappearing textual apparatus are not problems at all. Research libraries and many college libraries collect scholarly editions with their textual apparatuses intact, so that those who want to study textual fluidities can do so as an academic enterprise separate from ordinary or even close classroom reading. But the idea behind fluid-text editing is to inculcate a new kind of critical analysis and a new kind of reading that can be performed at home, or in class, not just in the stacks.

Reading Historically and the Pleasure of the Fluid Text

To return to Tanselle's yardstick of convenience as a measure of the effectiveness of an apparatus, we can readily agree that, if the coded abstraction we call a textual apparatus is the only option we have, it matters little where we put it. Whether inclusive or appended, it is equally inscrutable, so it might as well be placed where it is placed for convenience's sake. But, why, may we ask, must we settle for this inhibiting "barbed wire" (as Lewis Mumford put it decades ago) at all?[22] Less generous souls will suggest that textual apparatuses are the shibboleths of textual scholarship; they are to be "mastered," and one's mastery of them announces one's academic authority. Others might argue, too, that in the elite domain of textual scholars and critics who handle and preserve rare books and manuscripts, the textual apparatus is a sign that says Do Not Enter.[23] But most scholars I know cringe at such false accusations, even as they admit to the rarified nature of their profession. Increasing readers' access to arcane materials—often the basis for establishing textual fluidities—is at the very heart of textual scholarship, for it is the best way to increase access to past mental workings of the writer's mind and to enhance rather than close off our discourse upon those workings. Thus, the choices in shaping a textual apparatus are finally not options based on convenience. They are choices determined by one's commitment to the immediate contact with fluidity and to the heuristic use of an edition to engage readers more deeply in the ways of reading historically. To do this, the apparatus must, in some sense, be pushed in the reader's face. It will always be interruptive of regular reading, and, as likely as not, it will be inconvenient. But it must not be recondite, inhibiting, or alienating. The idea is to devise editorial strategies for combining text and apparatus for a given literary work that entice readers into the pleasures of the fluid text.

However, there is always a resistance to such enticement, for while

the pleasures of the fluid text may play upon our desire for some narra-
tivized history of the text, we are as often repelled by the actualities of
the real past from which the narrative descends: the relentless record of
change, the complex of causation, and the bewildering alternative speculations about the past. A text on a page is bewitching. If we let ourselves go, we fly with the argument or story or image in the text, lose
track of time and space, and for a moment we are caught in this illusory
but, to our mind, very stable narrative "past" in the text itself. The
power of language is such that we forget that this imagined past *in* a text
is not the actual past *of* a text. Indeed, the whole point of a well-written
text is to make us forget we are reading words. But a fluid text, when we
become aware of it *as* a fluid text, reveals to us an additional, and altogether different, kind of narrative, a very concrete narrative of the
writer's revision, which breaks the spell of the pleasures of everyday
reading. Although the pleasures of a fluid text are finally more compelling for what they reveal about both art and culture, they are pleasures that we do not anticipate nor long endure.

When first perceived, a textual fluidity invariably strikes us as
charming. In the first edition of *Typee,* Melville originally had Tommo
say of Fayaway: "I made a dress for [her]." But in revision this is
changed to "A dress was made for [her]." Readers who cannot tell you
what distinguishes active from passive voice, and who would not necessarily see the intimacy of the former clause without comparing it to the
latter, instinctively smile when both texts are placed side by side. A fruit-
ful discussion of revision strategies (not to mention grammar, not to
mention sex ensues).

In purely aesthetic terms, the *effect* of the passive version (which
appears in the standard NN print-text) is to emphasize Tommo's awareness in the modification of Fayaway's appearance; it implies a kind of
communal validation of their affair, in that Tommo recognizes that
some agent other than he has prepared the dress to acknowledge their
relationship. Such conclusions can emerge as we read Tommo's use of
the passive without knowing of the phrase's earlier, active version, and
little in that text urges us to question the rhetoric of the usage. But once
we learn that Melville had originally used the active construction, the
question of voice is immediately problematized. Readers cannot avoid
posing questions that place the effect of the passage in the context of the
causes related to revision. The passive becomes more clearly a strategic
choice; Melville intended it over the active voice, and suddenly this revi-

sion site—a material reification of authorial intentions—becomes a critical hot spot in which shifting intentions necessarily impinge upon our interpretation. But this new perspective on causation poses new critical problems concerning who and why. Did Melville or his editor make this change? If Melville, did he opt for the passive to conceal his island intimacies at the behest of or in deference to his mother, fiancée, or future father-in-law, or all three? Or did he simply erase a bawdy little joke best removed for the sake of future parlor readers? Or was this one of John Wiley's editorial expurgations? Speculations abound, and a charming fluid text begins now to remind us that we cannot really know the past, or anything, or ourselves; and spiraling down this abyss of uncertainty we can easily decide not to spend more time pursuing the past, or fluid texts.

As you can see, the initial charm in witnessing Melville's shift to the passive devolves into crisis as this new focus upon the causes of change intensifies. The pleasures of the fluid text are real and many, but we are often ill-equipped to enjoy them. What often can happen when readers experience some small measure of textual fluidity is a natural retreat from reading the fluid text historically into what I have in a different context already referred to as "aesthetic" reading in which readers allow themselves to shelve their questions about the text's historicity and pursue those matters that can be said to transcend the historical moment of creation. This aestheticizing occurs even when questions naturally arise that can only be answered satisfactorily by a plunge into the text's historical moment. Thus, the frustration of not being able to read historically leads to the further, but often unacknowledged, frustration of reading aesthetically. For decades in our critical studies and classrooms, we have settled for aesthetics over history in our reading and teaching of texts largely because we have not developed ways of reading historically that are as pleasurable as our ways of reading aesthetically. A fluid-text edition must counter this practice and help readers familiarize the processes of reading textual fluidities that are the concrete manifestation of a text's movement through history. Reading historically is a pleasure that leads to pain; however, we need to find ways in our editing of fluid texts to convert that pain into a deeper pleasure.

If the ultimately speculative nature of a fluid text means that the charm of reading devolves into discomfort, it can nevertheless induce a kind of self-affirming negative capability that allows us to continue speculating if only to feel for ourselves the potentialities of the past. Once again, Melville's play in *Typee* with the words *native, islander,* and *savage* illustrates the point. In print, these words are used dozens of times, and one can study their seemingly indiscriminate print placement and impact on readers both aesthetically and with an eye to their historical relevance. But the manuscript revisions reveal that Melville consciously discriminated and manipulated these terms as he wrote, and his strategy in doing so more precisely indicates not only Melville's growing ideology vis-à-vis colonialism but his complex relation to Toby.

In an early comic scene, the sequestered Tommo and Toby are approached by a party of revelers and invited to eat ("ki ki") from a trencher of mystery meat they think might be human. Toby typically overreacts:

> "Ki ki! is it?" said Toby in his gruff tones; "well, cook us first, will you?—but what's this?" he added, as another *savage* appeared, bearing before him a large trencher . . . containing some kind of steaming meat. (94)

Some days later, after Toby escapes, Tommo registers his anxieties but also the reactions of the Typees:

> The conduct of the *islanders* appeared inexplicable. All reference to my lost comrade was carefully evaded, and if at any time they were forced to make some reply to my frequent inquiries on the subject, they would uniformly denounce him as an ungrateful runaway, who had deserted a friend. (109)

In comparing these passages, readers can readily see that the word *savage* in the first episode clearly augments Toby's exaggerated fears of cannibalism. Polynesians bearing succulent viands equal *savage,* and we laugh. However, Melville's use of *islanders* in the second episode is not so remarkable. *Islander,* like *native,* is a neutral signifier, a kind of place-holding referent that identifies a population by its geography (or birthplace), not its cultural (or "moral") condition. *Islanders* in this case does little to augment the more sobering sense of betrayal in this scene.

But in the writing of both scenes, Melville had initially considered different words. The manuscript version of the comic scene of "savage" feasting shows that Melville had originally called the meat-bearing Typee a "native" but then revised that word to "savage." Conversely, in the second, more sober, psychological scene the inexplicable "islanders" had originally appeared as "savages."

The meaning of these revisions is readily articulated. In the first case, Melville adds the word *savage* to intensify Toby's anxiety. By doing so he confirms the reader's expectation of Polynesian savagery, which in turn enhances the comic effect. The second revision is more complicated, for the neutral term *islander* does not so clearly call attention to itself, as we read it in print. But once we know that in an earlier version the word *islander* was actually *savage* and that Melville consciously removed that culturally loaded term, we know that this neutral spot is really a hot spot. At the very least Melville's intention here is to elevate the Typees' reliability in their take on Toby's alleged desertion. These are not the views of savages, which we may discount; these are islanders speaking—islanders like the inhabitants of Britain or Manhattan who, if we choose to see them that way, are familiar hence credible respondents—and their judgment affirms, indeed articulates Tommo's anxious doubts about his friend. Who, then, is the savage: these worshipful island friends or the comrade (Toby) who deserts you?

We can easily go this far in interpreting the Δ*savage* fluidity in *Typee*. And further: for as we have noted from the beginning of this book, it is not simply that the revised words have meaning; it is also the case in fluid-text analysis that the *fact* of revision, itself, has even deeper, interpretable meaning. Melville clearly knows the power of the word *savage,* but the manuscript shows when he learned, through the writing process, how to use that power and what it could do rhetorically for both himself and readers. As we know, in most cases, the manuscript shows that Melville converted his initial use of *savage* to the two more neutral terms, *islander* and *native.* This suggests that Melville first used the term conventionally without much sense of its full cultural impact. But as he wrote and became more deeply engaged in the explicitly announced even repeated problem of Western culture's misapplication of the word *savage* to the Polynesians (NN *Typee* 27 and 125), it is likely that his own sensitivity to the word grew. He began to see how loaded the word is. His revision strategy (savage → islander) suggests his ideological growth from imperialist to cosmopolite and his desire to treat Typee culture more respectfully. But he knows, too, that this unfolding has advanced him beyond his readers' conventional views, and that the word *savage* is now all the more loaded, for in his hands it has now become a tool for audience manipulation. Thus, in reading the scene historically and in the context of the Δ*savage* fluidity, the reverse revision strategy of native → savage, in the comic scene, strikes us as all the more meaningful. Melville is clearly willing to use the infamous word to play on readers' fearful stereotypes even as he hopes in other places to instruct them in seeing the word's infamy. Is this a sacrifice of principles, or a subtle put-down of his reader's sensibility, or part of a plan to bring readers along to an as yet unrealized new awareness of cultural pluralism? And these problems further rebound on the meaning of the savage → islander strategy in the betrayal scene in which Melville seems equally willing to downplay his savage game to reinforce his own submerged (and savage) resentment of Toby. Is Melville's growing ideology and manipulation of readers toward an equivalent enlightenment as ironically manifested in the native → savage gambit finally nothing more than a self-serving rhetorical attack on Toby in its reverse (and dominant) savage → islander mode?

The answer to these questions is not as important here as what the new ability to pose such kinds of historicizing questions may mean to readers. Without any awareness that these two scenes in print are actually hot revision sites in manuscript, readers can and will read them aesthetically with at most a sense that *savage islander native* seem to be randomly interchangeable words in Melville's lexicon. But once the text is historicized through a revelation of its fluidity in these sites, the reader cannot avoid considering Melville's rhetorical condition as he wrote *Typee.* And if Melville as writer unfolded politically, artistically, and rhetorically as he revised, then how so might we as readers unfold along with him, or in reaction to his unfolding? Melville's struggle with Δ*savage* speaks to our own postcolonial condition, for our liberal democracy stumbling toward multiculturalism has yet to resolve its own relation to the "other," and like the n-word, *savage* is not obsolete.

My point in this brief foray into fluid-text analysis is not to suggest that we resist these kinds of questions in our reading of a text once they are posed—in fact, students invariably increase their interest in a text when they discover it is the locus of revision—but that exposing readers to a fluid text such as Δ*savage*—through the physical complexities of the change itself—requires a high degree of editorial guidance. One cannot "read" native → savage without placing it in the context of savage → islander, or vice versa; and it is hard enough to read the one fluidity or the other by itself, let alone then having to connect one to the other situated as they are fifteen pages apart. As noted before, the chances are that readers reading conventionally are not inclined to read historically without frustration. And simply adverting to fluidities in an editorial preface, or listing them in coded apparatus, will not suffice as editorial aids to the new kinds of reading required of us in reading fluid texts historically.

Tanselle states that the pursuit of history "appears to be one of the distinctive urges of the human mind," but he also contends that "one has no obligation to look backward, if one's temperament does not allow the looking to enhance one's sense of human possibilities and of self-fulfillment."[24] In arguing that one has no obligation to follow the distinctive urge to historicize, he hints at the paradoxical resistance to the pleasures of reading historically when readers are exposed to fluid texts. A fixed single reading text carries us forward; its narrative flows, and we are pleased to float in it with little regard for the past condition of the text itself or whether the word *islander* was always *islander* or at one time something else. But a textual fluidity, paradoxically, does *not* flow; it represents a place in the text where multiple alternative words vie for our attention. It is an apparent synchrony within the diachronic text; thus, it interrupts our easy linear reading and bears us down into historical speculation upon the causes of texts. If this is so, it may mean that no matter how alluring an edition and its textual apparatus can be made to be, the reading experience of a fluid text will be interruptive and inhibiting, and readers operating under a quite forgivable pleasure principle will retreat from historicism and fluid texts.

Even so, it is my belief that "looking backward" or reading historically is not simply a process reserved for those temperamentally disposed to do it. We are all disposed to historicize. "I desire the writer," Barthes tells us. "I need his figure."[25] To go further: We desire genesis; we need revision.

Let us then resolve: The past does not frighten me. Its scents emerge when, holding a text that is itself an object from the past, I activate its words by reading them, and in reading, give them a present flavor distinct from flavorings created by other readers around me now, or by previous generations of readers, or even the originating writer. An awareness of the distance between our sense of the text that is only a reflection of me and that of the text that is not me naturally comes as we read. We might be of a temperament to deny this distance and refuse to read it, and we may read as if with blinders against the inherent historicism of a text, as if the text were all me and only me. But this willful act of blindness does not erase the realities of genesis and revision, of authorship and cultural pressure, that have material presence if only we, as editors, choose to offer them to readers. Pleasurable or not, to read is to read historically.

In a post-Emersonian democracy of self-reliance and the now, we declare ourselves independent of the past and imagine it so, despite our unbreachable attachment to the past and despite our desire to know it better. Fluid texts are a means by which readers can begin to forge more supple relations between their dynamic past and dynamic now. Readers may have no "obligation" to read historically; then again, they have no obligation to breathe or know themselves. But inevitably they do and try. Scholars, critics, and teachers are, however, obliged to facilitate readers to read historically, to help them feel the pleasures of the fluid text. In practical terms, this means that we must convert heavily coded and alienating textual apparatuses into the pleasurable narratives of revision that they in fact encode. The following chapter proposes an agenda for fluid-text editing.

CHAPTER SEVEN

Editing the Fluid Text

Agenda and Praxis

*Our minds, like our bodies, are in
continual flux. . . . Do not suffer life to
stagnate; it will grow muddy for want of
motion: commit yourself again to the
current of the world.*

—Samuel Johnson, *Rasselas*

Midway through *Scholarly Editing in the Computer Age,* Peter Shillingsburg adopts a kind of millennial pose when he envisions "the word
definitive . . . banished from editorial discussion":

> Critics will learn how to use scholarly editions when they stop
> mistaking the clear-reading text of a scholarly edition for the
> work itself and when they stop regarding the textual apparatus
> as a repository of discarded and superseded variants preserved
> by pompous pedants. When critics will learn that, I cannot
> guess, since many editors who should know better have yet to
> learn it.[1]

The confusion among critics that Shillingsburg identifies is real. Many
critics, even some scholars, do not distinguish an edited text and the
work it represents. As exasperating as this may be, it is not entirely surprising considering that edited texts are far more concrete than the inef-
fable past process or "working" from which they are derived. Indeed,

141

the only way to access "the work" is through one's personal attempts to "construct" it or through someone else's constructed editions and "reading text," and, given the labor-intensive nature of gaining personal access to manuscript and rare first editions, we are more than happy to acquire a certain critical amnesia and forget that the texts we read cannot be "definitive" but are nothing more than an editorial version of a writer's work. And, of course, decades of literary theory and practice have valorized this amnesia. Thus, the problem of our persistent confusion about nonexistent "definitive texts" cannot be resolved simply by wishing everyone's consciousness to be higher. The problem is systemic and requires some radical rethinking of editorial and publishing practice.

Part of the problem has to do with the way books are conceived of and marketed. Commercial publishers have a vested interest in "authenticity," and they do what they can to assure readers of the impossible: that their product is equivalent to the writer's work. They gain the confidence of readers by giving them "genuine articles"—uncluttered, "definitive" reading texts—that are not only cheap to produce but fulfill a reader's false notion and expectations of a single, fixed literary work. Critics and scholars are no less inclined to conventional expectations; they expect the editing process to yield clear reading texts. Although in reality an eclectic critical edition is a collection of texts—not only the scholarly version of authorial intention that is the emended copy-text, but also added features such as a textual note, and an array or record of variants—it showcases the clear reading text, which becomes the inheritable, "definitive" feature of the project, despite all disclaimers to the contrary. As we have seen in chapter 6, subsequent reprints aid and abet in the culture's systematic reduction of the many texts of a critical edition to the one it chooses to inherit and call definitive. Unless an intelligible critical agenda involving the aesthetic and cultural relevance of textual fluidity takes hold, new ways of reading that can accommodate multiple versions will not develop, instructors will not bring fluid texts into the classroom, publishers will not have incentive to issue variant versions or more comprehensive fluid-text editions, and readers will continue to confuse an editor's reading text for the total "working" *(travaille)* of a literary work *(oeuvre)*.

Nor is it enough, as Shillingsburg suggests by his admirable pluralistic approach, simply to wait for the editorial establishment to produce different editorial versions of the same work, affixed with more accessible textual apparatuses. The hope is that these versions presented with clearly defined critical principles that establish their difference from one another will coexist in scholarly arenas, if not the marketplace.[2] This would be a good step toward Donald Reiman's notion of "versioning." Indeed, multiple, edited versions of *Lear, Frankenstein,* the poems of Dickinson, Whitman, and Eliot, and of *Ulysses,* to name a few, may be seen as harbingers of this pluralism. But this approach does little to countermand the system's tyranny of the single reading text or the phenomenon of the disappearing apparatus previously discussed. Critics, even scholars, will read a single version of a work as *the* text because invariably that version will appear in book form *as* the text, and they will ignore the appended apparatus (if it survives) because the clearness of a clear reading text urges them to do so. And the pleasures of the fluid text invariably accede to the pleasure of the clear reading text. More adventurous readers seeking textual fluidity are on their own to develop strategies of reading, usually with the plurality of edited versions perched precariously on their laps. Simply put, the pluralistic approach lacks practical direction or even an agenda for pulling the plurality together. It is the editor's job to guide readers through the plurality of textual fluidities.

By way of supplying an agenda for the editing of fluid texts, I want to present some general principles and specific ingredients for the construction of a reasonably pleasurable, reasonably heuristic fluid-text edition, using the example of *Typee* along the way. It goes without saying that while *Typee* is a particularly instructive fluid text, it is, like all fluid texts, unique; and I do not mean for it to be a template for other fluid-text editions. Each literary work will necessarily dictate the peculiar features of its fluid-text edition. Indeed, editing any particular fluid text will require an imaginative rather than formulaic approach in order to lure readers into textual fluidities and facilitate their reading. At the outset I also want to stress that fluid-text editing (like all critical editing) is not an end in itself but a means of enhancing fluid-text reading and analysis. Nor can the fluid-text editor succeed without enlisting the help of book designers, computer whizzes, publishing firms, literary critics and historians, teachers in the classroom, and poets.

Some Principles of Fluid-Text Editing: The Synergy of Book and Screen

The focus of fluid-text analysis is not on texts but on the distance between texts: the changes. And, thus, as noted in chapter 6, fluid-text editing must of necessity forsake the pleasure of clear reading texts.

Fluid-text editions will be interruptive of conventional reading processes, and yet they must not alienate; they must be pleasurable in their own right. They must display unfamiliar materials in a familiarizing way. They must tease coax entice readers into that destabilizing space between two versions, give them a comfortable way of confronting just so much fluidity but not so much as to confuse, and yet provide opportunities for returning home or plunging ahead into more variants and more spaces. To achieve this complex level of comfort, editors must be willing to become *narrators of revision;* that is, they must convert the bewildering array of data in their encoded textual apparatuses into pleasurable *revision narratives*. With this in mind, let's see if we can affirm the following four principles.

Fluid-text editing is critical editing. The purpose of a fluid-text edition is to showcase revision. In the terms we have previously developed, such editions manifest the energy or work that individuals and a culture put into the changing of a text from variant to variant and version to version. Fluid texts must be edited critically because the means by which we transcribe manuscripts, distinguish authorial and editorial variants, infer versions, and hypothesize revision sequences are all acts of judgment. But more than this: because the forces that drive revision are speculative, a fluid-text edition is not so much an imagined thing as it is an interpretation, a map for reading shifting intentions as revealed through variant sequentialized versions. We cannot present the revision sites of this map nor the revision narratives that explain them without their being shaped by critical agendas and ideologies. Rather than mask these subjectivities, the fluid-text edition must announce them and encourage debate.

Fluid-text editors are pedagogues. The strategy of a fluid-text edition is heuristic not rhetorical: it is designed to enable readers to discover textual fluidity, analyze its potential meanings, and learn among other things the nature of textuality, the interpenetration of individual intentions and social texts, and the relation of past language events to our present lives. It is not designed to promote a single interpretive reading of the work itself, although it will propose hypotheses about the composition and creative "working" of the work that will necessarily derive from and shape interpretation. Accordingly, and given the critical nature of editing, the complexity of multiple versions, and the miasma of alternative speculations on a particular revision sequence, fluid-text editors should take the lead in proffering their own judgments in a clear and distinct manner, but in the context of divergent hypotheses. The idea is to invite readers into the discourse on textual fluidity and enable them to consider alternatives of their own design. To the extent that fluid-text editors use their editions to engage readers in new and/or old problems about texts, they should see themselves as pedagogues: scholar-teachers.

Fluid-text editions must be comprehensive. Conventional critical editions that temporalize authorial or editorial intentions (early or late) do so with expressed disregard for certain unauthorized versions and adaptations, or what we here call cultural revisions. But if fluid-text analysis of genesis and revision allows us to gain a sharper sense of the energies of literary work as the locus of interaction of individual and society, then the idea of an "edition" must be expanded to include nonauthorial materials as well. A fluid-text edition is more than a volume of selected versions; it is a library with "reading rooms" for the inspection of intended and social texts as well as cultural adaptations.

Fluid-text editions are a synergy of book and screen. The principles outlined above can best be realized, perhaps *only* realized, through the extraordinary hypertextual features of the electronic medium; but it would be imprudent to reject the codex out of hand. Fluid-text editions should attempt to create a dynamic coupling of book and computer screen.

In theory, pulling these four principles together into a coherent editorial whole should not be the fantasy of utopian vision. Much work in many fields—medieval, Shakespeare and the Renaissance, Romantic, Victorian, and modern in both British and American studies—is currently under way to approach new plateaus of textual scholarship upon which editors and readers can more effectively interact to make textual fluidity more accessible and critically intelligible. Most of this new work involves electronic texts; thus, the last of these four principles—combining the strengths of book and screen—is our most immediate concern here.

　　To begin with, how do book and screen technologies truly differ? To those who have already sung their elegies on the passing of the book, this question may seem oddly phrased for in the presence of the all-powerful computer, the book seems to be a quaint corpse. There is, however, still some life, and utility, left in books, enough, too, to match the computer. In some regards, a book in hand is more convenient than a computer that has to be turned on, and books can also be highly hyper-textual devices. Indeed, from before the time of Gutenberg, book tech-nology has developed an astonishing range of graphic and typographical conventions designed to guide readers through texts and move them from one text to another. There are the familiar and serviceable table of contents and index, the indispensable quotation mark, footnote, and bibliography, as well as the appendix and more formidable textual appa-ratus. Each of these lowly devices is a remarkable mechanism allowing us to flip from one set of texts to another, by word, or topic, or page, or chapter. Books also contain such extras as illuminations, illustrations, charts, graphs, sidebars, marginalia, and targums. There are playful pop-ups, foldouts, and transparencies as well. In general, these hypertextual book features, which are models for many electronic features, are acti-vated by quick, eye-and-thumb coordinations that are at times handier than the buttons and menus of electronic technology. Electronic texts, by and large, emulate these book features so that one may click on a table of contents heading and move instantly to that section of the elec-tronic text. One might also place a mouse icon over a highlighted word and a corresponding footnote or graphic will instantly pop into view. But these miracles are merely quicker (or seemingly quicker) versions of the organizational headers, footnotes, and illustrations that makers of textbooks have for centuries incorporated into their book designs. The issue, then, is what can computers do for readers that books cannot.

Obviously, electronic texts can perform a number of astonishing functions. They can generate word searches and concordances in no time, and assemble various extratextual materials (primary sources and secondary resources) all on one screen. Although much strategizing, programming, and coding in the markup languages of SGML or XML must be done to enable such hypertext surfings to occur, the user-end ease of access is worth the enormous front-end labor of, and cost to, edi-tors. The benefit of such electronic features is that they extend access of fluid texts to more people (or at least to those who can get on-line). And more: they enable readers to perceive the variants within a fluid text. Before the computer age, we were forced to balance books on our laps and finger our way (by means of patient collation) through textual dif-ference, or if such collations had already been performed, our task was to decode heavily encoded textual apparatuses. Now with computers, such inhibiting codes are invisible, and variant texts like *savage/islander* in *Typee* can be inspected directly on-screen, in context, and/or side by side. Thus, computers can present textual evidence with a facility that was unimaginable to preceding generations of scholars, and one can only hope that this new ease of access will encourage critics to use fluid texts more often in their work. But will critics, students, and general readers as quickly recognize the relevance of textual fluidity simply because of this remarkable new facilitation of the displaying of fluid texts, without some coherent critical approach to fluid texts in general? Moreover, it strikes me that simply placing fluid texts side by side on a screen is little more than a perfunctory transference into electronic form of what we can also find in print. The problem, then, is how to use computers to develop new ways of reading and talking about fluid texts, beyond the mere display of fluid texts.

If electronics were to do nothing more than facilitate access, speed up the hypertextuality already available in books, hasten certain time-intensive textual jobs like collation, or make textual apparatuses less inhibiting, its importance to readers of fluid text would be merely *mechanical*. How, we must ask, can electronic texts be *functionally* different from our experience of books. Screen versions of fluid texts must be more than just faster and more convenient ways of delivering what can be delivered by books. Fluid-text editors must consider what electronic technology can do qualitatively that book technology cannot.

At the very least, an electronic archive can assemble all versions of a work in one place so that the comprehensive "library" aspect of a fluid-text edition can be achieved on a disk, or better, on a secure, always updatable web-site. And beyond this important aspect of assemblage, computers can provide new ways of reading, by emulating textual fluidity itself. The problem to be resolved by our computer gurus and textual scholars is how to create programs that allow readers to follow the sequential stages of revision in the creative process as it extends from manuscript into print and on into adaptation. Rather than surf the net, let's surf the morphings of textuality.

The problem is not easily resolved and requires paying considerable attention to the limits of readers, the painful pleasures of fluid texts, and the critical agenda one might be pursuing. Despite the title of his book on editing in "the computer age," Shillingsburg seems less than sanguine about the use of the electronic medium as the solution to the problem of analyzing and editing textual fluidity. One can put two texts side by side in a book or on screen, but readers cannot read the two simultaneously,[3] and this ingrained linearity of mind cannot be denied to accommodate the simultaneity of vision seemingly required by the reading of fluid texts. As one geneticist put it, one needs to read textual variants synchronically while moving diachronically along with the narrative flow.[4] And while this kind of bifocal reading can be contemplated abstractly or poetically, doing it with either book or screen can induce the migraine. Consequently, fluid-text editors need to devise programs that convert the bewildering, apparent simultaneity of variants into a more comfortable linearity. Eventually I shall argue that this is best achieved through the editorial construction of the revision narrative.

The creation of a more comfortable linearity should not be difficult because, in fact, variants and versions are not really synchronous at all; they are sequential and grow in linear fashion. Writers compose one word at a time, and while they may revise recursively and at different times in apparently random fashion, they nevertheless do so one event after another. Fluid-text editors must necessarily theorize about the growth of a text through its compositional and revisional stages, and computers can help them *visualize* their theory and the revision codes of their fluid texts, allowing users to watch the theoretical progression of events unfold on screen. Moreover, this flowing of a fluid text can be linked to graphic and voice-over renditions of the editor's revision narrative pertaining to the growing text in question. This kind of electronic program can be used to analyze single or multiword variants in differing print versions, but it is a particularly useful technology for analyzing heavily revised working drafts such as the *Typee* manuscript, which (as a document) contains multiple, inferred versions and numerous revisions within each version.

Computers, then, are exciting for the qualitatively different reading experiences they can provide. As school districts and institutions of higher learning put more on-line computers into the classroom and libraries, instructors will be able to promote fluid-text analysis more readily but only if they can develop programs capable of manipulating the electronic texts and enabling readers to read the fluidities.

But will the technology evolve to such an extent that computers will entirely supersede book technology? Probably the one element that militates against this is the simple pleasures found in books. At present, books are lighter than computers, easier on the eye, more portable in and out of libraries, and even into bed. Cybernauts assure us that in due course and barring socioeconomic cataclysm, the computer with its light bursting from each tiny pixel will become as ubiquitous, more user friendly, and portable as the handheld book I carry with me to class or rest on my stomach. But computers, it seems, are forever hurrying to move me somewhere else in hyperspace, and, without waxing poetic, I appreciate a book's solid grounding and patience as it allows me to slow down and warm up in the reflected, not bursting, light of its pages.

But the importance of books in fluid-text editing goes beyond creature comfort. The physical limitations of books have the benefit of forcing book versions of fluid-text editions to be selective, critical, argumentative, and pedagogical. And this would be a good thing. Let me explain:

Pleasurable fluid-text editions must combine the most useful hypertextual features of both book and screen. The two must interact synergistically, as microcosm and macrocosm. The electronic version should be primarily archival. The logic of its construction should resemble a library with comfortable "reading rooms" for textual research and play, including the kind of surfing of fluidities just discussed. This electronic library should be a macrocosmic collocation of all materials related to the fluid text in question, a world of its own. The book version should be a critical and heuristic selection of materials from the archive, a microcosmic representation, a friendly visitor from that other larger world, one that can effectively use but not overextend the hypertextual capabilities of bookmaking and book design.

The book cannot contain all the information that can fit into an electronic archive; it cannot, for that matter, let you surf. It can, however, be an instructive, representative sampling of the entire fluid-text edition located on-line. By this, I mean that the editor's "selected book version" would be designed to demonstrate a particular version of the total "global" revision narrative witnessable in the electronic library. It might offer crucial strategic moments of revision but not, let's say, all or even any minor occurrences of tactical revision. Advanced elements of book design should be used to enhance the reader's ability to perceive the editor's selected fluidities, if not at a glance then in a meaningfully, not frustratingly, disruptive way. The idea is to showcase, generally on two-page spreads, parallel columns, sidebars, graphic boxes in wide margins, only the more demonstrative variants, revision sequences, and their narratives. Material judged less relevant may remain in electronic storage waiting to be seized upon and made more relevant by a future scholar-critic-teacher in another book version.

In the case of *Typee,* for instance, the strategic Δ*savage* pattern would be mapped out in full, whereas such tactical shiftings as the revision of *which* to *that,* if taken to be merely mechanical, might be selected out. This editorial strategy aims to reduce the overwhelming complexity of textual fluidities that are bound to bewilder readers and retard their engagement with revision. (Textual fluidity is too much for "our infirm Delight," and fluid-text editors must "dazzle gradually" in carefully selected portions, "Or every man be blind.") The further aim of the heuristic book version is to induce readers to get out of the book to seek further information on the screen. Thus, readers will be prompted throughout the book to dial up the on-line version for more detail about a particular revision site, or more material concerning other sites noted in the book but not fully discussed.

The book version of a fluid-text edition can be carried into both conventional and wired classrooms. Instructors might use the book solely for the close reading of what I call the edition's *base version,* upon which revision sites are mapped (see below). But if the book is properly designed, both student and instructor will inevitably turn to the selected revision sites mapped on the base. Students might then be asked to go on-line to explore the full range of revision sites or textual fluidities found in the electronic library version. Essentially, the representative book version would be a gateway to the fuller screen version on-line.

Instructors conducting class in a computer lab or wired classroom might also conduct class discussion directly from the screen. In such cases (and soon enough, most colleges and universities will be equipped for on-line instruction), one wonders if the book edition has any utility in class. One advantage of the book, however, is that it can be carried anywhere out of the classroom, whereas the on-line version can only be accessed through a monitor. (I am not convinced that handheld devices have the screen size to do the trick.) Students can study important aspects of textual fluidity and perform edition-related assignments just as readily in the book as on-screen, especially if they do not have immediate access to a screen. Moreover, books with properly designed elements can emulate certain selected on-line features, such as the sequencing of revisions, so as to give readers a more immediate (though book-bound) sense of the text's fluidity. Indeed, the more a fluid-text edition, as a book, draws from strategies we find in textbooks (with graphics, variant fonts, boxes, sidebars, etc.), the more powerful it can be in guiding readers through a series of revisions and moving them toward on-line use.

The on-line site itself archives all relevant materials and includes several more advanced features of textual editing and text manipulation, such as magnifiable facsimiles of manuscript, a text lab for the collation and searching of multiple texts, and a revision workshop in which users may construct their own revision narratives. And just as the book version of a fluid-text edition urges readers to become users of the archive, the archive can suggest ways in which users can return to the book for various reasons: not simply to rest the eyes a bit or reclaim the tactile experience of book reading assumed by all prehypertext authors but also, since the book version will showcase the editor's main critical ideas (embodied in his/her revision narrative), to gain a more concrete sense of his or her selection process, critical approach, and ideology. The synergy between book and screen reminds us that the on-line archive is itself a critically inert warehouse of data valuable for its storage and the management of textual fluidity, but its more selective book partner is the enactment of a heuristic narration of a critical selection of textual fluidity from the warehouse.

Elements of the Fluid-Text Edition

With these four principles of critical editing, pedagogy, comprehensiveness, and book/screen synergy in mind, let's also consider the more practical matter of how to display a multiplicity of variants and versions in a readable fashion and what revision codes might be employed. We have already weighed (in chapter 6) the merits of appended and inclusive apparatus, and they, like the encrypted footnotes of a variorum, do not truly facilitate fluid-text analysis. Nor is the solution of side-by-side textual display as helpful as we might wish, for readers must bounce between the end points of revision—from this variant to that, then back—and the exertion of so much bouncing dissipates the energy we need to direct ourselves toward the causes of revision rather than the revised texts alone. A better method of display, I feel, uses a *base version* of the literary work upon which one may map *revision sites* (the hot spots of revision) that in turn are associated with an enumerated *revision sequence* and an explanatory *revision narrative* that relates the causes of that sequencing.

A Rationale of Base Version

The conventional eclectic edition emends a copy-text version of a work with borrowings from other versions to approximate a writer's intention (in most cases) at one (usually final) moment in the creative process. A fluid-text edition, however, is designed to track the full course of revision (authorial or otherwise) from version to version. But unlike Gabler's genetic approach that conflates all textual versions and renders variants in an encoded, inclusive apparatus, the fluid-text edition uses a single base version upon which to "map" all revision sites, that is, those places in the base that have been revised in earlier versions or will become revised in later versions. Since it is not the aim to construct a text to match an imagined temporalized intention but rather to show the sequencing of shifting intentions by various agents, the rationale for selecting a base version is not so much a matter of intentionality as it is two other concerns: the editor's critical and heuristic goals and the size and scope of revision (the textual terrain) to be covered.

With the first concern, a base version reflects the editor's announced critical position. With *Typee,* for instance, an editor stressing Melville's various intended texts generated through authorial revision might be tempted to use a transcription of the working draft manuscript as a base, allowing that particular constructed text to serve as a surface upon which to map out all physical revisions and any of a number of inferred hypothetical versions created before, during, or after the composition of the manuscript itself, as well as any appearing in subsequent print versions. But the choice of the *Typee* manuscript as a base version presents serious inconveniences because this particular manuscript consists of only three chapters, and much editorial masonry would have to be applied to make the base version adequate to the task of providing a ground for the many inferred authorial revisions found beyond the range of the manuscript terrain. The editor might, therefore, find the British edition of February 1846 (the first print edition following the manuscript stage) to be a more effective base version.

Turning from authorial to editorial revision, a fluid-text editor stressing the social texts of different collaborations (including some found on the manuscript) might also choose the first British edition, or a later printing in which "The Story of Toby" was added, or either of Wiley's American editions, including the infamous expurgated version, or even the posthumous Stedman edition of 1892. Good cases might be made for any of these. However, if an editor also focusing on *Typee* as a social text were to gravitate toward the American revised edition for the base text, the problem of size would emerge once again, for the very thing that makes this edition interesting—its expurgations—is what makes it inadequate for a convenient display of textual fluidity. The absent materials would have to be editorially restored in order to make the fact of expurgation comprehensible, and this is not only cumbersome but reverses rather than simulates the initial act of censorship. A fuller base version, then, would be needed.

Thus, once one has determined a critical focus, the second concern in the rationale for a base version is quite simply the fullness of the base. A base version should be the physical, not inferred version[5] that offers up a playing field large enough to display the largest number of revision sites and to accommodate the full gamut of revisions leading up to and following the composition of the base version itself. If all the working that goes into a fluid text could be compared to a cathedral in Genoa that began as a cellar and grew over the centuries to include nave, side chapels, and tower but lost a wall or room here and there to earthquake or war, the base version of that work would be that state in which the cathedral was quite simply the biggest. Thus, to return to *Typee,* a late printing of Murray's 1846 edition, which accepts no expurgations but adds "The Story of Toby," would be a serviceable base version for most fluid-text editions of Melville's work, including studies of creative process and social text—for while it does not contain by itself all the language associated with *Typee,* it does offer all the "places" where revision occurred, whereas this is not the case for either the manuscript or the American revised edition, both of which are fragmentary.[6]

Using this rationale, an editor in search of a base version for a fluid-text edition of *Lear* would look to the longer and earlier first Quarto version, not the shorter later Folio;[7] however, an edition of *Leaves of Grass* might use the 1881 seventh edition, which is the last edition to revise individual poems, or the 1892 deathbed edition, which includes subsequent "annexes" to 1881, rather than any of the manuscripts or the 1855 first edition.[8] Since little of Dickinson's poetry was published in her lifetime, and since subsequent editions have grievously underrepresented her writings and overmanaged the verse, a plausible base version for Dickinson's working would be a transcription of the manuscript fascicles, letters, and other "open folios."[9] Similarly, a fluid-text edition of Eliot's *Waste Land* would use the complete typescript version, not the first print edition. *Frankenstein* presents an interesting base version problem. The novel has a fascinating record of authorial, editorial, and cultural revision, and as one of our most enduring fluid texts has left furrows on the high and low brows of almost two centuries. Its manuscript is large but nevertheless a fragment,[10] and its two major print versions, the 1818 and 1831 editions, are quite different in important places but of similar length. In such cases in which significant versions of indifferent size must be confronted, fluid-text editors should probably choose the later option, with the assumption that it is finally easier for readers to assess the growth of revision up to the version at hand rather than up to and away from it. This would make the 1831 edition the more serviceable base version.

Finally, it should be noted that the practical technologies employed in conventional critical editing apply to fluid-text editing, especially for establishing the copy-texts of base versions, if not to render emendations. All relevant documentary witnesses of manuscript and print versions should be collated and their textual and bibliographical variants recorded to determine if variations within a version are in any way intentional or the accidents of transmission. Accidents (as far as they can be determined to be such) should be corrected to enhance readability. Substantial variations should be regarded as revision sites to be mapped. The only significant textual variants in Murray's later version of *Typee* is the change of title and the addition of "The Story of Toby"; any other changes in the text are the result of printing accidents.

Since the *Typee* manuscript is the only extant witness to the compositional stage it represents, it cannot be collated with any other witnesses to that stage. However, its cancellations and insertions can be taken as a set of instructions for the creation of a clean textual version of the stage in question, and we can create a fair copy of that clean text as if on Melville's behalf. In the fluid-text edition of the *Typee* manuscript in *Melville Unfolding,* I have followed Melville's revisional instructions to create such a fair-copy reading text as the manuscript edition's base version.[11] Not surprisingly, Melville's instructions were not perfect, and there are about half a dozen inadvertencies (such as repeated words due to faulty cancellation). However, I have not corrected these errors, nor have I added any clarifying punctuation. I have chosen to do this in order to more faithfully simulate the pre-house-editing condition of this version. This reading text, then, is readable, although rough in a few spots and thus not a "clear" reading text.

A Map of Revision

The purpose of a base version is to provide a textual surface upon which the editor may lay a "map" of revision. The map itself is a simple set of designations indicating (on the surface text of the base version) the placement of the *revision sites*. (The screen version of the fluid-text edition would display all revision sites to be found throughout all of the work's versions; a book version would of necessity present a critical selection of the revision sites.) The map should be clear enough to make its presence known as a kind of overlay on the base text, but it should not unduly interrupt a reader's reading of the base version, if he or she should choose simply to read without reference to revision.

The map may be little more than a consistent set of numbers and the boldfacing of relevant revised words in the text. Whether the base is a reading text of an early manuscript or a later print version of the work, the mapping on it will include sites for both *intraversional* revisions within the manuscript as well as sites of *interversional* alterations between manuscript and subsequent print versions. Accordingly, each site should be coded to indicate the stage of revision at that site. With manuscript revisions, each revision site should be accompanied by a readable, graphic *transcription* of the intraversional revisions at that site, placed beside the revision site in the margins of the book edition. In on-line versions, these marginal transcriptions can be brought into view in pulldowns or subscreens. In addition to each transcription, the editor should provide a sequential list that further relates steps (actual or hypothetical) the writer or editor made in revising. This *revision sequence* is constructed out of variant texts associated with the site in question and enough of the surrounding invariant context to make each step in the sequence pleasurably readable by itself. Each step in the sequence is numbered, and in order to make the steps linguistically accessible for readers, each step repeats enough unrevised words of the previous step to allow readers an immediate sense of what is at stake in each revision and how meanings are altered within a particular revision site. (See fig. 1.)

In this approach, typographic simulations of revisions replace cumbersome abbreviations and codes (such as brackets, braces, half brackets, etc.) indicating various modes of cancellation and insertion, and the actual wording of each step of revision is literally spelled out. The repetitiousness of the revision sequence in this approach is bound to annoy practiced textual scholars accustomed to the codings of their craft. Repeating unaltered language in each of the steps in a revision sequence takes up page space and is more costly to print than the barebones variants and abstract codes typically found in manuscript transcriptions and lists of print variations. But one benefit of the revision sequence is that it walks readers through each numbered step of a particular revision,

Reading Text of Manuscript
Revision Site 111

—¶ "Ki Ki, is it? said Toby in his gruff tones —
"well cook us first will you" — but what's this"
he added, as another **savage**[111] appeared bearing
before him a large trencher of wood, containing
some kind of steaming meat ...

Revision Transcription,
Sequence and Narrative

RS111. but what's this" he added, as another ~~native~~ savage
appeared bearing before him a large trencher of wood
   1. as another **native** appeared
   2. as another **savage** appeared

RNms111: Generally, HM's revision strategy is to reduce
his usage of "savage" by altering it to one of two more
neutral options: "native" or "islander." Here in a
proofreading phase, he reverses that trend changing
"native" to "savage," which intensifies the sailors'
lingering fears of cannibalism and plays upon the reader's
presumed expectation of Polynesian savagery.

Fig. 1. A revision site in the fluid-text edition of the *Typee* manuscript. In this example, revision site 111 is "mapped" (numbered
and boldfaced) on the manuscript reading text, or "base version,"
in the left column. To the right, the corresponding lines from
revision site 111 in the graphic transcription of the manuscript are
followed by the two-step revision sequence, which contains
sufficient contextual wording to make the shifts in meaning more
apparent. Following the revision sequence is the revision narrative
for the site, which takes the reader through a rationale for each
revision step. Thus, in the left column, we read Melville's final
intention for the manuscript state and can readily recognize the
revision sites mapped on the text without serious disruption of
the reading experience. However, readers wishing to find out
what is happening at the revision site can move to the right column to learn that Melville had revised *native* to *savage* and why.

performing for them each step so that each of Melville's sequential
workings can be visualized immediately as the reader reads. The larger
benefit emerges, however, with more complicated revision sites than the
one sampled here. In such cases, which may involve a dozen or more
steps, readers confronting the transcription only are quite naturally dis-
possessed by the miasmic cascade of separately canceled and inserted
words, and they cannot be expected to work out on their own the dozen
steps of revision embedded in the manuscript, no matter how graphically rendered they are in the transcription. But with the steps of revision
carefully sequenced and fully contextualized at such revision sites, read-

ers are able to read the revision site and apprehend the revision strategy hidden behind the manuscript's cryptic cancellations and insertions. Of course, more likely than not, the editor's sequencing at any site with multiple revision steps will be hypothetical, and editors are obliged to offer alternative hypotheses. Readers are asked to accept the editor's primary hypothetical sequence as a starting point, but once they have grown accustomed to the analytical process of sorting out a revision, they will be ready to develop hypotheses of their own.[12]

Since the revision sequences in a revision map are in most cases hypothetical, they must be argued for and cannot stand independent of argumentation. This truism seems obvious especially in the case of agency when we move from intraversional to interversional revision. With intraversional revisions found on a single manuscript document, there is little doubt that the revisions are performed by whoever composed them. The fact of their authorship is in the handwriting.[13] Thus, on this score, no further argumentation is generally required. But with interversional revision between, let's say, the final reading text of a manuscript and the first print edition, or between a first print wording and the variant wording in a subsequent edition, there are no identifying hands to distinguish the agent of one print variant from another. Unless external evidence tells us otherwise, we cannot know for sure if the revision in any interversional case was performed by writer or editor. Thus, we can only speculate on who made the many changes found in step 5 in the example of revision site e298 (see fig. 2). Interversional revision sequences, while they can never be displayed in anything other than a two-step sequence, must, nevertheless, involve an added layer of hypothesis concerning agency not generally required in intraversional revision sequences. In either case, the point quite simply is that no revision sequence can by itself tell the whole story. A revision sequence is only the skeleton upon which an explanatory and necessarily argumentative *revision narrative* hangs.

The Revision Narrative

In preparing a fluid-text edition, the editor will want to provide the fullest narrative of revision possible.[14] The fundamentals of the work's compositional and publication history will appear in an overarching introduction to the edition that provides biographical details and publisher's transactions as well as discussions of the writer's creative process and patterns of revision, the vectors of external influence, and an eluci-

Reading Text of Manuscript
Revision Site ms318 e298

& [**apprehending** that ere long we might fall victims to some **sudden caprice on the part of the savages** ^{ms318} **I now abandoned all thoughts of success & became a prey to the most gloomy imaginings.**] ^{e298}

Revision Transcription ,
Sequence, and Narrative RSms298e318.

& apprehending that ere long we might fall victims
  on the part of the savages   abandoned all thoughts ~~for~~ +of success &
to some sudden caprice of ~~the natives~~ ∧ I now ∧ became a
prey to the most gloomy imaginings.

1. apprehending that ere long we might fall victims to some sudden caprice of the natives I **now** became a prey to the most gloomy imaginings.
2. apprehending that ere long we might fall victims to some sudden caprice of the natives I now **abandoned all thoughts for success &** became a prey to the most gloomy imaginings.
3. apprehending that ere long we might fall victims to some sudden caprice of the natives I now abandoned all thoughts **of** success & became a prey to the most gloomy imaginings.
4. apprehending that ere long we might fall victims to some sudden caprice **on the part of the savages** I now abandoned all thoughts of success & became a prey to the most gloomy imaginings.
5. **apprehensive** that ere long we might be expose to some **caprice** on the part of the **islanders** I now **gave up** all **hopes of recovery** & became a prey to the most gloomy **thoughts**. [RSe298: English edition]

RNms318&e298. Originally, HM wrote: "apprehending that ere long we might fall victims to some sudden we might fall victims to some sudden caprice of the natives I now became a prey to the most gloomy imaginings" [step 1]. The exact sequence of revisions at this site is not certain. In one proofreading phase, Melville placed a caret after "now" and inserted "abandoned all thoughts for success &" to emphasize his sense of personal abandonment [2] and perhaps include a Dantean allusion to "Abandon all Hope." Probably at the time of making this insertion, he also revised the preposition by writing "of" over "for" [3]. In another proofreading phase, Melville canceled "the natives," placed a caret after "natives," and inserted "on the part of the savages" [4] thus making one of the few strategic revisions of "native" to "savage" (see RSms111). But evidence in the first English edition indicates that Melville continued to revise this passage from any time after completing his manuscript draft on up to the publication of the English edition [5]. Most notably, "savages" is changed to "islanders." Chances are that in first revising natives to savages in manuscript [2], Melville was attempting to heighten the sense of anxiety Tommo is feeling at this low point in his emotions. Revising savages back to the more neutral islanders [5] — and it seems likely that this is Melville's revision not Gansevoort's or Murray's — suggests a willingness on Melville's part not simply to tone down the emotions for the print version but regain for himself a distance from the darker emotions he has projected in manuscript through Tommo. In addition to this revision, "sudden" is dropped from "sudden caprice," "abandoned all thoughts of success" has been altered to "gave up all hopes of recovery," and "gloomy imaginings" has been revised to "gloomy thoughts" (step 5, see also NN *Typee* 10-4.19). These tinkerings (aided perhaps by Melville's editor) may be a further dance with Dante.

Fig. 2.   Revision sites ms318 and e298. In this example, the revision sites are numbered and boldfaced in the manuscript reading text to the left to indicate changes to text in both manuscript and English edition, respectively. To the right, the graphic transcription of the manuscript at that site is followed by the five-step revision sequence with sufficient contextual wording to make the interversional manuscript shifts and the intraversional shift to the English edition more apparent.

dation of the text's stages of development through its various physical and inferred versions from earliest draft to printings and bindings. However, the editor must also prepare individualized and informing revision narratives for each revision site. Each revision narrative is keyed to and elucidates the possible agents and motives behind each numbered step of a revision sequence, whether they be aesthetic or simply grammatical, broadly political and/or sexual, or rhetorical with a more localized agenda in mind.

Succinct but readable, a revision narrative may be utterly routine in describing a tense shift or pronoun modification, or it may tell a complex tale of intentions and maneuvers with novelistic intensity and suspense. One need not forsake editorial restraint for poetic subjectivity in crafting these narratives, but one should relate the events in an intelligible, pragmatically pleasurable way in order to familiarize readers with the processes of revision. For readers, the revision narrative can be an exemplary pattern for the kind of historical reading discussed in chapter 6. It is the ultimate contextualization most effectively rendered in narrative form. To read the revision narrative is essentially to read the fluidity of a fluid text.

Like any other narrative, a revision narrative will have plot (the revision sequence and motives), character (writer and editor), and ideas (aesthetic strategies and cultural intervention). In addition, its peculiar focus on the making and changing of words requires the elucidation of more specialized elements, or *revision codes.* A revision narrative clarifies the *mechanics* of change: cancellations, insertions, transposition of text. It will naturally indicate or speculate upon the *agent* of revision as well as the *phases* of revision, whether a change was performed in the midst of composition or later in a tinkering or proofreading phase or during a moment of more radical reconceptualizing. With this in mind, the editor must also explicate his or her sense of the *direction* in which a revision takes an idea.[15] Accordingly, he might also consider (as I do in *Melville Unfolding*) broader *modes* of revision that may be linked to certain inferred versions. In the case of *Typee,* such modes include the *transcription* of the memories of personal events on to the page, the *transformation* of personal narrative into a more unified, dramatized work, and the *translation* of text into more socially acceptable or rhetorically useful forms.

In assessing the mechanics, agents, phases, direction, and modes of revision, the editor will inevitably speculate upon the strategies that dictate revision. A *revision strategy* may involve the micromanipulation of words for stylistic ends or the broader, modal reconceptualizings of the social and rhetorical impact of the work that may be evidence of inferred versions. Thus, the editor will naturally use the revision narrative as an opportunity to distinguish tactical phases of revision from strategic stages of composition. As such, each narrative tells a story of revision and initiates discourse about that story.

To some extent, the revision narrative is the fluid-text edition's equivalent of the more conventional critical edition's "Discussion of Emendations." But its function goes far deeper and is far more central to the editorial agenda of fluid-text analysis. The revision narrative is an editor's most direct means of contact with readers. It is the heart of an edition, for it leads readers into, and familiarizes them with, the spaces between variant texts, and it asks them to contemplate in those silent spaces the intangible "springs and motives," the personal and cultural forces, the energies of change. Here, out of the fragments of the author's text and the gropings of editorial judgment, the editor gives voice to this energy and thereby in essence creates a text, or rather transcript, of the work's textual fluidity. The full set of revision narratives should obviate the barbed wire of conventional textual apparatuses; it should flow with the parent text's fluidities and articulate the instabilities of the text in a stabilizing way; it should induce in readers a pleasure of its own. Here, in the discourse of this narrative script that runs from one revision site to the next is where readers come to read historically. Here, too, is where they may discover the reality of textuality, the interpenetration of authorial and cultural intentions, and the critical relevance of textual scholarship.

If the organizing principle and ingredients of a revision narrative are beginning to sound too artistic, too subjective, too unscientific; so be it. There is, however, nothing in the crafting of a narrative that precludes analysis, judgment, restraint, and editorial accountability. In fact, any narrative, if it is to be taken as reliable, must incorporate these very elements in credible ways. Editors of fluid texts, then, must be prepared to develop a narrative voice that is itself reliable, one that can articulate complex maneuverings succinctly but pleasurably, that can speculate without arrogance, and that above all can empower readers to question speculations but enable them to speculate themselves.

The fluid-text editor's narrative voice should also serve as a link between book and screen. The book version of a fluid-text edition will supply only a critical sampling of the revision sequences and narratives. And this sample will be representative enough for the book to give readers a good start on their fluid-text analysis. The on-line version, however, may be the users' first contact with the full edition, and they may need as much or surely more guidance from the editor in navigating the sites, sequences, and narratives. Moreover, the electronic version will have significantly more resources at hand so that the editor-narrator must also become an editor-narrator-librarian of the fluid text "reading room" wherein all full texts of all versions of a work are stored. And still more: to channel electronic features toward empowering readers to become more familiar with and adept at textual scholarship's techniques, editors need to create a text lab and revision workshop for users. These "rooms" (down the hall from the electronic archive of versions, sources, and secondary materials) will teach users to perform the spadework of textual criticism on their own.[16] The text lab would allow users to search texts, collate versions, assemble variants, craft concordances, and make editions. It would allow for the comparison of not only variant manuscript and print texts (as with *Lear, Frankenstein,* or *Typee*), let's say, but also scenes from Shelley's novel and its numerous adaptations, or illustrations from modern editions of *Typee* and its comic book version.

The revision workshop would focus on different skills, allowing users to locate and map the revision site of a base version, establish revision sequences, and then compose revision narratives to elucidate revision strategies. Students could build portfolios in both text lab and revision workshop to compare their editorial work with that of others. The more textual scholars can do to expose general readers to procedures still thought of as arcane, the more they will be able to induce participation in the study of textual fluidity.

The Example of Typee: *An Agenda*

To conclude, I would like to imagine what a larger, fluid-text edition of *Typee* as a whole might entail. As is often the case in such projections, my imaginings begin with questions. Why bother with *Typee*? Where and in what form will the fluid-text edition appear? What might its relation be to a Melville Electronic Library (MEL)? What do I want the fluid-text edition to do?

Why Typee?

As a collocation of a full range of literary and sociological materials, the work called *Typee* provides examples of all phases of revision (authorial, editorial, even cultural) and accordingly is one of the best candidates among Melville works, or all early American works, for a fluid-text edition. Its manuscript, although fragmentary, is the earliest recorded instance of Melville's creative process, and it is large enough for us to construct and substantiate credible theories of the growth of the entire work (as I do in *Melville Unfolding*). Markings on the manuscript and the variations between manuscript and first edition further suggest early editorial collaborations, just as the two American editions reveal later, more complex censorings and self-censorings. *Typee* was not the best-seller we might like to think it was; it sold only around twenty thousand copies during the author's life (NN *Typee* 298), but it made Melville's reputation, and its popularity endured, much to his chagrin (at first), and even outlived him, much (I suspect) to his approval. Critics have always sustained a cautious admiration of *Typee*. Today, the book has become the focus of new historicists and postcolonialists who, in finding a link in *Typee* between personal narrative and cultural narrative, have added new vigor in our appreciation of Melville's first novel.

Probably the most significant cultural fact of *Typee*, though, is not its present-day topicality, but the simple material fact that its two print versions existed side by side, in equal-sized print runs by both authorized publishers and pirates, well into the twentieth century, so that as an artifact it records a long-standing and varied audience response to an evolving post-Puritan, postcolonial Victorian culture. And the record of variant versions did not stop with the first British and American editions. In the months before his death, Melville himself gave instructions for a new edition of *Typee* that varies from both the novel he first published in England and the revised American edition he consented to in 1846. This edition was never realized and exists as an inferred version. Approximating it, however, is the posthumous, 1892 edition, edited by Melville's literary executor, Arthur Stedman. Thus, even up to the late hours of Melville's life, *Typee* continued to reflect the artist's personal interactions with his audience. Finally, the relevance of *Typee* as an exemplary fluid text is also revealed in its twentieth-century manifestations. *Typee* has appeared in numerous modern reprintings, several illustrated editions, the NN scholarly edition prepared along Gregian lines, the Penguin Classics teaching edition, two screenplays, and a comic book.

For various reasons, *Typee* exceeds other Melville texts as a fluid text. *Moby-Dick* was expurgated (in this case by the British) and therefore exists in two versions, and it has had a much deeper cultural impact than *Typee*, but unlike *Typee* not a shred of *Moby-Dick* manuscript survives. Published posthumously, *Billy Budd* is all manuscript and something of a mirror image bookend to *Typee*, for as a kind of working draft combination of successive fair-copy drafts, it represents a late phase of development in Melville's final years as a writer, whereas the *Typee* fragment is an early draft of Melville's earliest book. Out of its complex manuscript, the text of *Billy Budd* has been constructed into at least four modern versions, each different and none supervised by Melville, including the most reliable Hayford and Sealts's version of 1962. It has been transformed into a play, opera, and film. But unlike *Typee*, it did not go through years of editorial revision during the writer's lifetime. Although *Typee* may rank in magnitude beneath *Moby-Dick* and *Billy Budd*, it is the more serviceable Melvillean fluid text, and in this regard is on par with the likes of *Lear, Frankenstein,* and *Ulysses.*

Where Will It Appear?

An agenda for the construction of a fluid-text edition of *Typee* begins with the principles of comprehensiveness and book-screen synergy already noted in this chapter, and with the fact that the edition will be housed in a larger electronic archive or Melville Electronic Library (MEL) comprised of several interlinked "rooms" holding certain texts and allowing for various activities. One room will hold fully searchable facsimiles of the manuscript, a full transcription of the manuscript, and all print versions of *Typee* (including the NN critical edition). Another room will contain a fully annotated text linked to various source studies (such as Anderson's *Melville and the South Seas* and *Melville Unfolding*), and original source works such as Charles Stewart's *Visit to the South Seas* and David Porter's *Journal of a Cruise,* also searchable with links to passages in *Typee* that borrow from these texts. There will also be an art gallery for the display of visual images related to *Typee,* including early engravings of Polynesians and Polynesian life, modern illustrations of the novel, the Classics Illustrated comic book, and recent photographs of relevant sites on Nuku Hiva, Melville's Marquesan island retreat. If retrievable, videos of the two films based on *Typee*—*The Last of the Pagans* and *Enchanted Island*—will be located in a viewing room. Yet another room will contain secondary research materials, works of

Melville scholarship such as *Melville's Correspondence, The Melville Log, Melville's Contemporary Reviews, Melville Dissertations, A Companion to Melville Studies,* and so on, as well as critical studies of *Typee* (such as Herbert's *Marquesan Encounters*). There will also be activity rooms, such as a *Typee* text lab and a *Typee* revision workshop, in which users may generate their own editorial versions of *Typee* as either an intended, social, genetic, or fluid text. But the centermost room would hold the electronic fluid-text edition of *Typee*.

What Might a Fluid-Text Edition of Typee *Do?*

This query is linked to the more exacting question of what position or role the fluid-text edition can play in an electronic archive such as MEL. Essentially, the edition should be a device that can employ all features found in all other rooms of the archive. Users should be able to access the base version of *Typee* as a clear reading text that provides further access to annotations, sources, letter, reviews, and commentary as well as illustrations and other visuals. But the primary function of the fluid-text edition is to squire readers from one version to the next, and, above all, to showcase revision. In this regard, a simple click would place (metaphorically speaking) an electronic web over the base version, which supplies readers with a map of all revision sites of *Typee*. Scrolling through the mapped base version, readers can then click on a given revision site and a window opens revealing the revision sequence for that site and its accompanying revision narrative. (See fig. 3.) If a sequence begins with revisions in manuscript, a facsimile and transcript of the manuscript site also appears. Readers may also access from the fluid-text edition both the text lab and revision workshop rooms, where, on the one hand, they can bring up and collate any combination of the versions of *Typee* and, on the other hand, conjure up their own revision narratives for a particular revision site.

Clearly, the screen version of the fluid-text edition of *Typee* is designed to give users full access to the gathered materials associated with Melville's novel. But an archive is just a gathering, and all gatherings are shaped by principles of selection. Editions are similarly determined through selection and judgment. The fear is that users of electronic archives will assume that the size of the archive constitutes its catholicity when in fact they include only what the designers include. In addition, the map and revision narratives of an on-line fluid-text edition of *Typee* will similarly reflect the editor's sensibilities. A fluid-text editor needs, then, to remind screen users of these subjectivities in the way the revision narratives are composed and also in the way all materials are presented. Users should be encouraged to question the selection principles. And while the screen edition should be designed for ease of access and comfortable usage (with aids to prevent one's becoming lost in hyperspace), it should also be designed to move readers out of the archive, to get them off the screen.

The book version of the screen fluid-text edition can be used to reinforce this notion of the archive's selectivity (see fig. 4). Because of its limitations in size and page spread, the book itself can be nothing other than a critical selection of materials. Its principles of selection will be more clearly restrictive than the screen's seemingly all-encompassing display. The fluid-text editor will naturally choose those revision sites and revision narratives in *Typee* that seem most representative of the entire field but also most supportive of the editor's larger critical hypotheses concerning composition and the text's cultural significance and meaning. It is, of course, any editor's obligation to "socratize" these matters, to make interpretations as provisional hypotheses for readers to test through their own questioning and analysis. To this end, the fluid-text edition of *Typee* should encourage readers to generate revision narratives of their own, either as revisions (as it were) of the editor's work, or as narratives of new problems. And while the book version should be designed for ease of access and comfortable usage (with aids to help reader's stay focused on the revisions on a given page), it should also be designed to move readers beyond the book, to get them off the page and into the raw materials themselves, the documents.

Finally, both screen and book versions should encourage readers to get into the real world, of which both screen and book are mere facsimiles.

What Do You Want Your Typee to Do?

The mapping of revision and revision narratives depend upon the editor's heuristic aims and a simple set of queries: What will your *Typee* do? How will it represent the whole body of revision materials? How will your edited version demonstrate a critical perspective? How does it vary from other possible fluid-text editions of *Typee*? While a screen version has the opportunity to include many such *Typee*s, the more selective book version will necessarily present a more focused critical interpretation of the work's development, or what I call in *Melville Unfolding* a

Writing
Typee

MS **Transcript**   **EDITIONS OF**   **LATER EDITIONS**   **REVISION NARRATIVE**

First English   First American   American Revised   Second English   1846   1892   1968 NN   MS   Print

MANUSCRIPT
Page 30

Photo of MS
Page 30

426

427

428

←   Go To MS Page   →

TRANSCRIPTION
MS Page 30

426

taken hi{mself}1 off to that vile & detestable place
"Nuiheiva." — {¶} But now that Δ the ↑my companion↓ was gone, the|¶| Δ
↑savages ◊islanders◊| appeared to multiply|+|ied their acts of kindness
towards ↑ |But whatever they might have Δ◊been◊ thought of my
companion; now that he ◊the fate that Toby had received◊ ◊at their hands,
the natives◊| ◊now that he was gone the natives◊|
m|e|+|self Δ ↑myself↓ showering upon me a degree of attention they
could hardly have surpassed had the object of
their devotion been some celestial visitant. **Kori Kori**
never for [a?]|+the moment left my side Δ **without** ↑unless↓ it
were to execute my wishes. The faithful fellow
twice every day, in the cool of the morning |at|+& at the
~~during the s~~{hade} when the shades of evening where
descending over the valley insisted on carrying me
to the stream & bathing me in its waters. Oftentimes

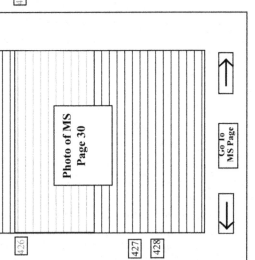

Transcription
Symbols

[A line by line transcription of the entire manuscript page
to the left with Revision Site 426 highlighted. The reader
can access a pop-up menu explaining the transcription
symbols by clicking on the box provided. To access the
revision narrative screens for this particular site, the
reader simply clicks on the Revision Site number.]

Typee

	MS		EDITIONS OF 1846				LATER EDITIONS			REVISION NARRATIVE	
	Transcript	First English	First American	American Revised	Second English		1892	1968 NN		MS	Print
	▨	☐	☐	☐	☐		☐	☐	▨	MS	☐ Print

Revision Site 426

TEXT PASSAGE . . .   In Manuscript

◊] But now that Λ he ⎰my companion⎱ was gone—they[Λ
⎰savages ◊islanders◊⎱ appeared⌐to multiply⌐‑ied their acts of kindness
towards ↑him Λ ⎰But whatever they might have Λ◊been◊ thought of ↑my
companion, now that the ◊the fate that Toby had received◊ ◊at their hands◊
the natives◊ ◊now that he was gone the natives◊⎱
m[e]⌐‑yself Λ ↑myself◊ showering upon me a degree of attention they
could hardly have surpassed had the object of
their devotion been some celestial visitant.

REVISION NARRATIVE   Voice Over

Step 1

In Manuscript

HM first wrote "But now that he was gone, they appeared to multiply their acts of kindness towards me showering upon me....celestial
visitant." Quite possibly the trigger for the wholesale revision in
this site was the desire to eliminate the repetition of "me" in "towards me showering upon me." HM altered "me" to "myself" by
writing "yself" over "me," but he then canceled the cobbled word,
writing "myself" afresh above the line for clarity. At this time, he
also made the routine change of "he" to "my companion" and the
more problematic change of "they" to "the savages."

---

1. [▨] But now that he was gone, they appeared to multiply their acts of kindness towards me showering upon me a degree of attention they could hardly have surpassed had the object of their devotion been some celestial visitant.

2. [2] But now that my companion was gone, the savages appeared to multiply their acts of kindness towards myself showering upon me a degree of attention they could hardly have surpassed had the object of their devotion been some celestial visitant.

3. [3] But now that my companion was gone, the islanders multiplied their acts of kindness towards myself showering upon me a degree of attention they could hardly have surpassed had the object of their devotion been some celestial visitant.

4. [4] But whatever might have been the fate that Toby had received at their hands[,] now that he was gone the natives multiplied their acts of kindness towards myself showering upon me a degree of attention they could hardly have surpassed had the object of their devotion been some celestial visitant.

5. [5] But whatever might have been his fate[,] now that he was gone the natives multiplied their acts of kindness towards myself showering upon me a degree of attention they could hardly have surpassed had the object of their devotion been some celestial visitant.

Fig. 3. Storyboard for a fluid-text edition of the *Typee* manuscript.

"global narrative of revision." One approach to this creative selectivity is to ask, "Which set of 'unfoldings' in the history of the work's many unfoldings will you stress?"

In *Typee*, for instance, I can isolate at least four major unfoldings during Melville's lifetime, each associated with a distinct set of versions. The 1845 manuscript and 1846 British edition constitute one unfolding in which the author may be seen composing both in isolation and in collaboration with various familial and professional editors. This represents Melville's first mediated intentions for his book. A second unfolding, focusing on the revised edition of 1846, involves a significant socially engendered series of reconceptualizations with Wiley's expurgations and Melville's assent to the expurgation coupled with his own additional revisions, including "The Story of Toby." A third unfolding may be seen as a period of conflicting texts throughout most of the latter half of the nineteenth century. Murray's refusal to accept the expurgations meant that British and American versions coexisted for decades in these two widely variant, but equally authorized texts (The Routledge and Gibbs piracies of 1850 used the British and American texts, respectively.) Finally, a fourth period of authorial unfolding involves the inferred version of *Typee* that Melville requested late in life, in which certain passages were to be restored, a paragraph on seaman debauchery dropped, and "Buggery Island" changed to "Desolation Island." These revisions were not fully honored by Arthur Stedman in the posthumous edition of 1892 he prepared, but a fluid-text editor would follow the writer's instruction to construct Melville's last version in comparison to Stedman's 1892 edition, to clarify Melville's final unfolding even though it was never materially realized.

Different editors will be drawn to different eras of unfolding in order to establish a grounding for certain critical concerns about *Typee* or about the historical period in question, and each will compose a narrative of revision accordingly. My *Typee* stresses the artist's struggle to unfold sexually and politically within himself as revealed in manuscript. In this case, as I demonstrate in *Melville Unfolding*, we find unfoldings within unfoldings. In contrast, your *Typee* might stress Melville's struggle with editors to maintain artistic integrity while trying to get published for the first time in 1846 or stress a later artistic integrity in Melville's suggested revisions for a last publication of *Typee*, eventually realized in 1892, a year after his death. Each approach has its valid critical view. But if these editorial constructs simply promote a mutually exclusive critical agenda, they will be merely isolated, rhetorical *editions imaginaires*. In time you and I might agree to collaborate on a third fluid-text edition of *Typee* that stresses both perspectives. An ideal fluid-text edition would attempt to embrace, as much as possible, all periods of fluidity, but most importantly it invites readers to discover patterns of revision on their own so that they may experience for themselves the dynamics of fluid texts.

To help readers read *Typee* this way is to enable them to observe an artist and culture unfolding. This is an event we rarely allow ourselves to imagine. We can watch Melville playing with the proper placement of *native, islander,* and *savage,* and recognize in that complex set of revisions that the young man confronting his language is also confronting his culture's deepest anxieties, some of which he cannot himself fully deny. In the same vein, he is using language to define himself. Readers can watch his unfoldings, construct them in their own terms, and by thus participating in Melville's re-self-definitions, we will find ourselves considering the fluid condition of self, language, and culture beyond the moment of 1845, up to our own present tense. Melville's unfolding is a version of our own unfolding.

Fig. 4. Book version of a fluid-text edition of the *Typee* manuscript. In side-by-side pages, the reader would find *(a)* a photo-reproduction of each manuscript leaf and *(b)* the graphic transcription of that leaf. On subsequent pages, the reader would be able to view *(c)* the reading text of the manuscript, which consists of a "base version" with numbered lines corresponding to the transcription, the mapping of all revision sites, and selected revision sequences and revision narratives. *(following three pages)*

Toby "Ki Ki" (cont) — "He had not addressed us until
he had assured himself
he perceived that we were both awake, at which he

seemed somewhat surprised. Probably for fear of dis-
turbing our slumbers he had approached us thus cautiously.
"Ki Ki, is it? said Toby in his gruff tone — "Were
cook us first will you" — but what's this "he added,
as another servant appeared bearing before him a large
accompany some kinds of steamy meats from the oven is diffusing
trencher of wood which he deposited at the feet of
Nehei' — "A baked baby I dare say — but I will
taste none if it never mind what it is — a pretty
fool I should make of myself indeed, to be
waked up here in the middle of the night,
stuffing & guzzling to make a fat meal for
a parcel of bloody cannibals one of these pleasant
salubrious mornings, No, I see what they are
after very plainly, so I am resolved to starve
myself into a bunch of bones & gristle & them — if they
serve me up, they are welcome — But I say Tomo,
you are not going to eat any of that inferior stuff
there in the dark are you? "
Kori Kori why how can you tell what it is? "
"By tasting it to be sure" said I, masticating a morsel
that Kori Kori had just placed upon me — "& excellent
good it is too, very much like veal. "
"A Baked
baby, by the soul of Captain Cook!" but faith
Toby with amazing vehemence — "Veil! Why there
never was a calf on the island till you landed —
I tell you —
you are bolting down mouthfulls from a dead
as sure as you live
Hapaa's carcass, that you & no deception!"
Emetics & luke warm water! What a sensation in the
abdominal regions! Sure enough, where could
the fiends incarnate have obtained meat — but I would
satify myself at all hazards, & turning to Nehei
I soon made them ready understand that I
wished a light to be brought. When the tapers came, I
gazed eagerly into the vessel & recognized the mutilated
remains of a genuinely deceased porker!

1   Toby Ki Ki" (eat) — He ~~did~~ ∧ not address+ed us until

2   he ~~perceived~~ that we were both awake, at which he

3   seemed somewhat surprised. Probably for fear of dis=

4   turbing our slumbers he had approached us thus cautiously

5   —¶ "Ki Ki, is it? said Toby in his gruff tones — "well

6   cook us first will you" — but what's this" he added,

7   as another ~~native~~ appeared bearing before him a large

8   trencher of wood ∧ which he deposited at the feet of

9   Mehevi — "A baked baby I dare say — but I will

10 have none of it, never mind what it is — a pe+retty

11 fool I ~~would~~ ∧ make of myself indeed, to be

12 waked up here in the middle of the night,

13 stuffing & guzzlling ∧ to make a fat meal for

14 a parcel of bloody cannibals one of these ~~pleasant~~

15 salubrius mornings, No, I see what they are

16 after very plainly, so I am resolved to starve

17 myself into a bunch of bones & gristle & then if they

18 serve me up, they are welcome — But I say Tomo,

19 You are not going to eat any of that, ~~are infernal stuff~~

20 there in the dark are you, +?" ~~This question was put,~~

21 ~~as Kori-Kori~~ why how can you tell what it is?"

22 —¶ "By tasting it to be sure" said I masticating a morsel

23 that Kori Kori had just forced upon me — "& excellent

24 good is +t is too, very much like viel."— ¶ "A Baked

25 baby, by the soul of Captain Cook!" burst forth

26 Toby with amazing vehemence — "Veil! why there

27 never was a calf on the island till you landed —

28 — ∧ you are bolting down mouthfulls from a dead

29 Hapaa's carcass, ~~that you~~ & no deception!"

30 — ¶ Emetics and luke warm water! What a sensation in the

31 abdominal regions! Sure enough, where could

32 the fiends incarnate have obtained meat — but I ∧ ~~will~~

33 satisfy myself at all hazards, & I turn~~ed~~ +ing to "Mehevi"

34 & +I soon made the ready ~~savage~~ understand that I

35 wished a light to be brought. When the taper came, I

36 gazed eagerly into the vessel & recognized the mutilated

37 remains of a prematurely deceased porker!

Reading Text

1 Toby Ki Ki" (eat) — He [**had not addressed**]ms109e92 us until
2 he **had assumed himself**ms110 that we were both awake, at which he
3 seemed somewhat surprised. [Probably for fear of dis-
4 turbing our slumbers he had approached us thus cautiously] e93
5 —¶ "Ki Ki, is it? said Toby in his gruff tones — "well
6 cook us first will you" — but what's this" he added,
7 as another **savage**ms111 appeared bearing before him a large
8 trencher of wood **containing some kind of steaming meat [from]**e94 **the
   odors it diffused &**ms112 which he deposited at the feet of
9 Mehevi — "A baked baby I dare say — but I will
10 have none of it, never mind what it is — a **pretty**ms113
11 fool I **should**ms114 make of myself indeed, **to be**e95
12 waked up here in the middle of the night,
13 stuffing & guzzlling **& all**ms115 to make a fat meal for
14 a parcel of [bloody cannibals]e96 one of these
15 [**salubrius**]ms116e97 mornings, No, I see what they are
16 [after]e98 very plainly, so I am resolved to starve
17 myself into a bunch of bones & gristle & then if they
18 serve me up, they are welcome — But I say Tomo,

RSms111: as another ~~native~~ savage appeared
1. as another native appeared
2. as another **savage** appeared

The Confidence-Man.

RSms115-16e96-97: stuffing & guzzlling ∧ & all to make a fat meal
for
a parcel of bloody cannibals one of these ~~pleasant~~
salubrius mornings
1. stuffing & guzzlling to make a fat meal for a
   parcel of bloody cannibals one of these
   pleasant
2. stuffing & guzzlling to make a fat meal for a
   parcel of bloody cannibals one of these
   salubrius mornings
3. stuffing & guzzlling **& all** to make a fat meal
   for a parcel of bloody cannibals one of these
   salubrius mornings
3. stuffing & guzzling, and all to make a fat meal
   for a parcel of **bloody-minded** cannibals one
   of these salubrius mornings [RNe96]
4. stuffing & guzzling, and all to make a fat meal
   for a parcel of bloody-minded cannibals one
   of these [...] mornings [RNe97]

RNms111: Generally, HM's revision strategy is to reduce
his usage of "savage" by altering it to one of two more
neutral options: "native" or "islander." Here in a proofreading phase, he reverses that trend changing "native"
to "savage," which intensifies the sailors' lingering fears
of cannibalism and plays upon the reader's presumed
expectation of Polynesian savagery

RNms115-16e96-97: Toby's voice is that odd combination of educated and low-class dictions typical of
the eccentric gentleman type found in the amiable hu-
mor of the day, a precursor to HM's "genial misan-
thrope" in his last novel *The Confidence-Man*. Revisions at this site show HM modulating this combination. Initially,
HM has Toby say "stuffing & guzzlling to make a fat meal for a
parcel of bloody cannibals one of these pleasant" with the intention
of continuing on with "pleasant mornings" [step 1]. However, as
soon as he inscribed "pleasant" HM upgraded the adjective to the
more pretentious (and charmingly misspelled) "salubrius mornings"
[2]. In a proofreading phase, HM later added the colloquial "& all"
[3] to emphasize Toby's "gruff tones" established eight line up.
RNe96: Revising "bloody cannibals" (offensive to British ears) to
"bloody-minded cannibals" may have been a concession HM made
himself in the fair copy stage, or an editorial change he silently accepted during the preparation of the English edition.

Cont. RN page 35

CHAPTER EIGHT

Coda: America as Fluid Text

*And with restored scorn his back he turn'd
On those proud Tow'rs to swift destruction
   doom'd*

—John Milton, *Paradise Lost*, Book V

*What is the great globe itself but a Loose-
Fish? And what are you, reader, but a
Loose-Fish and a Fast-Fish, too?*

—Herman Melville, *Moby-Dick*

*A cosmopolitan, a catholic man; who,
being such, ties himself to no narrow tailor
or teacher, but federates, in heart as in cos-
tume, something of the various gallantries
of men under various suns.*

—Herman Melville, *The Confidence-Man*

My purpose in writing *The Fluid Text* is both professional and—I suppose for lack of a better word, I'll say it—moral. I want to address the academic community—scholars, critics, and pedagogues alike—with the idea of reminding ourselves of a fundamental reality: texts are mutable and the measure of their mutation is a record of the interpenetrations of artist and culture. But if this fundamental is easy enough to accept, the deeper concern is how we may use textual fluidity to find deeper truths about creativity: about ourselves, our lives, our culture. And here is the moral dimension. The fluid text crystallizes for us the fact of change, and no other factor in our lives contributes to so much fear, joy, and anxiety as change. If we can come more to grips with the fluidities of language and the writing process (elements so vital to our existence), it stands to reason that we can prepare ourselves for better understanding social change.

Melville's struggle with *savage, native,* and *islander* is not a problem that lends itself to any editorial fix; it is not strictly speaking a "problem" at all, but a fluidity, which once seen as a fluidity, reveals the tensions of an artist and of a culture working toward the expression of a moment in time. We cannot edit the fluidity away; in fact, we are obliged to edit it into existence, to showcase it for readers, and to help readers pleasurably read it so that they are better equipped to comprehend its reality and to make of it what they will. This editorial and readerly enterprise inherent in fluid-text editing is a professional concern, but it is finally a moral one, too. And one that takes us to the heart of America's clearest challenge of the twenty-first century: How can a multicultural society grow to become at pleasure with itself.

Culture is a text we collectively revise; it is a fluid text. If we are to learn to read a culture, we must learn how this text is written down, whose words combine to convey the text, and how to read historically. The Declaration of Independence is a revision of Locke; the Constitution a series of emendations, our people always in search of identity. America has its myth of a unified genesis and presumptions of racial purity, and yet its frequent revolutions and ineluctable mixings make multiculturalism our inevitable, cosmopolitan end. Our culture is a fluid text, but we want to read it as a fixed thing, never seeking to find the dynamics of its changing but always to discover the authority of its imagined fixity, its nonexistent past purity. The strict constructionist makes present judgment upon the wisdom of a past moment and intention, and fails to recognize that the past, too, is a fluid text that we revise as we desire, as we must. Culture flows as history flows as text flows.

We can deny fluidity in culture and text, or celebrate it for its own sake, but these conservative and relativist poses have little social or aesthetic utility. Fluidity is a condition we need to engage directly. We cannot cure the condition, for fluidity is not a disease and requires no cure. Rather, our obligation is to understand the causes and currents of fluidity. And find out what it means.

Here, today, on January 18, 2001, as I write that "culture is a fluid text," I wonder about baseball, and jazz, and election ballot chads; about Serbia, Bosnia, and the Bronx; about my newest daughter, born in China of Chinese parents lost. Each summer I watch her turning browner as I grow gray. America is difference and distance brought close together; it is the Lost and Found. We need a vocabulary to aid in our expression of our multicultural life so that when my daughter says, as she will in a few years, I am China, I can say, so am I. And we together are more.

And here, today again, on December 11, 2001, three months after the terrorist attack on the World Trade Center, just south of my home, as I revise this book, thinking on the words "And we together are more," and the words "culture is a fluid text," I consider the New York skyline, so cruelly revised, and a minor consequence reflected in an October 25, 2001, letter to the *New York Times.* In that letter, comedian and film director Ben Stiller responds to complaints about the release of his most recent movie *Zoolander,* a burlesque on the fashion industry which included footage of the skyline, doctored so as to obscure the once-proud now demolished Twin Towers. The complaints were not about the appropriateness of releasing a comedy on the heels of the disaster, but about Stiller's presumption in "Editing the Towers" (as the *Times* staff put it). He explains that for the sake of audiences seeking comic escape, he did not want the image of the towers in two crucial shots to complicate the effect of his scene. "I decided," he writes, "to edit out one shot, and to obscure the towers in another."

But viewers and (worse for Stiller) reviewers of the film did not react as anticipated. Instead, they experienced a grim "fluid-text moment." While viewing the edited film, they became conscious of Stiller's revision of the skyline; they "saw" the towers' exclusion, and called the revision "execrable": an attempt to "pretend they were never there." Stiller had tried to preserve a comic mood by removing a bit of text that had now, suddenly, become a threat to that tone, but in doing so he triggered the very passions he had hoped to avoid; in fact, he incited even deeper passions, a resentment over his presumption and an anger at his power to revise a cultural icon itself, ironically, already revised out of existence, if not memory. Bemoaning his no-win situation, Stiller concludes, "I only assert that I was trying to do the right thing."

Stiller, it seems, was damned no matter what he did; but damned, we should add, the moment he had decided to become a filmmaker, and hence a film editor, that is, one who has no choice but to "make cuts," rearrange bits of text, and revise. And just as sure as Stiller must edit and revise in order to create, his audiences are just as certain to react deeply to his revisions, when made aware of them. More to the point, the fluid-text moment Stiller triggered with his "editing of the tower" is only symptomatic of a deeper condition of culture.

First, let us be clear: Stiller did not "Edit the Towers"; he only edited an image he had made of the towers. The terrorists were the primary editors; they made the deeper cut. This is not to trivialize the horror and injustice of their deed. The still smoldering graveyard they made—in one instant consigning 3,000 lives to an unspeakable death—has triggered a fluid-text moment the world shall not soon forget. Like all fluid-text moments, this one has awakened us to a simple, knowable, but often denied truth. Like any text, culture is fragile, mutable, constantly revisable. It is fluid and always has been. The New York City skyline has changed over the centuries with growth spurts and reductions from forest, field and rock to spires and towers. Its material presence has achieved iconic status. But the fatal appeal of an icon is its ability to lure us into delusions of power, stability and permanence, when no city is permanently powerful or stable, and no city's skyline should ever be anything but an icon of change. After the terrorist attack of September 11, after the towers were "edited," pundits and citizens alike agreed that "everything is changed now." But the reality is that everything always was changing. America did not need a criminal attack to learn this reality. But the attack came, and the question is what to make of change.

People will shape their lives in response to the change they perceive. Filmmakers will make their cuts; advertisers, merchants, brokers, and economists will promote "sales" to honor the dead; memorialists and real estate dealers will propose new towers; mayors and presidents will root out "evil"; lawmakers will suspend liberty. But the analyst of fluid texts will explore the causes of change and seek out the sources of influence that shape and trigger cultural revision. Their search will take them beyond the material and iconic text of the skyline and even past the text of the Quran into the rage of minds that cheered the fall of "those proud Tow'rs site to swift destruction doom'd." They will find explanations, not justifications, and they will write their narratives of revision.

And here, today yet again, I sit now with my oldest blue-eyed daughter, newly wed, and my new brown-eyed son-in-law, he born of

Milwaukee, the son of a Pakistani father and Anglo-Irish mother, both citizens of America. They have read this Coda in its earlier version replete with my copy editor's "suggested" revisions, and they agree to the necessity of my adding the foregoing paragraphs on editing the towers. Their thought, too, is that this final section, if not the entire book, should be printed up with the copy-editor's electronic copy-editing cancellations and insertions intact so as to demonstrate to readers the material fact of revision as I attempt to make concluding remarks on revision, texts, and culture. Very postmodern. And ~~I am thinking~~ maybe they have a good idea. But as I watch them reading together on my couch, my thoughts are on what may be the color of my grandchildren's eyes, and of the possibilities of brown. Families are also fluid texts.

I wonder how next I shall greet my students. Shall I offer them some text to read and then a variant version and watch the discussion as it flows? Will I wait to ask: What is the meaning of the way you now must read, once confronted by these variants? Are these words "fast-fish," the fixed, immutable possession of the literary work, or are they, as Ishmael suggests, "loose-fish," free now fast later and loose again? Are not these loose-fish textual fluidities the vestiges of a changing mind, shifting intentions, and social pressure? If this fluid text signifies a writer's condition, and if you are a writer—and write we must—then is this fluid text not an emblem of our own condition as well? Are we not revising ourselves, always, to find the flow of ourselves, and then too the mixings and revisions of our culture?

We may ignore the fluidity of texts and of culture; we may insist upon fixity or simply yield out of exhaustion to the tyranny of single-text editing, single-text reading, and single-text thinking. But the inevitability of a global community and multiculturalism requires a new cosmopolitanism in our analysis of literary works. For in learning the meaning of the revision of texts, we discover a new kind of critical thinking based on difference, variation, approximation, intention, power, and change; a kind of thinking to ready us for the shifting sands of democratic life, if democracy should ever finally come.

Notes

Introduction

1. Joseph Grigely, *Texualterity: Art, Theory, and Textual Criticism* (Ann Arbor: University of Michigan Press, 1995).

2. According to Peter Shillingsburg, "The word *definitive* should be banished from editorial discussion." *Scholarly Editing in the Computer Age: Theory and Practice*, 3d ed. (Ann Arbor: University of Michigan Press, 1996), 90.

3. No one, I think, would deny the general truth of this assertion, and support for it would involve a monumental footnote, which we may happily forgo except to give brief mention to those in the field of textual scholarship who have written effectively on "process editing": George Bornstein, Paul Eggert, Hans Walter Gabler, Jean-Louis LeBrave, Stephen Parrish, Donald Reiman, Jack Stillinger, and Peter Shillingsburg.

4. Jack Stillinger provides a voluminous list of multiversioned works or fluid texts in the appendix to his *Multiple Authorship and the Myth of Solitary Genius* (New York: Oxford University Press, 1991).

5. Hans Walter Gabler notes, "Instability is an essential feature of the text in progress." And while he argues that an editor should not use this "instability" as evidence of a movement toward "the fulfillment of its real or assumed teleology" or final intention, he does not address the implied teleological connotations in the use of *instability*. See "The Text as Process and the Problem of Intentionality," *Text* 3 (1987): 111.

6. George P. Landow, *Hypertext: The Convergence of Contemporary Critical Theory and Technology* (Baltimore: Johns Hopkins University Press, 1992), 88–89.

7. W. K. Wimsatt Jr. and Monroe C. Beardsley, "The Intentional Fallacy," in *The Verbal Icon* (Lexington: University Press of Kentucky, 1946), 3–18.

8. Stillinger, *Multiple Authorship,* 189.

9. Jacques Derrida, "Structure, Sign, and Play in the Discourse of the Human Sciences," in *The Structuralist Controversy,* ed. Richard Macksey and Eugenio Donato (Johns Hopkins University Press, 1972); rpt. in *Criticism: Major Statements,* ed. Charles Kaplan and William Anderson (New York: St. Martin's Press, 1991), 533.

10. As Peter Shillingsburg notes, with some frustration, "[I]t is curious that deconstructionists have failed to take up [the question of the indeterminacy of

documentary texts] as one inextricably linked to the question of indeterminate meaning." *Resisting Texts: Authority and Submission in Constructions of Meaning* (Ann Arbor: University of Michigan Press, 1997), 38.

11. In trying to suggest that textual criticism operates more in sympathy with than against deconstruction, I am following the lead of two others, G. Thomas Tanselle and D. C. Greetham. In "Textual Criticism and Deconstruction," Tanselle bemoans de Man's naive confusion of text, document, and work despite the fact that he and other poststructuralists are clearly attuned to the inherent intangibility of language and should know better (see "Textual Criticism and Deconstruction," *Studies in Bibliography* 43 [1990]: 17). Greetham acknowledges Tanselle's concerns and pursues further deconstructionist principles in intentionalist textual criticism, but tempers Tanselle's response by stressing more positive interconnections between editorial and deconstructionist theories. He states, for instance, that textual criticism "employ[s] the Derridean inversion of absence over presence in seeking to discover the present author who is manifest only through the marks or 'traces' of absence in the documentary remains—in 'writing,' or *'écriture'*" (20). Greetham concludes that "[t]he successful textual critic is, like the successful deconstructor, one who can perceive both the raveling and the unraveling, the singularity and the heterogeneity, the construction and the dissolution." "[Textual] Criticism and Deconstruction," *Studies in Bibliography* 44 (1991): 20, 29. See also his recent volume *Theories of the Text* (New York: Oxford University Press, 1999).

12. Michel Foucault, "What Is an Author?" in *Contemporary Literary Criticism*, ed. Robert Con Davis and Ronald Schleifer (New York: Longman, 1989), 275.

13. Herman Melville, *Correspondence,* ed. Lynn Horth, Harrison Hayford, Hershel Parker, and G. Thomas Tanselle (Evanston: Northwestern University Press; Chicago: Newberry Library, 1993), 193.

14. See my "Herman Melville: A Writer in Process," in *Tales, Poems, and Other Writings by Herman Melville* (New York: Random House, 2001). This volume also contains innovative fluid-text displays for portions of *Typee* and *Billy Budd* as well as for the poems "Art" and "Camoens."

Chapter 1

1. Of textual scholarship D. F. McKenzie has written that bibliography in general is "the only discipline which has consistently studied the composition of, formal design and transmission of texts by writers, printers, and publishers; their distribution through different communities by wholesalers, retailers, and teachers; their collection and classification by librarians; their meaning for, and—I must add—their creative regeneration by, readers." *Bibliography and the Sociology of Texts* (London: British Library, 1986), 4. McKenzie's final emphasis upon the power of readers to reshape the texts they read significantly extends the discipline of bibliography into the social forces that contribute to the fluid text.

2. G. Thomas Tanselle, "A Checklist of Editions of *Moby-Dick,* 1851–1976" (Evanston: Northwestern University Press; Chicago: Newberry Library, 1976), 1.

3. Hershel Parker, *Herman Melville: A Biography,* vol. 1 (Baltimore: Johns Hopkins University Press, 1996), 363.

4. Herman Melville, *Typee: A Peep at Polynesian Life,* ed. Harrison Hayford, Hershel Parker, and G. Thomas Tanselle (Evanston: Northwestern University Press; Chicago: Newberry Library, 1968), 277–302.

5. G. Thomas Tanselle, "The Text of Melville in the Twenty-First Century," in *Melville's Evermoving Dawn: Centennial Essays,* ed. John Bryant and Robert Milder (Kent, Ohio: Kent State University Press, 1997), 334.

6. For a fuller discussion of this point, see my "Politics, Imagination, and the Fluid Text," *Studies in the Literary Imagination* 29, no. 2 (1996): 89–107.

7. Hershel Parker provides this date for Melville's proposal of marriage in *Herman Melville: A Biography,* vol. 1, 450.

8. G. Thomas Tanselle, *A Rationale of Textual Criticism* (Philadelphia: University of Pennsylvania Press, 1989), 93. Hereafter cited parenthetically in the text as *Rationale.*

9. Jerome J. McGann, *Social Values and Poetic Acts: The Historical Judgment of Literary Work* (Cambridge: Harvard University Press, 1988), 240, 131.

10. McGann, *Social Values,* 26, 47, 55, 72.

Chapter 2

1. R. M. Davis makes this familiar point about the writing process in "Writing as Process: Beyond Hershel Parker," *Literary Research* 12, no. 4 (1987): 179–86.

2. Jack Stillinger refers to the goal of the Greg-Bowers line of editing to be "the Platonically perfect realization of an author's final intentions in a work" (*Multiple Authorship,* 198). Although Peter Shillingsburg notes that a work is the product of the imagination and not a Platonic ideal, he also uses the word *ideal* somewhat loosely, as in the following passage: "The only real alternative to a multiple, nonlinear text for scholarly editions is the creation of an ideal text based on frankly acknowledged critical principles" (*Computer Age,* 42, 90). Hans Walter Gabler flatly affirms that "the edited text fulfilling the author's final intentions is, as everyone avows, an ideal text" (see his introduction to *Contemporary German Editorial Theory,* ed. Hans Walter Gabler, George Bornstein, and Gillian Borland Pierce [Ann Arbor: University of Michigan Press, 1995], 3–4). And Tanselle, himself, perhaps ill-advisedly, adopts the term in his review essay "Textual Instability and Editorial Idealism" but defends eclectic editing by saying that it "is not attempting to construct a single, final, ideal ahistorical text but to reconstruct what was intended at a specific time" (*Studies in Bibliography* 49 [1996]: 17). Just as Shillingsburg rightly calls for the banishment of the word *definitive,* I would appreciate a moratorium on *ideal text.*

3. I put this expression in quotation marks to indicate its problematic nature. Since documents are by their physical nature susceptible to intended and unintended variation, it is misleading to call even unintended textual variation "corruption" because the term implies the existence of some form of the text that is

uncorrupted or perfect, and this is both impossible in the physical world and limiting in hermeneutics.

4. For texts and discussions cf. Herman Melville, *Moby-Dick,* ed. Harrison Hayford and Hershel Parker (New York: Norton, 1967), 349 and 493 with Herman Melville, *Moby-Dick; or, The Whale,* ed. Harrison Hayford, Hershel Parker, and G. Thomas Tanselle (Evanston: Northwestern University Press; Chicago: Newberry Library, 1988), 416 and 892–93.

5. Michael Sadleir's 1922–24 Constable edition, despite its importance in the Melville revival, offers no discussion of editorial principles and even contributed one famous typo: the so-called "soiled" rather than "coiled fish" that flummoxed F. O. Matthiessen's analysis of *White-Jacket.* Nevertheless, the Constable edition was cited as "standard" well into the 1970s. See G. Thomas Tanselle, "Melville and the World of Books," in *A Companion to Melville Studies,* ed. John Bryant (Westport, Conn.: Greenwood Press, 1986), 808–9. As of this writing, two volumes (published poems and late manuscripts, including *Billy Budd*) of the now-standard NN edition remain to be published.

6. The versions of *Typee* are the subject of this book, and the British and American versions of *Moby-Dick* have already been mentioned. Melville's tales appear in magazine and book versions as well as one fair-copy text; his unpublished poems (including the posthumously published *Weeds and Wildings*) appear in working draft and fair-copy states; and *Billy Budd* exists as a polished but not finished manuscript and three published versions of that document, including Hayford and Sealts's 1962 edition, which shall be the version used in the NN edition of that novel.

7. Letter to Duyckinck, July [30?] 1846, NN *Correspondence,* 60. The Duyckinck letter to which Melville is responding has not been found; however, the context of Melville's response suggests that Duyckinck had referred to the shortened version to be released as an "Expurgated Edition" and that in calling "Expurgated" an "Odious word," Melville was good-humoredly steering Duyckinck back to his preferred term, which he underlines in the letter: "The *Revised . . .* Edition of Typee." Melville's ironic insistence upon the euphemism clearly reveals his desire to place a positive light upon the expurgation of his text while conceding its problematic nature.

8. NN *Correspondence* 56, his emphasis. Melville was drawn, at this time, to the word *narrative* as the designation of a genre of truthful personal tale, or what he refers to in a letter to Alexander W. Bradford, supportive editor of the *Albany Argus,* as "a genuine narrative" (38). On the other hand, he was not pleased with Murray's original, rather journalistic title for *Typee—Narrative of a Four Months' Residence Among the Natives of a Valley of the Marquesas Islands*—preferring the "strangeness and novelty" of the island name, which is "naturally suggested by the narrative itself" (57). Clinging to a sense of truthful narration, Melville was from the beginning pushing the notion of narrative to include the strangeness of the novel or romance.

9. Parker expresses the standard critical view that in arguing for the expurgation of *Typee,* Melville "had even rationalized that it improved the unity of the book" (*Herman Melville,* I:453). But as Bryan C. Short argues, Melville's so-called

rationalizations make aesthetic sense. See "'The Author at the Time': Tommo and Melville's Self-Discovery in *Typee*," *Texas Studies in Literature and Language* 31 (fall 1989): 386–405; rev. in *Cast by Means of Figures: Herman Melville's Rhetorical Development* (Amherst: University of Massachusetts Press, 1992), 23–41.

Chapter 3

1. See, in particular, G. Thomas Tanselle, "Textual Criticism and Literary Sociology," *Studies in Bibliography* 44 (1991): 83–143; "Editing without a Copy-Text," *Studies in Bibliography* 47 (1994): 1–22; "Textual Instability and Editorial Idealism," *Studies in Bibliography* 49 (1996): 1–60; and "Reflections on Scholarly Editing," *Raritan* 16, no. 2 (fall 1996): 52–64.

2. *Studies in Bibliography* 17 (1964): 228.

3. Fredson Bowers, "Authorial Intention and Editorial Problems," *Text* 5 (1991): 53.

4. Bowers, "Authorial Intention" 55, 61.

5. Forcing a parallel between Gregian editorial theory and eugenics, Joseph Grigely then imputes a causal relation: "the textual-critical strategies of eclectic editing were strongly influenced by the residue of eugenic ideology surviving in the discourse of mid-century idealism" (*Texualterity*, 26). Less audacious but equally disappointing is Gary Taylor's celebration of his idea that textual criticism "is always *ad hominem*." In "The Rhetoric of Textual Criticism," *Text* 4 (1988): 39–56, he favorably contrasts his self-consciously "disruptive" and "personal" mode of textual argumentation to Tanselle's "characteristically assimilative, synthetic, diplomatic, and impersonal" discourse (54). This postmodern romanticizing of one's self-conscious subjectivity—my rhetorical mask is better than yours because, unlike you, I am aware that my mask is a mask—is at best self-serving and at worst, well, ad hominem.

6. As we shall see in chapter 6, Parker's so-called Kraken edition of Melville's *Pierre* puts this theory into practice.

7. James Thorpe, *Principles of Textual Criticism* (San Marino, Calif.: Huntington Library, 1972), 31.

8. Jerome J. McGann, *A Critique of Modern Textual Criticism* (Chicago: University of Chicago Press, 1983), 55 and 8.

9. McGann, *Critique,* 42, 51.

10. Stillinger, *Multiple Authorship.*

11. McGann, *Critique,* 48.

12. McGann, *Critique,* 62.

13. D. F. McKenzie's familiar articulation of this idea appears in *Bibliography and the Sociology of Texts.*

14. McGann, *Critique,* 62.

15. Jerome J. McGann, *The Textual Condition* (Princeton: Princeton University Press, 1991), 21.

16. McGann, *The Textual Condition,* 11, 15.

17. McGann, *Social Values,* 42–43.

18. McGann, *Social Values,* 72,

19. McGann, *The Textual Condition,* 15.

20. Stillinger, *Multiple Authorship,* 185.

21. Tanselle minimizes the relevance of bibliographical codes, arguing that writers generally expect publishers to manage bibliographical formats and therefore that bibliographical codes are generally not a feature of authorial intention ("Text of Melville," 341–42). From McGann's reader-response perspective, the issue of an author's expectations is beside the point.

22. McGann, *The Textual Condition,* 30–31. McGann's current editorial project is a hypermedia version of the works of Dante Gabriel Rossetti. This "decentered approach" avoids issues of copy-text or continuous production texts, giving the user access to a "set of electronic facsimiles" to be navigated however the user may wish. See Jerome J. McGann, "The Complete Writings and Pictures of Dante Gabriel Rossetti: A Hypermedia Research Archive," *Text* 7 (1994): 100–101.

23. McGann, *The Textual Condition,* 60, 61.

24. Herman Melville, *The Confidence-Man: His Masquerade,* ed. Harrison Hayford, Hershel Parker, and G. Thomas Tanselle (Evanston: Northwestern University Press; Chicago: Newberry Library, 1984), 183.

25. Raymond Williams, *Marxism and Literature* (Oxford: Oxford University Press, 1977), 198.

26. Williams, *Marxism and Literature,* 210.

27. Clifford Geertz, *The Interpretation of Cultures: Selected Essays* (New York: Basic Books, 1973), 131.

28. McGann, *The Textual Condition,* 79.

29. Tanselle argues in several places that intentionalism and social text theory are complementary, if not entirely compatible ("Textual Criticism and Literary Sociology," 140; "Text of Melville," 342).

30. Tanselle welcomes "recent interest in the process of textual metamorphosis," especially as it is discussed in James McLaverty's notion of utterance, discussed in chapter 2. See Tanselle's "Textual Instability and Editorial Idealism," *Studies in Bibliography* 49 (1996): 25, 49. Peter Shillingsburg is more sanguine in applauding the efforts of German geneticists and what is called "process editing," the goal of which is "to make the process visible by some means that distinguishes between the various agents of change and evaluates the changes, not only according to the perceived effect made by the change but according to the 'authority' of the agent of change" ("Text as Matter, Concept, and Action," *Studies in Bibliography* 44 [1991]: 37). My point in stressing Energy is not to dismiss the idea of Process but to expand its scope beyond authorized change to include what in chapter 5 I call authorial, editorial, and cultural versions of a work.

Chapter 4

1. Central to D. F. McKenzie's opening argument for his sociological definition of bibliography is his own highly ironic, "fluid-text moment" involving Wimsatt and Beardsley's use of a Congreve text, which in the modernized version

they use supports their notion of "intentional fallacy," whereas, in fact, the original version of Congreve conveys exactly the opposite view (*Bibliography*, 9–16).

2. Gabler, "Text as Process," 111; Gunter Martens draws upon Adorno's notion of "'the spirit of the work of art' [that] exists in the tension between its elements seen as a process" to make this point. See "(De)Constructing Texts by Editing: Reflections on the Receptional Significance of Textual Apparatuses," in Gabler, Bornstein, and Pierce, *Contemporary German Editorial Theory*, 132.

3. Gabler, introduction to *Contemporary German Editorial Theory*, 2.

4. Hans Zeller, "Record and Interpretation: Analysis and Documentation as Goal and Method of Editing," in Gabler, Bornstein, and Pierce, *Contemporary German Editorial Theory*, 29.

5. The actual display of variants may differ among editors. Gerhard Seidel's display of variants of a poem by Brecht sits on the page in chart fashion and is even more of a challenge to standard linear reading practice than Gabler's synopsis. See "Changing Intention in the Process of Writing: A Poem by Bertolt Brecht on Karl Kraus in a Historical-Critical Edition," in Gabler, Bornstein, and Pierce, *Contemporary German Editorial Theory*, 233–72.

6. Hans Walter Gabler, afterword to *Ulysses: A Critical and Synoptic Edition*, vol. 3, ed. Hans Walter Gabler, Wolfhard Steppe, and Claus Melchior (New York: Garland, 1986), 1895.

7. Zeller, "Record and Interpretation," 106.

8. Louis Hay, "Does 'Text' Exist?" *Studies in Bibliography* 41 (1988): 71, 74.

9. Zeller, "Record and Interpretation," 104.

10. Gabler, "Text as Process," 112.

11. Siegfried Scheibe, "Theoretical Problems of the Authorization and Constitution of Texts," in Gabler, Bornstein, and Pierce, *Contemporary German Editorial Theory*, 175.

12. Zeller, "Record and Interpretation," 113.

13. Scheibe, "Theoretical Problems," 176.

14. Hay, "Does 'Text' Exist?" 73.

15. John Wenke, *Melville's Muse: Literary Creation and the Forms of Philosophical Fiction* (Kent, Ohio: Kent State University Press, 1995), 80.

16. Jack Stillinger, *Coleridge and Textual Instability: The Multiple Versions of the Major Poems* (New York: Oxford University Press, 1994), 119.

17. Donald H. Reiman, "'Versioning': The Presentation of Multiple Texts," in *Romantic Texts and Contexts* (Columbia: University of Missouri Press, 1987), 169.

18. Stillinger, *Coleridge and Textual Instability*, 131.

19. Stillinger, *Coleridge and Textual Instability*, 133–34.

20. Reiman also restricts the study of social text versions this way. In his *Study of Modern Manuscripts* (Baltimore: Johns Hopkins University Press, 1993), he notes that critical editions of works will have to be published from time to time, and "In such instances, I would favor basing the texts on versions that the author accepted as his or her public texts once they were circulated rather than on prepublication manuscripts" (111). The Reiman reason for this preference of circulated versions can be found in his broader analysis of manu-

scripts, which he categorizes as private, confidential, and public. Public and confidential documents may not, indeed probably were not, intended to be circulated to the general public, and editors must be aware that this factor alters the nature of the author's self-conscious presentation of self (68). Thus, if a working draft version of a text is classifiable as private or confidential (or is attached to such documents, such as a version of a poem embedded in a love letter, let's say), then the editor may consider not reproducing that private or confidential version. Regarding Joyce's randy letters to Nora, Reiman even goes so far as to say: "I might well decide to destroy parts of that record rather than have it disseminated without discretion" (81). What Reiman leaves unstated is the method of destruction he might use.

21. Shillingsburg, "Text as Matter," 74.

22. Shillingsburg, *Computer Age*, 44.

23. Shillingsburg, "Text as Matter," 50.

24. Shillingsburg, "Text as Matter," 68.

25. McGann, *The Textual Condition*, 51.

26. The puzzle is as follows: If the Mona Lisa hangs in the Louvre, where is the text of *Hamlet*? The point is that while a painting is a single, material object, the text of a literary work, like language in general, is an intangible thing manifesting itself in variant physical versions. *Hamlet* is a fluid text; *La Gioconda* is not.

27. James McLaverty, "Issues of Identity and Utterance: An Intentionalist Response to 'Textual Instability,'" in *Devils and Angels: Textual Editing and Literary Theory*, ed. Philip Cohen (Charlottesville: University Press of Virginia, 1991), 137.

28. James McLaverty, "The Mode of Existence of Literary Works of Art: The Case of the *Dunciad* Variorum," *Studies in Bibliography* 37 (1984): 82–105.

Chapter 5

1. One caveat: In fluid-text analysis, meaning is constructed out of the contemplation of revision and of the textual differences between versions of a literary work. Individual versions necessarily yield their share of varied interpretations, but we should not slip into the habit of referring to one's interpretation or reading of a version as an actual or material version of the text itself. While versions are textual constructs based on physical difference, our differing interpretations are different arguments we might construct about the meaning of a version. However, Peter Shillingsburg argues, cogently and rather compellingly, that since reading itself is a creative act, a literary work "is a conceptual entity resulting from a reception performance" (*Resisting Texts*, 40). This performative notion of the act of reading as a generator of the work might further suggest that any given reading is, contrary to my view, a version of the work, but I would argue that such a performance has no practical reality until it is transformed into a material textual alternative to the work. The word "version," then, should be used to refer to the transformed text, not the critical interpretation upon which it is based.

2. McGann, *Critique,* 51.

3. Joseph Grigely supplies a good example of such response to a text in his cultural analysis of the *Reader's Digest* version of *Tom Sawyer:* "In as much as I am interested in how different textual states reveal the complex and sometimes quirky machinations of cultural production and consumption, I am in this sense concerned with how textual consciousness is an integral part of the experience of reading cultural texts—not just literature" (*Texualterity,* 45).

Chapter 6

1. Peter Shillingsburg parallels this view when he identifies various aspects of the creative and production processes in book-making as "the developing *division of labor* into literary agents, publishers, printers, wholesalers, and booksellers. Each of these matters should be thought of as a *force field* influencing what the work became" ("The Autonomous Writer, the Sociology of Texts, and the Polemics of Textual Criticism," in Cohen, *Devils and Angels,* 30; emphasis added).

2. Shillingsburg argues that the editorial mission of creating a "single text edition" masks the "force fields" of social influence at the expense of what is taken to be the writer's autonomous vision; this leads to a "polemical view of editing," whereas what in fact is needed is a more "comprehensive textual criticism" ("Autonomous Writer," 40). My point throughout, of course, is that fluid-text editing aims for the kind of authorial and sociological comprehensiveness Shillingsburg is calling for.

3. In Shillingsburg's words, "To do a contextual reading right we would have to do it all" ("Autonomous Writer," 29, 41). His point is that contextualizing is not simply placing the text in conjunction with the history-book events of the historical period in which it was composed (i.e., my notion of "time line" contextualizing). Rather, it also means tracing the composition and reception histories of a text from its beginning to the present.

4. Hayden White, "The Burden of History," in *Tropics of Discourse: Essays in Cultural Criticism* (Baltimore: Johns Hopkins University Press, 1978), 49–50. White goes on to adopt the spirit of this historicist approach by eschewing those histories that impose "a specious continuity" and by concluding that "we require a history that will educate us to discontinuity" (50).

5. According to Tanselle, "critical editors—by definition—always produce an 'imagination' or 'reconstruction' of a past text" ("Textual Criticism and Literary Sociology," 107).

6. As Shillingsburg succinctly puts it, "[T]he contexts we identify as relevant to the text we read determine our interpretation, and the interpretation we adopt determines the text we establish or edit" ("Autonomous Writer," 39).

7. The early dawnings of this idea appear in Parker's two essays "Why *Pierre* Went Wrong" (*Studies in the Novel* 8 [spring 1976]: 7–23) and "Contract: *Pierre,* by Herman Melville" (*Proof* 5 [1977]: 27–44). A 1978 piece with Brian Higgins, "The Flawed Grandeur of Melville's *Pierre,*" in *New Perspectives on Melville,* ed. Faith Pullin (Kent, Ohio: Kent State University Press; Edinburgh: Edinburgh Uni-

188 ∽ NOTES TO PAGES 116–33

versity Press), foregrounds the likelihood that blowups with Duyckinck and Harpers initiated disastrous revisions of *Pierre* and elaborates upon the aesthetic inconsistencies in the novel that are derivable from those last-minute reorientations. See also their 1983 introduction to *Critical Essays on Herman Melville's "Pierre; or, The Ambiguities"* (Boston: G. K. Hall), and their 1986 chapter on "Reading *Pierre*" in *A Companion to Melville Studies,* ed. John Bryant (Westport, Conn.: Greenwood Press).

8. Herman Melville, *Pierre, or The Ambiguities.* The Kraken Edition, ed. Hershel Parker, pictures by Maurice Sendak (New York: HarperCollins, 1995), xxxv.

9. See James Duban, *Melville's Major Fiction* (DeKalb: Northern Illinois University Press, 1983), 181; and Robert Milder, "Herman Melville," in *American Literary Scholarship, 1981* (Chapel Hill, N.C.: Duke University Press, 1983), 60.

10. Hershel Parker, *Flawed Texts and Verbal Icons: Literary Authority in American Fiction* (Evanston, Ill: Northwestern University Press, 1984).

11. Higgins and Parker, introduction to *Critical Essays on "Pierre,"* 268, and "Reading *Pierre*," 215.

12. Martens, "(De)Constructing Texts by Editing," 138.

13. Hans Zeller, "Structure and Genesis in Editing: On German and Anglo-American Textual Criticism," in Gabler, Bornstein, and Pierce, *Contemporary German Editorial Theory,* 20.

14. Zeller, "Structure and Genesis," 41; Hans Walter Gabler, "Textual Criticism and Theory in Modern German Editing," In Gabler, Bornstein, and Pierce, *Contemporary German Editorial Theory,* 6.

15. Jerome J. McGann, *Social Values and Poetic Acts: The Historical Judgment of Literary Work* (Cambridge, Mass.: Harvard University Press, 1988), 181.

16. Albert J. von Frank has made a case for exploring the "grammar (or hypergrammar) of manuscripts and genetic texts," as a means of accessing a "correspondingly special poetics, in which authorial intention plays a more important and less problematic role than it ordinarily does in literary criticism." "Genetic versus Clear Texts: Reading and Writing Emerson," *Documentary Editing* 9, no. 4 (1987): 8.

17. Tanselle, "Textual Criticism and Literary Sociology," 108–9.

18. G. Thomas Tanselle, "Critical Editions, Hypertexts, and Genetic Criticism," *Romanic Review* 86 (1995): 586.

19. Tanselle, "Critical Editions, Hypertexts," 590.

20. Examples of this approach are Valerie Eliot's edition of *The Waste Land* manuscript and Charles Robinson's magisterial *Frankenstein Notebooks,* 2 vols. (New York: Garland, 1996).

21. Shillingsburg repeatedly calls for more accessible and useful textual apparatuses that reveal the development of a work, who might have created a variant, and under what circumstances (*Computer Age,* 91, 116, 119).

22. Lewis Mumford, "Emerson behind Barbed Wire," *New York Review of Books,* January 18, 1968, as qtd. in Tanselle, "Critical Editions, Hypertexts," 583.

23. As Tanselle notes, the limitations of apparatus reflect the limits of the codex format and the cost of book publication. That is, you can only fit so much information about variants and versions on a page without creating highly expensive page layouts.

24. Tanselle, *Rationale*, 90, 92; the latter quotation also appears in "Reflections on Scholarly Editing," 59.

25. Roland Barthes, *The Pleasure of the Text*, trans. Richard Miller (New York: Noonday Press, 1975), 27.

Chapter 7

1. Shillingsburg, *Computer Age*, 90.

2. Shillingsburg, *Computer Age*, 91, 100.

3. Shillingsburg, *Computer Age*, 89.

4. Zeller, "Record and Interpretation," 106.

5. It should go without saying that an inferred version whose historicity may be real but whose physicality and precise textuality can only be hypothesized may not be a good candidate for a base version, for if a record of revisions (some of which are intangible, such as manuscript expansions made on lost leaves but appearing in a print version) is to be comprehensible and credible, it must be grounded on a tangible text. Thus, the Kraken edition of *Pierre*, which uses a hypothetical inferred version as its base, is not (for whatever other merits it may have) a useful fluid-text edition. Tanselle offers a measured discussion of this problem in his "Editing without a Copy-Text," *Studies in Bibliography* 47 (1994): 1–22.

6. A case could be made for the posthumous 1892 edition of *Typee*, edited by Arthur Stedman. While this is largely based on the longer British text and seems to include Melville's latest revisions, it is minus at least two major passages (NN *Typee* 314).

7. René Weis, introduction to *King Lear: A Parallel Text* (London: Longman, 1993), 3.

8. James E. Miller Jr., introduction to *Complete Poetry and Selected Prose by Walt Whitman* (Boston: Houghton Mifflin, 1959), xxix–xxx.

9. Marta L. Werner, *Emily Dickinson's Open Folios: Scenes of Reading, Surfaces of Writing* (Ann Arbor: University of Michigan Press, 1995). See also Ellen Louise Hart and Martha Nell Smith, eds., *Open Me Carefully: Emily Dickinson's Intimate Letters to Susan Huntington Dickinson* (Paris Press, 1998), as well as R. W. Franklin's edition of *The Poems of Emily Dickinson* (Cambridge, Mass.: Harvard University Press, 1999), based on Dickinson's manuscripts and Smith's electronic version of Dickinson's manuscripts (University of Maryland).

10. Robinson, *The Frankenstein Notebooks: A Facsimile Edition of Mary Shelley's Manuscript Novel, 1816–1817* (New York: Garland Publishing, 1996).

11. This may seem to contradict my earlier statement that a fluid-text edition of *Typee* should use the British first edition as base version, but my intention in *Melville Unfolding* is to focus on the fragmentary working draft. Space and critical focus prohibit a complete fluid-text edition of *Typee;* hence the use of the smaller reading text of the manuscript.

12. For instance, in the example in fig. 2, I assume that the insertion of "abandoned all thoughts for success" is a Dantean allusion that in effect "triggers" one of Melville's rare revisions of *native* to *savage*, rather than the reverse notion in

which the revision to *savage* triggers the insertion of abandonment. Nothing in the physical document itself suggests that this second alternative is any less plausible than the first; however, I opt for the first because the use of *savage* as a projection of Tommo's anxiety onto the natives seems to be a strategic reinforcement of Tommo's sense of abandonment and gloom.

13. In manuscript, authorships can be distinguished. The *Typee* manuscript, for instance, is largely written in Melville's hand; however, it is also evident that Melville's brother Gansevoort inscribed marginal suggestions for revision in pencil.

14. While the locution *revision narrative* might be new, the idea behind it is not extraordinary. In *Whitman's Manuscripts: Leaves of Grass (1860)*, Fredson Bowers set a model for the kind of explication of revision discussed here. His edition provides reading texts of manuscripts affixed with easily read notes designed to lead readers through Whitman's revision steps. As he put it, "[B]y a series of notes I have attempted in a partly narrative manner to reconstruct in these manuscripts the revisory progress from first inscription to the finally achieved version" (University of Chicago Press, 1955, vii). My approach takes Bowers model a couple of steps along, by including revisions of all versions associated with the *Typee* manuscript throughout the life of *Typee,* by offering revision sequences as a visual component of revision narratives, and by creating full, not partial, narratives that hypothesize upon motives of revision.

15. In some cases, editors may not be able to discern a precise strategy because they cannot, interestingly enough, fully determine the direction of a revision. With *Lear,* for instance, a case can be made that the 1623 Folio version represents revisions of the earlier 1608 Quarto versions; however, René Weis argues for a possible counterdirection. It is possible that manuscript material dropped from the Quarto may have been *restored* to the Folio. Without a surviving manuscript, the available documents are not enough to prove a case for either revision of Quarto or restoration of Quarto, so we cannot reasonably establish the *direction* of textual fluidity in *Lear.* It may, then, be said in some abstract sense that the *Lear* variants oscillate back and forth in our minds as textual options. In cases of *oscillating variants,* the editor should try to establish how and why this oscillation may have meaning in lieu of the more concrete meanings we can gather from textual fluidity that have a determinate direction. At the very least, one may say that the scene of oscillation symbolizes a moment of cultural debate.

16. Versions of a text lab are already being devised. Charles Ross of the University of Hartford, for instance, has developed a HyperCard program that allows his students to collate versions of D. H. Lawrence's short stories, mark variants, attribute motives to them, and construct new versions of each tale.

Index

Abridgment, 92
Access, to textual fluidity, 9
Adaptation, 62, 108; as mode of production, 93. *See also* Cultural revision
Adorno, Theodor, 185n. 2
Agency, 39, 41, 42, 157
Anderson, Charles Roberts, 163
"Annabel Lee" (Poe), 32
Archive, 150–51; electronic, 147; as library, 145. *See also* Melville Electronic Library
Arnold, Matthew, 82
Array, of documentary data, 51, 71. *See also* McGann
"Art" (Melville), 95; fluid text edition of, 132
Author, 10, 11; death of, 13. *See also* Writer
Authorization, 73, 104. *See also* Geneticism
Autopoiesis, 48, 49, 99
Avante-texte, 72

Barthes, Roland, 112, 139
"Bartleby" (Melville), 18
Base version, 150; for map of reading, 152; rationale of, 151–54
Beardsley, Monroe C., 179n. 7
Beaumont and Fletcher, 45–46
Beggar's Opera (Gay), 105
Bible, 3
Bibliographic code, 49, 52, 53, 60, 66, 184n. 21; inadequacy of, 58–59
Billy Budd (Melville), 92, 109, 116, 182n. 6; fluid text edition of, 132; Hayford-Sealts edition of (1962), 127–28; as heuristic edition, 130; and *Typee,* 163
Blake, William, 49
Bloom, Harold, 51
Book: as heuristic fluid text, 150–51;

pleasure of, 148–49; as technology, 146
Borges, Jorge Luis, 17
Bornstein, George, 179n. 3
Bowdlerization, 92, 100
Bowers, Fredson, 22, 44–46, 127, 183n. 3, 190n. 14
Bradbury, Ray, 110
Brecht, Bertolt, 185n. 2
Bryant, John, 180n. 14; editor of Melville Society, 118, 181n. 6

"Camoens" (Melville), fluid text edition of, 132
Carver, Raymond, 3, 100; and editorial collaboration, 7
Case of the Disappearing Textual Apparatus, 122, 130–31
Censorship, 100
Chaucer, Geoffrey, 3
Circulating draft, 91
Clarel (Melville), 116
Clear reading text, 123, 125, 141, 142, 143; of *Typee,* 9, 24, 50
Clotelle (William Wells Brown), 3, 80
Cold War, 110
Collaboration, 7, 62
Companion to Melville Studies, A (ed. Bryant), 164
Computer. *See* Electronic editing; Electronic text; Synergy of book and screen
Confidence-Man, The (Melville), 53, 173
Conflated edition. *See* Eclectic edition
Constitution of United States, as fluid text, 174
Construct vs. *reconstruct,* 37
Continuous manuscript text, 125. *See also* Gabler
Copy-text, 21, 71; of *Typee,* 24. *See also* Base version

191

Cosmopolitanism, 137, 177
Creative process, 90–92
Critical edition, 22, 114, 127–28, 154; agency and moment, 39, 41, 42; as conception of historical moment, 37–38; and dehistoricizing of text, 22, 27; eclectic, of *Typee*, 40– 42; historicity of, 28; and ideology, 39; perpetuation of textual fluidity, 26; as polemic (Shillingsburg), 115. *See also* Edition; *Edition imaginaire*
Critique genetique, 72. *See also* Geneticism
Critique of Modern Textual Criticism (McGann), 47
Cultural revision, 93, 108–10; as misnomer, 109, 110. *See also* Adaptation
Culture, as fluid text, 9, 173–77; Geertzian view of, 54

Davis, R. M., 181n. 1
Declaration of Independence, as fluid text, 174
Deconstruction, 10, 180n. 11
Definitive text, problem of, 2, 22, 27, 66, 130, 142
Delta Δ function. *See* Revision code
Democracy, 113
Derrida, Jacques, 10, 179n. 9
Dialectic, 51. *See also* Array
Dickens, Charles, 87
Dickinson, Emily, 3, 30, 96–97; base version of her poetry, 153; and editorial collaboration, 7; multiple editions of, 143
Difference, 66, 89, 114; reading of, between versions, 62
Diplomatic edition, 20, 52, 127–28. *See also* Edition
Distance, between versions, 114, 123. *See also* Difference
Doctorow, E. L., 101
Document, 32; unreliability of, 32–33
Donne, John, 3
Dreiser, Theodore, and editorial collaboration, 7

Duban, James, 188n. 9
Duyckinck, Evert, 31, 40, 41, 117, 182n. 7

Eclectic edition, 21, 40–42, 47, 50. *See also* Critical edition; Edition
Edition, 20, 66; popular idea of, 65. *See also kinds of editions:* Critical; Diplomatic; Eclectic; *Edition imaginaire;* Facsimile; Fluid text; Genetic; Heuristic; Rhetorical; Variorum
Edition imaginaire, 114–22, 169; rhetorical and heuristic, 61, 115, 119, 121, 122, 123
Editor, 6; and collaboration, 7; as set of strategies, 108; as transcendent collective, 107–8
Editorial collective, 107–8
Eggert, Paul, 179n. 3
Einstein, Albert, 61
Electronic editing, 122, 145; emulating fluid text, 147, 148
Electronic library. *See* Melville Electronic Library
Electronic text, 122, 145, 161, 184n. 22; as archive, 149
Eliot, T. S., 3, 91, 100; and editorial collaboration, 7; multiple editions of, 143
Emendation, 21; of *Moby-Dick*, 33, 131; of Fayaway, 25; of *Typee*, 24–26, 34
Emerson, Ralph Waldo, 90
"Empedocles on Etna" (Arnold), 82
Enchanted Island (film of *Typee*), 163
Energy, 59–63. *See also* Work
Expurgation, 92, 105; of *Typee*, 40–41, 57, 58

Fabbro, 100
Facsimile edition, 20. *See also* Edition
Fair copy, 91
False start, 19. *See also* Transcription (of a document)
Faulkner, William, 3, 100
Fayaway: Northwestern-Newberry emendation of, 25; revision of, 134–35

Typee (Melville) (*continued*)
Toby," 23; text lab and revision
workshop, 164; and textual debate,
23–28; Tommo's bath scene,
53–59; as travel narrative and
romance, 91
Typescript, 91
Typographical error: and intentionality, 67–68
Tyranny of the single reading text. *See*
Single Reading Text

Ulysses (Joyce), 71–72, 125; Gabler's
edition of, 125–29, multiple editions of, 143
Uncle Tom's Cabin (Stowe), 109
Utterance, text as speech act, 84. *See
also* McLaverty

Variants, 72–73; single, 75; not synchronous, 148. *See also* Version(s)
Variorum edition, 21. *See also* Edition
Version(s), 61, 66; always linked, 89;
and authorization, 89; base, 150,
151–54; as critical construct, 90;
degree and manner of variation in,
70; direction of, 89–90; distance
between, 123; "essayed" (Shillingsburg), 81; fluid text definition of,
88–90; functional unity, 82; as independent work, 85–87; inferred, 69,
72, 77; limited access to, 4;
McLaverty's "continuity," 83; physical and inferred, 88; and physical
document, 76, 77; as revision, 89;
rhetorical impact, 90; "unities"
(Shillingsburg), 81; and work (as
concept), 86
Versioning, 76, 143. *See also* Reiman
Visit to the South Seas (Stewart), 163
von Frank, Albert, 188n. 16

Waste Land, The (Eliot), 91, 100; base
version of, 153

Weeds and Wildings (Melville),
182n. 6
Weis, René, 190n. 15
Wenke, John, 75
"What Is an Author?" (Foucault),
11–12
White, Hayden, 51, 113, 187n. 4
Whitman, Walt, 3, 67, 127; *Leaves of
Grass,* 6; manuscripts of *Leaves of
Grass,* 190n. 14; multiple editions
of, 143
Wiley, John, 23, 26, 38, 100, 105
Williams, Raymond, 54
Wimsatt, W. K., 179n. 7
Wolfe, Thomas, 100; and editorial col-
laboration, 7
Woolf, Virginia, 3
Word vs. wording, 32. *See also*
Text
Wordsworth, William, 3, 6, 85
Work: author's conception vs. "ideal,"
31 (*see also* Intentionalist approach;
Tanselle); as concept, 31; as energy
(*travaille*), 59–63, 66, 112; energy
of revision, 94; as event, 48, 50; as
object (*oeuvre*), 61
Working draft, 91, 94. *See also Typee,*
manuscript
Wright, Richard, 64; and editorial col-
laboration, 7
Writer: absence and presence of,
12–13; vs. author, 11; as first reader,
10, 98
Writing: historicizing of, 37; as
process, 3
Writings of Herman Melville. See
Melville, Northwestern-Newberry
edition of

Yeats, William Butler, 3
Young Frankenstein (film), 109

Zeller, Hans, 70, 73–75, 124–25
Zoolander (film), 175